Renzo Piano Building Workshop

Space – Detail – Light

Edgar Stach

Renzo Piano Building Workshop

Space – Detail – Light

Birkhäuser
Basel

Editorial support and drawings
Brad Blankenbiller, Philadelphia
Clara Bucar, Philadelphia
Stephanie Connelly, Philadelphia
Nicola Taylor, Philadelphia
Rachel Updegrove, Philadelphia

Layout
Edgar Stach, Philadelphia
Alexandra Zöller, Berlin

Cover design and typesetting
Alexandra Zöller, Berlin

Project management
Henriette Mueller-Stahl, Berlin

Copy editing
Esther Wolfram, Hamburg

Production
Heike Strempel, Berlin

Paper
120 g/m² Amber Graphic

Lithography
bildpunkt Druckvorstufen GmbH

Printing
optimal media GmbH

Library of Congress Control Number: 2020952005

Bibliographic information published by the German National Library
The German National Library lists this publication in the Deutsche Nationalbibliografie; detailed bibliographic data are available on the Internet at http://dnb.dnb.de.

ISBN 978-3-0356-1460-2
e-ISBN (PDF) 978-3-0356-1457-2

German Print ISBN 978-3-0356-1461-9

P.O. Box 44, 4009 Basel, Switzerland
Part of Walter de Gruyter GmbH, Berlin/Boston

9 8 7 6 5 4 3 2 1

www.birkhauser.com

Table of Contents

Preface

> *Light has not just intensity, but also a vibration, which is capable of roughening a smooth material, of giving a three-dimensional quality to a flat surface.*[1]
>
> Renzo Piano

The Italian architect Renzo Piano is perhaps the world's most prolific museum designer. He and his practice Renzo Piano Building Workshop (RPBW) are known for their sensitive and poetic creation of space, delicate and refined architectural details, and transparent and natural light. In 1998, Renzo Piano was awarded the Pritzker Prize, with the Jury comparing him to Leonardo da Vinci, Michelangelo and Brunelleschi, highlighting "his intellectual curiosity and problem-solving techniques as broad and far ranging as those earlier masters of his native land."[2]

In his early career, Renzo Piano worked for the architect Louis I. Kahn,[3] the master of natural light. Kahn believed that architecture began with the "making of a room" and that "a room is not a room without natural light."[4] These are values Renzo Piano embraced throughout his entire career. At the age of 34, Renzo Piano and Richard Rogers won the design competition for the cultural Centre Pompidou in Paris, one of the most avant-garde and iconic high-tech buildings of our time, designed in a then-radical fashion to create column-less, flexible interior space for exhibitions. In 1981, he founded Renzo Piano Building Workshop and in 1986, he made his debut with The Menil Collection, his first museum design, which is a manifesto for the synthesis of form, space, structure and light.

One of the most powerful aspects of Renzo Piano's museum architecture throughout his career is his endeavor to bring natural light into the interiors in the most imaginative ways. Piano's lighting is modulated, calm, dynamic, accentuated, contemplative or bright, depending on the artwork and the ambience needed to support the art.

The sensitive design with space and light creates contemplative spaces in which visitors can comfortably and creatively experience paintings and sculptures. Renzo Piano describes a museum as a "magical place … a place where you have to cry or lose your head, it's true, a museum is a place out of the world. It is actually about physics, metaphysics, above physics, above this world, not in this time. You take a piece of work that is so fragile, build, protect the piece of art, and put it in a different dimension that is timeless: this is the spirit. The museum is a place that is of metaphysics … You really create a new dimension; creating the museum is creating a place for the experience of a new dimension, above the world."[5]

This book is an introduction to RPBW's ideas about daylight in museum architecture. It decodes the relationship between space, structure and light in some of the most important contemporary art museums in the world. An analysis of nine unique museums developed over the last 25 years by RPBW reveals an intimate relationship between the exhibition space, the artwork and the natural lighting conditions. RPBW uses innovative and subtle solutions for modulating natural light through a highly complex set of construction layers in the roof and ceiling. Each project showcases a distinct different architectural and constructive approach and a built solution that has been fine-tuned to the physical location, cultural context, artwork and required luminescence. Collectively, the book contains a wealth of technical details explaining and categorizing the spectrum of daylight modulation techniques from glass ceilings, over skylights and fixed shading systems, to highly complex technical solutions. At the same time, each project is described individually in terms of the design parameters

1 Renzo Piano, *Logbook*, The Monacelli Press, New York 1997.
2 https://www.pritzkerprize.com/laureates/1998
3 Renzo Piano worked at Louis I. Kahn's office in Philadelphia between 1965 and 1970.
4 Louis I. Kahn, *Drawings for City/2 Exhibition: Architecture Comes from the Making of a Room*, 1971.
5 Renzo Piano, *Logbook*, The Monacelli Press, New York 1997.

space, construction detail and daylight. The photometric investigation and daylighting analysis unlocks the superb lighting qualities of each project.

These nine buildings illustrate the mastery of RPBW when it comes to creating architecture through space, detail and light, ultimately making magical spaces in which to experience artwork. The use of natural light and the idea of lightness are essential to his practice. The unique design solutions and technologies are executed with such craftsmanship and attention to detail that they can maintain a sense of simplicity and purity. RPBW's buildings convey truthfulness to materials that can be breathtaking yet remain neutral. This allows the building to provide a truly magical environment that enhances the experience of interacting with the artworks. In looking at each project, RPBW's process is revealed, showing how each of the spaces is unique to its location and art collections. Each building has mythical spaces and is responsive to its given site; each one presents in a unique manner of integrating the building with the landscape, while still maintaining a dialogue with the specific collection of artworks.

This publication is the second in a book series unlocking the relationship between space and construction by analyzing key works from famed architects. The first book, *Mies van der Rohe: Space – Material – Detail* (Birkhäuser 2018), described 14 projects spanning from Europe in the 1920s to the United States in the late 1960s, and analyzed the interrelation between construction and design expression. Mies van der Rohe's design and planning concept is based on the mutual influence of space, construction and material. Like Mies van der Rohe decades before, Renzo Piano embraces in his architecture the synthesis of form, space, structure and detail infused with light. Each of his museum buildings in its entirety represents a continuum that coherently incorporates all spatial, construction and perception requirements.

This publication is intended for architects, exhibition designers, lighting professionals, conservation scientists and in particular anyone involved in museum planning and/or artwork display. It aims to give the reader a level of understanding for different daylighting systems, the visual effects of lighting and conservational considerations of artwork. The first part of the book introduces the museum buildings, while the second part analyzes different daylighting solutions using simulation tools, and presents recommendations based on their comparison.

My special thanks go to Stefania Canta from RPBW, who has supported this publication by providing photos and vital project information. I was advised by several consultants in the fields of daylight simulation, museum lighting and museum management.

This book has been made possible thanks to the contributions of many individuals and institutions, to all of whom I wish to express my sincerest gratitude. I am indebted to The Menil Collection and Cy Twombly Pavilion for providing valuable daylight data. I would like to thank the Beyeler Foundation, the Zentrum Paul Klee, the High Museum and the Broad Contemporary Art Museum for providing me with invaluable materials and documents. I also wish to thank the administration of the Nasher Sculpture Center, Jean-Marie Tjibaou Cultural Center and the Morgan Library and Museum.

Further thanks go to Professor Christoph Reinhart, Ph.D., from MIT for helpful advice about the DIVA lighting analysis, Prof. Dr.-Ing. Uta Pottgiesser at TU Delft for practical suggestions, Shrikar (Shri) Bhave from Transsolar Energietechnik for his valuable advice and Matt Franks from the ARUP Lighting Group for insightful suggestions. Special thanks to Julian Siggers, Ph.D., Director of the Penn Museum at the University of Pennsylvania, for his experience and invaluable insight into museum architecture. Special thanks to Michael Esposito from Integral Group and his expert criticism in helping shape the form and content of the lighting analysis.

This book would not have been possible without the editorial expertise of Henriette Mueller-Stahl from Birkhäuser who guided the book through publication.

Beyeler Foundation

I gratefully acknowledge Thomas Jefferson University for the unparalleled support for this publication. I cannot begin to express my thanks to Jennifer Wilson and Christianna Fail from Thomas Jefferson University for their language editing. Special thanks to my students who collaborated on generating the analytical drawings.[6] I would especially like to thank Rachel Updegrove for her deep editorial support and Stephanie Connelly for the factual review and technical editing of the manuscript.

Edgar Stach
Philadelphia, January 2021

6 All analytical drawings were generated by the author and his students.

The Menil Collection

Introduction

Space – Detail – Light

Renzo Piano's love for spaces created by light is evident in all of his buildings, both on a large scale and when embedded in the details. From his earliest projects, such as the Centre de Pompidou, to his newest museums, high-rises and laboratories, light orchestrates concept, functionality, comfort and beauty. Light has the dramatic ability to completely change spaces, unite spaces, hide spaces or showcase spaces.

> *Light is the most important for architecture ...*
> *The next is water – water is magic because it is never the same.*[1]
>
> Renzo Piano

Interior of the Kimbell Art Museum West Lobby, Kimbell Art Museum, Fort Worth

In Renzo Piano's early years as an architect, he worked as a student under Louis I. Kahn when the iconic Kimbell Museum was being designed. Kahn saw light as the interplay of sun and shadow. At the Kimbell Art Museum, light was the theme:

> *We knew that the museum would always be full of surprises. The blues would be one thing one day; the blues would be another thing another day, depending on the character of the light.*[2]
>
> Louis I. Kahn

Much like Kahn, Piano started his own practice, the *Renzo Piano Building Workshop*, known today for nearly 50 years of museum, lighting and cultural designs. Nearly 35 years after working briefly for Louis I. Kahn, Renzo Piano was called back to expand on the work of his teacher, Kahn's Kimbell Art Museum. No longer an apprentice, Piano had his own practice and his own themes, and was a Pritzker Prize laureate. Evolving through his practice, Renzo Piano has always kept space, detail and light in focus – these are Piano's "themes."

Light is understood and studied by Piano in terms of lightness and transparency. Focusing on opportunities to use and diffuse natural lighting, "the workshop's preoccupation with transparency, beauty and lightness extends to a striving for 'weightlessness'."[3] For Piano, the meaning of light is dimensional – light brings not only visibility, but a feeling of force, weight, or the lack thereof. Lighting is not only a tool within his architectural palette,[4] but also a specific part of the environmental, contextual and public space within which he designs.

To create spaces, Piano "use[s] immaterial elements like transparency, lightness, the vibration of the light. [He] believe[s] that they are as much a part of the composition as the shapes and volumes."[5] Often Piano's spaces seem to be lifted or "floating", allowing the space to interact with the people, the light and the air[6] as they would have naturally, had a building not been there. He is sensitive to the context of place and site informing the created space, through listening and studying the surroundings. Piano called this the Genius Loci.[7]

The details that Piano regards to create a space of light and lightness are considered to be a technique of components or pieces. This technique "generate[s] an emotion, and it does so with its own specific language, made up of space, proportions, light and materials."[8] Because of his unique technique of thoughtful and integrated pieces, his details are multifaceted and grounded. While he considers individual themes of space, detail and light, these themes do not exist in isolation, but in relational unison to one another and their contexts.

1 Martin Filler, *Makers of Modern Architecture, Volume II: From Le Corbusier to Rem Koolhaas*, New York Review Books, New York 2013, p. 174.
2 Nell E. Johnson and Louis I. Kahn, *Light is the Theme: Louis I. Kahn and the Kimbell Art Museum, Kimbell Art Museum*, Fort Worth 1975, p. 16.
3 http://www.rpbw.com/
4 Ibid.
5 https://www.pritzkerprize.com/sites/default/files/inline-files/1998_Acceptance_Speech.pdf
6 http://www.rpbw.com/
7 Ibid.
8 https://www.pritzkerprize.com/sites/default/files/inline-files/1998_Acceptance_Speech.pdf

Renzo Piano in Context

Renzo Piano was born into an Italian Genovese family of builders and engineers in 1937. Not following their footsteps, Piano did not want to be a builder, as he wanted to design lightweight structures and spaces of light. Many attribute his desire for lightness to his interest in sailing, as Genoa is a port city, but actually many teachers and colleagues have influenced who Piano is today: Richard Rogers,[9] Peter Rice,[10] Franco Albini,[11] Frei Otto,[12] Jean Prouve[13] and Louis I. Kahn. All of these teachers and collaborators are architects, engineers and inventors who pushed the technological and aesthetic envelope.

To understand Renzo Piano and where he came from, it is best to consider him amongst his teachers and his historically contextual counterparts: Louis I. Kahn, Mies van der Rohe and Steven Holl. This is not an attempt to competitively compare the success of these architects to that of Renzo Piano. It is a juxtaposition of viewpoints, from architects historically and contextually relevant to Piano, in dialogue with one another on the topics of space, detail and light.

The Kimbell Art Museum – Renzo Piano Pavilion, south facade

Learning from Kahn – Light and Landscape

Louis I. Kahn came from an era of architecture prior to that of Renzo Piano. In fact, when Louis I. Kahn was near the end of his career, finishing the Kimbell Art Museum in 1972, Renzo Piano was just getting started, working for Louis I. Kahn in 1968–1969 and designing the Centre Pompidou in 1971–1977. Renzo Piano first met Louis I. Kahn through a University of Pennsylvania professor of lightweight structures named Robert Le Ricolais.[14] Piano was taking a course taught by Le Ricolais, who collaborated with Louis I. Kahn as an engineer.[15] Piano was apprenticing with Kahn during the time that Kahn was working on the Kimbell Art Museum; however, Piano never got to work on the museum until he was hired for the expansion project in 2007. Regardless, Kahn was Piano's teacher, as evident in his architectural lightness.

Louis I. Kahn in front of the completed Kimbell Art Museum photographed on Aug. 3, 1972

Piano and Kahn have different approaches to achieving light or lightness. Kahn's light concept focuses on materiality and building geometry, whereas Piano's focuses on detailing and a layered light filtering system. In Kahn's Kimbell Museum, sunlight falls through a slot in the cycloid vaults and is reflected upwards by aluminum wings against the curved ceilings illuminating the galleries with a warm glow, contrasting with the beige travertine walls. In Piano's Kimbell Museum, a sophisticated roof system layers stretched fabric, the wooden beams, glass, aluminum louvers, and photovoltaic cells to create a controlled daylit environment. Louis I. Kahn was an architect known for the artful play of light and shadow. Site orientation, form and materiality were the factors and tools he had at his disposal to explore light and shadow:

> *A column and a column brings light between them. To make a column which grows out of the wall and which makes its own rhythm of no-light, light, no-light, light: that is the marvel of the artist.*[16]
>
> Louis I. Kahn

Kahn was an artist of dichotomies: light/no-light; solid/void; inside/outside; served/service.[17] He believed "structure is the giver of light."[18] Structure creates openings and opportunities for walls, roofs and floors to have natural light come in and create a moment of blended lightness, through the use of light and shadow. His craftsmanship allowed Kahn to use the material's properties to his own artistic advantage. When looking at Kahn's Yale University Art Gallery, the triangulated concrete slab represents this idea of structure giving light but also darkness, in the form of shadows. As natural and artificial lighting bounce within the space, there are areas of the floor slab that do and do not receive light. This is quite a dynamic experience throughout the day, with the sun's position changing how the space is perceived and felt.

9 1933–present, British-Italian architect.

10 1935–1992, Irish structural engineer and designer.

11 1905–1977, Italian architect and designer.

12 1925–2015, German architect and structural engineer.

13 1901–1984, French architect, designer and metal craftsman.

14 1894–1977, French-American structural engineer.

15 https://www.surfacemag.com/articles/renzo-piano/

16 Nell E. Johnson and Louis I. Kahn, *Light is the Theme: Louis I. Kahn and the Kimbell Art Museum*, Kimbell Art Museum, Fort Worth 1975.

17 Louis I. Kahn's definition of "served" and "servant" spaces is one of the most critical architectural theory contributions. According to this, served rooms are the rooms in a building actively used, and servant rooms serve the purpose.

18 Ibid., p. 21.

Because it is the light the painter used to paint his painting. And artificial light is a static light … where natural light is a light of mood. And sometimes the room gets dark – why not? – and sometimes you must get close to look at it, and come another day, you see, to see it in another mood – a different time … to see the mood natural light gives, or the seasons of the year, which have other moods.[19]

Louis I. Kahn

The Menil Collection

Piano's thoughts on light are similar and unique to that of Kahn's, as they are influenced by his partnership with and training from Kahn. Renzo Piano sees light as the "immaterial" tool: while natural light is not a literal or physical object, it is a dynamic and lively element that can be modulated into a unique experience. It has an aura and presence that can influence the "perception of volumes and … emotional response."[20] Kahn and Piano share this understanding of daylight, that it is unique, evolving, time specific and never a constant.

Unlike Kahn, however, Piano strives for lightweight structures and a sense of lightness. Kahn could have seen this removal or lightness in structure as a missed opportunity for light and shadow, believing a contrast is needed. Piano eliminates structural elements down to what is absolutely necessary.[21] This eliminates intense contrasts that would otherwise be provided by Kahn's view of light/no-light. Such elimination to the necessities allows for a transition rather than a hard line contrast of light and shadow.

The connection between the landscape and Piano's understanding of site specificity creates a contextually grounded building that appears to belong where it is situated. Piano's understanding of light, wind, terrain and context, whether natural or cultural, expresses his appreciation for the natural world's abilities and lessons it has to teach us.[22] The Beyeler Foundation displays the immateriality of light, the lightness of structure and its relation to landscape. The sectional qualities of the museum allow the outside and the inside to blend, using the linearity of the architecture to direct visitors' views out into a pool and then further to the landscape. The relation of the landscape, to the covered outside (portico), to the inside shows how "the space of architecture is a microcosm, an inner landscape."[23] Piano's layered glazed roof system allows visitors to still feel connected to the outside world visually, but filters the light to give a progressional sequence: from inside to outside, from shade to light.

Beyeler Foundation

When looking at the Kimbell Art Museum and the Renzo Piano Pavilion, the two architects' own architectural languages complement and converse with one another. Kahn's Kimbell Art Museum has a linear skylight coming through the center of the art gallery, pouring light into each room. The formal massing of the concrete material guides the warmth of the natural light throughout the space. After the natural light enters, it is contained and held within the space to stay, providing a feeling of shelter within the vaulted concrete roof and the exterior porticos. The Renzo Piano Pavilion, the expansion of the Kimbell, was executed sensitively and respectfully by Piano, creating meaning and relation to the existing Art Museum, while still allowing it to stand alone as an individual building. Piano's addition references pieces or detailed components of the Kimbell to inform his lighting strategy. In relation to Kahn's skylights, Piano uses the linear thinness and repetition in his addition's ceiling. But rather than the architecture forming the light, as with Kahn, Piano is using light to form the architecture. Through the use of a glazed roof system, the light informs the way the space looks and feels. Piano's layered approach has pieces of architecture from many different scales and weights, such as the lightweight structural members, vast glazed roof panels and thin cables, making visitors feel calm by blurring the lines that separate the inside and the outside.

19 Ibid., p. 17.
20 Roberto Brignolo, Kenneth Frampton and Renzo Piano, *The Renzo Piano Logbook*, Thames and Hudson, London 1997, p. 253.
21 Ibid., pp. 252–253.
22 Ibid., p. 254.
23 Ibid., p. 251.

Piano and Mies – Space and Detail

Mies van der Rohe, a German-American architect before the time of Piano, focused on craftsmanship, materiality, space, and detailing, and less on natural lighting. Many of Mies's projects, like the Crown Hall (1956) at IIT in Chicago or the National Gallery in Berlin (1968), focused on natural lighting only on the podium or the first floor. As evidence, Mies is known not only for his "Less is More,"[24] but for his concept of "universal space."[25] "The universal space is the ultimate expression of flexible space and can be modeled or adapted to fit almost any use … The supporting framework is both the basis and prerequisite for the free plan of the building."[26] In contrast to Piano, who wants the architecture to be a neutral backdrop to the artwork, Mies believes that the space is the exhibit. The New National Gallery is a prime example of "universal space," with the museum giving off the air of a temple, where viewers can walk through freestanding spaces as if they were the art. Mies is able to make such artistic spaces through his dedication to understanding materials, their context and their characteristics.[27] The Tugendhat and Barcelona Pavilion both expose the structural chrome-cladded cruciform columns; such use of material is efficient and non-confining, using a naturally strong material to carry the building's weight, while the chrome's visual characteristics make the buildings feel endless, light and suspended.

Crown Hall, Chicago History Museum, Ludwig Mies van der Rohe

> *We instinctively seek enclosure, a fixing of limits, in what is built. Space does not exist except insofar as it is precisely – and solidly – circumscribed … I have a less suffocating idea of space: the space of architecture is a microcosm, an inner landscape.*[28]
>
> Renzo Piano

Like Mies's thoughts on universal space, Renzo Piano has his views on space, as well. Piano does not want to overpower the art in the gallery spaces, whereas Mies's gallery spaces are the art. However, Piano's spaces are still dynamic and contextual, as the unique spatial locations of each gallery have their own situated environments. Mies's New National Gallery and Piano's Nasher Sculpture Center both feel like vast, endless extensions of weightless spaces, but for different reasons in the realm of materials.

New National Gallery, Ludwig Mies van der Rohe

Mies looks to use materials for their known physical or visual characteristics, such as strength, durability, water-resistance, or texture. This sense of materiality, which looks towards a classic craftsmanship of making, has allowed Mies to make such timeless creations. The New National Gallery was crafted carefully through a gridded structural system that allows the roof to cantilever out, supported by eight steel cruciform columns.

Piano focuses on the immaterial (visual and spatial) characteristics of materials. This is indicative of Piano's creation process, which is experimental and scientific. He believes architecture is science.[29] Through the creation of scaled to full-size mock-ups, Piano is able to test the performance characteristics of materials. Based on this experience of built models and realized projects, RPBW is continuously developing new technical solutions. "When you work in a circular way the technical aspect returns to its place at the center … experimenting serves to link together the idea and its material consequences … knowing how to do things not just with the head, but with the hands as well."[30] For example, RPBW developed a new type of shading system for the roof of the Nasher Sculpture Center, which spans the entire glass roof. RPBW developed a lightweight roof system with parametric shaped light scoops using analog and digital models and material tests. Combining a complete glass roof with a new type of shading element gives the single-story building light and spacious impression.

24 Edgar Stach, *Mies van der Rohe: Space – Material – Detail*, Birkhäuser, Basel 2018, p. 19.
25 Ibid., p. 11.
26 Ibid., p. 12.
27 Recorded in Werner Blaser's notes of conversations with the architect during his period in Chicago between 1951 and 1953.
28 Roberto Brignolo, Kenneth Frampton and Renzo Piano, *The Renzo Piano Logbook*, Thames and Hudson, London 1997, p. 252.
29 https://www.pritzkerprize.com/sites/default/inline-files/1998_Acceptance_Speech.pdf
30 Roberto Brignolo, Kenneth Frampton and Renzo Piano, *The Renzo Piano Logbook*, Thames and Hudson, London 1997, p. 18.

Nasher Sculpture Center

Piano and Holl – Lightness and Filigree

Piano's contemporary counterpart is Steven Holl. Both are masters of space making through their creative use of light, in their own respective ways. Steven Holl is known for his monolithic and cubistic forms that are activated and contrasted by dynamic lighting, normally through the use of light wells. Holl's Nelson Atkins Museum of Art best illustrates the cubistic forms and dynamic light wells that take over the interior of the art galleries and circulation by creating pockets of light, shadow and activation. Such extreme contrasts are compelling and keep the visitor interested and stimulated – going from a contained place of shadows to an open space with light.

> *The phenomena of the space of a room, the sunlight entering through a window, and the color and reflection of materials on a wall and floor all have integral relationships. The materials of architecture communicate through resonance and dissonance, just as instruments in musical composition, producing thought and sense-provoking qualities in the experience of a place.*[31]
>
> Steven Holl

With focusing so much on provoking the senses with light and darkness, there is no in between or transition from areas focused on lightness to areas focused on darkness. This hard contrast between darkness and lightness leaves spaces feeling heavy and objective. In contrast Renzo Piano uses materials varying in lightness, weight and scale to develop a balanced lighting scheme through various filigrees and masses. However, similarly to Holl, Piano works with contrasts, calling them "contradictions"[32] or "tensions":

> *The placeform and the produktform are the two terms between which the tension of architecture is created. I find this a good way of conveying the tension between the ground and the structure, the setting and the building, the local and the universal.*[33]
>
> Renzo Piano

While Piano and Holl are well known for museum design, they can be differentiated from one another by how they allow contrasts to perform. Renzo Piano's contrasting elements – such as light/no light, heavy to light, details to masses – all exist as a progression.

Nelson Atkins Museum of Art, Steven Holl

Renzo Piano's Beyeler Foundation displays this sense of progression through layered transitions that ease into one another: the interior gallery spaces are enclosed rooms but have a glazed plane looking to the outside, followed by a roof overhang that filters the light, and then a pond that follows this overhang and slowly dissipates as it extends out into the landscape. In this way, the gallery spaces are dynamic in the sense that they are connected to many different environments, such as the daylighting filtered from above, or the landscape out in the distance. These transitions, while subtle, allow the focus to stay on the artwork, which has a backdrop of consistent white walls. This subtle contrast is necessary to have the correct perception when looking at artwork.

The Nelson Atkins Museum of Art is complexly dynamic and could resemble Mies's concept of space itself being the exhibit. Through the weaving and meandering of circulation from gallery to gallery, Steven Holl blends spaces by making the viewer question what space they are in. His gallery walls, while monochrome and light, have light wells and sculptured masses above in the ceiling plane. When viewing artwork, this may be compelling to the observer, as the museum itself becomes artwork. However, contrast is necessary to know where to focus, so that one perceives depth perception and dimensionality correctly.

31 https://www.stevenholl.com/about
32 Roberto Brignolo, Kenneth Frampton and Renzo Piano, *The Renzo Piano Logbook*, Thames and Hudson, London 1997, p. 246.
33 Ibid., p. 250.

Piano and Space

Renzo Piano's concept of space, whether for a museum or tower, is always unique and informed by context and the building's physical location, which entails culture, people, the natural environment (including natural lighting) and the built environment. He believes:

> *There is no, thank heaven, "Piano sense of space." There is the spatiality of the church, the spatiality of the museum, the spatiality of the auditorium. When style is forced to become a trademark, a signature, a personal characteristic, it then also becomes a cage … The mark of recognition lies in the acceptance of the challenge. And then, yes, it does become identifiable: but by a method, not by a trademark.*[34]
>
> Renzo Piano

Cy Twombly Pavilion

For Piano, his projects are identifiable because of his process – while his process may be uniform as a working method, he contextualizes each project as its own. However, his spaces do have some uniformly recognizable traits because of how he treats each project through his process.

Generally, his spaces have a sense of lightness, as Piano looks to correlate the indoors to the outdoors by using natural lighting and the landscape.

Renzo Piano's design process takes into consideration the urban, social and environmental context, and uses these specific spatial typologies:
- Enclosed space: A spatial arrangement of separated individual rooms and polarity between inside and outside, e.g., Cy Twombly Pavilion
- Continuous space: A series of staggered and offset spaces with large openings to the garden interweaving indoor and outdoor spaces, e.g., Beyeler Foundation
- Free plan space: A single space structured only by freestanding wall planes, e.g., High Museum Expansion and the Broad Museum
- Universal space: The ultimate expression of flexible space; a long-span single-volume flexible enclosure, e.g., Nasher Sculpture Center

High Museum Expansion

Renzo Piano believes that museum space should not overpower the artwork. Museums as their own building typology require contextual attention to specific program requirements, as would any other building typology. Piano rationalizes this program's context by understanding the relationship of artwork, space and visibility. Focusing on acceptable light levels, contrast and shadow, aspects that impact visibility, Piano's museum spaces are often calm and feel serene. In the Zentrum Paul Klee, for example, the artwork is so delicate that any sunlight would have a damaging effect. Therefore, all light is electric and strictly monitored.

In another example, the Morgan Library has the light quality and atmosphere of an Italian piazza, with bright lights and a dynamic atmosphere. Yet another example, the Nasher Sculpture Center, shows sculptures in very bright daylight, almost as if the exhibit were outdoors.

Piano acknowledges the need for context to inform his architecture and space, working with anthropologists to better understand the culture, people and history. The Jean-Marie Tjibaou Cultural Center required knowledge of the cultural and environmental context of New Caledonia, as RPBW had not done a museum in this country before. Being in a new context comes with a new set of people and narratives, as well as the lighting position, climate, vegetation and building materials. "It meant taking off the mental clothes of the European architect and steeping myself in the world of the people of the Pacific … It was not feasible to offer a standard product of Western architecture, with a layer of camouflage over the top."[35]

34 Ibid., p. 255.
35 Ibid., p. 180.

Even projects such as the High Museum Expansion or the Kimbell Museum required sensitivity to the previous architectural context of Richard Meier and Louis I. Kahn, respectively. An understanding of past buildings was required to make a relationship for the future expansion, and therefore having the buildings of the past (Kahn and Meier) be in dialogue with those of the present (Piano). This is evident, after much debate, in the color choice of the High Museum being Meier's white,[36] but also in the paralleled and rhythmic parts of the Kimbell.

IBM Traveling Pavilion

Piano and Detail

The use of "immaterial" characteristics is how Renzo Piano approaches lightness and space, looking to non-physical elements that can influence perceptions of space. Some "immaterial" examples are: light, texture, color and transparency. These qualitative details impact the perception of space by modulating light in association with the complex roof assemblies designed by Piano.

Some complex roof assemblies are:

- Surface lighting systems – An entire plane, such as the ceiling, is a light source. The louvers can be fixed or dynamic, using the sun's ever-changing position from above to produce a dynamic movement of light throughout the day.
- Linear lighting systems – Light comes from a source in the shape of a line or bar. This system is fixed, curating light through a specific linear aperture, such as a saw tooth roof.
- Point lighting systems – The light source consists of an individual skylight in the roof. This passive system has fixed shading and is arranged in an organized pattern.

Cy Twombly Pavilion

Within this art of detailing such complex roof assemblies and lighting systems, he believes, "there is a degree of complexity that cannot be avoided. Excessive simplification is ridiculous. The architect works by bringing materials together, not by separating them."[37] Using a layered approach in many of his roofing systems, his details and assemblies still appear lightweight, despite having many layers. Each layer of the roof assembly serves a purpose and an action – to connect, to filter, to support – and the layers relate to one another, often serving dual purposes.

In the transparency of the Beyeler Foundation's roof assembly, the layered approach is clear: opaque glazed sunshading, double pane glass, aluminum louvers, structural members, glazing, and then an opaque screen. Many of these layers work to regulate thermal and visual comfort, using each layer as another measure of regulation to buffer the natural lighting's glare and brightness.

Piano and Light

Renzo Piano's museums harmonize light and space, without one overpowering the other. The light is balanced, natural and thus dynamic, allowing visitors to see the natural lighting change as the day goes on. Piano sensitively looks at lighting through many different lenses, another probable reason for a balanced presence of lighting. He looks at lighting as systems: the natural environment as a system of day and night, light and dark; the perception of light as a person moves through space, light is projected, received, processed, and then perceived by the viewer; natural lighting systems such as sunlight and electrical systems such as light bulbs in spotlights.

Many of Piano's detailed roof assemblies are designed to maximize comfort (reducing glare by using diffused light) and natural lighting (through sensitivity of the site and its climate). As a result, Piano's lighting levels are balanced, not flat, creating enough contrast between light and shadow for depth perception, allowing viewers to see dimensionality. But Piano's fascination with light also surpasses the connotation of the ability to see, and moves towards the connotation of weightlessness – the ability not

36 https://www.nytimes.com/2005/10/30/arts/architecture-lovely-museum-mind-if-i-redesign-it-for-you.html
37 Roberto Brignolo, Kenneth Frampton and Renzo Piano, *The Renzo Piano Logbook*, Thames and Hudson, London 1997, p. 249.

to weigh down but to suspend, by having little to no weight. Because Piano's spaces feel balanced, having the right amount of contrast of light and shadow between spaces, the museum spaces begin to blur the lines between the outside and inside; the lighting and the shadows ("shade") feel calm, as if the spaces are lightweight and airy, not heavy and contained.

When looking at The Menil Collection, Piano's experimentation with materiality in the fiber cement leaves of the roofing system brings to life a dynamic space of weightless light. He uses the natural lighting as "immaterial element(s) such as transparency, lightness and the vibration of light in the architecture."[38] The way that the leaves integrate functions, such as enclosure, roofing, structure and filtration,[39] the lighting becomes even more integrated, contextually situated, grounded and thus calming and reflective.

The Menil Collection

Much can be learned today from Renzo Piano's museums, daylighting concepts and design process. By responding to the physical and environmental context, RPBW has curated this successfully grounded process through decades of practice. Looking at the details, where layered systems translate into larger-scaled performative architectural systems, inhabited spaces are illuminated with daily dynamic lighting that is comfortable for the users and the artwork.

> *Every time you take a new job, the one thing that's constant is the magic of light ... But everything else is different – the direction of sun, the energy consumed, the people you are working with.*[40]
>
> Renzo Piano

Renzo Piano's many milestones have informed his process, concepts and beliefs as an architect. His era began with the Centre Pompidou, as his first exhibit design, which contrasts with exhibits he creates today: while the Centre Pompidou's building systems are external, many of his subsequent projects integrate building systems into the interior of the building. The IBM Pavilion was his first prefabricated exhibit space, consisting of glazed arches unified into one large inhabitable vault. The Menil Collection was one of his first light explorations, where he anchored details into his architecture as a piece of art, using intricate leaves in his roof system to direct and filter lighting.

Kimbell Art Museum Expansion

As he perfected his practices with lighting and detail, the Beyeler Foundation is the benchmark where he exhibits his perfection in daylight – not just because of the beautifully curated light, but because of how the lighting connects the landscape and the architecture. This connection of site specificity carried over into his contextual understanding of culture, as evident in the Jean-Marie Tjibaou Cultural Center. After practicing for almost 50 years, Renzo Piano came back to build next to the architecture of his teacher, Louis I. Kahn, where light remained the theme, beautifying spaces through execution of integrated and insightful details.

38 Ibid., p. 74.
39 Ibid., pp. 72–74.
40 https://www.architectmagazine.com/design/buildings/art-plus-light_o

Part I

Nine Museums by Renzo Piano Building Workshop

The Menil Collection 1982–1986

Houston, Texas, USA

Geographical context within the USA

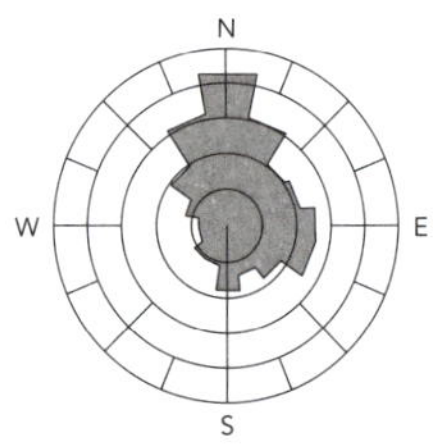

Wind rose: January

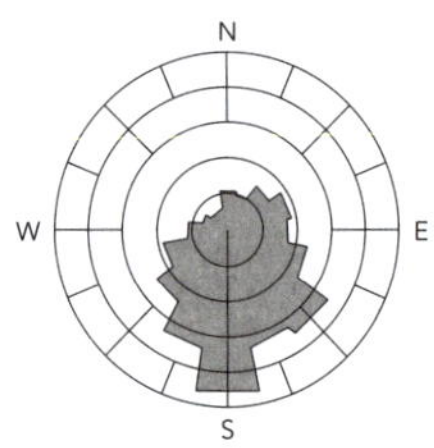

Wind rose: July

In 1982 Renzo Piano designed a new museum for the Dominique de Menil Collection of surrealist and primitive African art located in Houston, Texas, USA, on a 30-acre campus for the arts. The Menil Collection houses about 10,000 works of art in special exhibitions and the permanent collection. It anchors a campus with four other museum buildings, the Cy Twombly Pavilion (1995, architect: Renzo Piano), the Dan Flavin Installation (1996), the Byzantine Fresco Chapel (1997, architect: François de Menil) and the Menil Drawing Institute (2018, architect: Johnston Marklee). The museum opened in April 1987 and remains one of the most important collections of its kind in the world today. The museum is located in the Museum District in Houston's Montrose neighborhood. It respects the scale of the existing residential fabric by maintaining height considerations of the surrounding homes and through the use of carefully selected materials. The art campus features satellite gallery spaces and related cultural institutions with a park-like setting. In 2009, David Chipperfield Architects designed a new master plan for the Menil campus. The plan emphasized the park-like atmosphere and the dialogue between the arts pavilions and the neighboring residences.

> *I came up with a concept … we would rotate the works of art … The public would never know museum fatigue. Works would appear, disappear, and reappear like actors on a stage. Each time they would be seen with a fresh eye.*[1]
>
> Dominique de Menil

The Menil Collection is nearly 152 meters (500 feet) long but seems "small on the outside but large inside,"[2] with 2,787 square meters (30,000 square feet) of gallery. The gallery spaces are arranged on the north side of a long promenade, with preservation studios and offices located in the second-story wing to the south. The roofing system of The Menil Collection uses ferro-cement leaves to shade an outside arcade alongside the building while diffusing the sunlight that illuminates the sensitive artworks housed there.

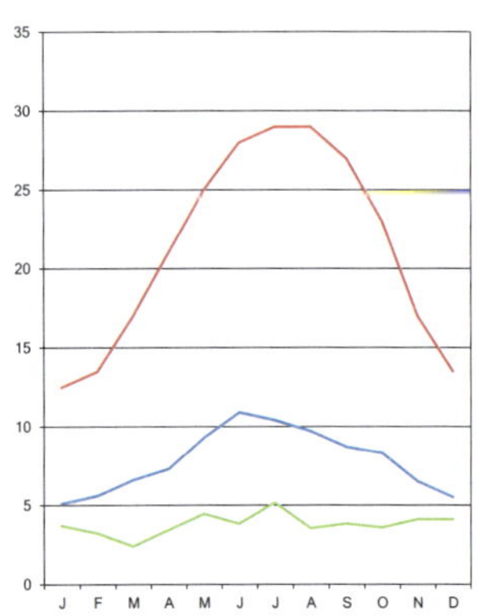

- Sunlight hours/day
- Temperature (°C)
- Average rainfall/month (in)

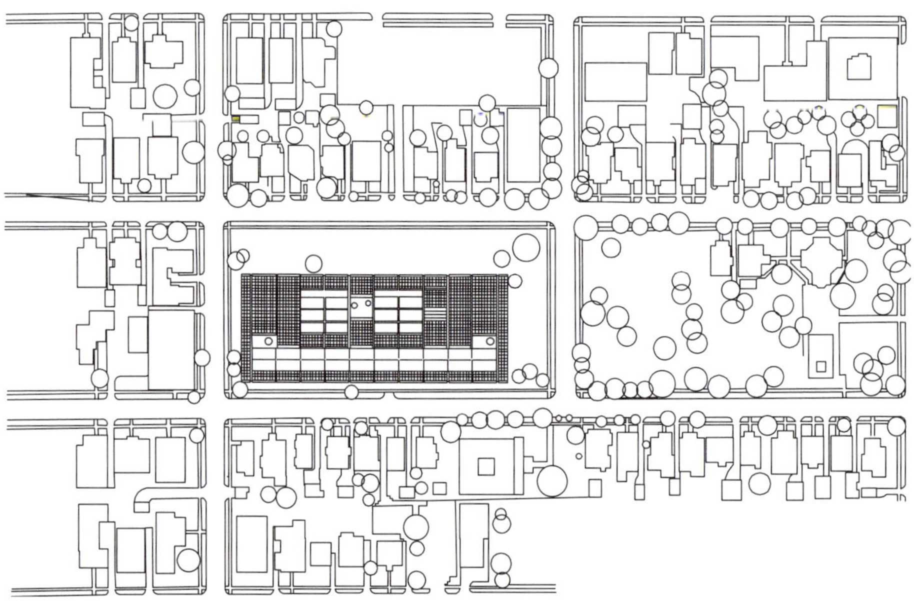

Site plan

1 https://www.menil.org/campus/main-building
2 Ibid.

An aerial view of the Museum District in Houston's Montrose neighborhood, with The Menil Collection being the central focus

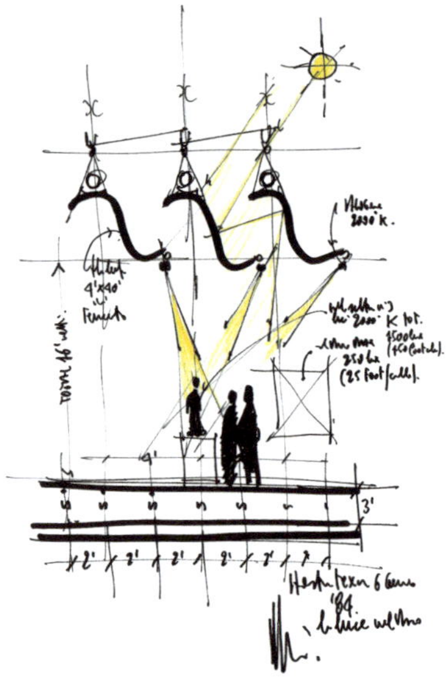

One of Renzo Piano's sketches of the roof, focusing on the daylighting that the shape of the roof will create

The museum has a modest appearance and scale. Its materiality recognizes the residential neighborhood with its gray cypress siding, white steel frame and glass. The interior spaces show black stained wood floors, white walls and floor-to-ceiling glass walls surrounding the interior garden courtyards. The only decorative detail of the elegantly discreet museum building is the ceiling above the galleries and arcade. The galleries are covered by a transparent horizontal glass roof and 300 ferro-cement wave-like curved prefabricated elements spanning across the gallery spaces to filter and diffuse natural light. The ferro-cement leaves form an 11.4-meter (37.5-foot) structural composite beam in combination with the ductile iron trusses. The leaves were prefabricated in a one-sided mold using a mix of white aggregate and cement, and vary in thickness.

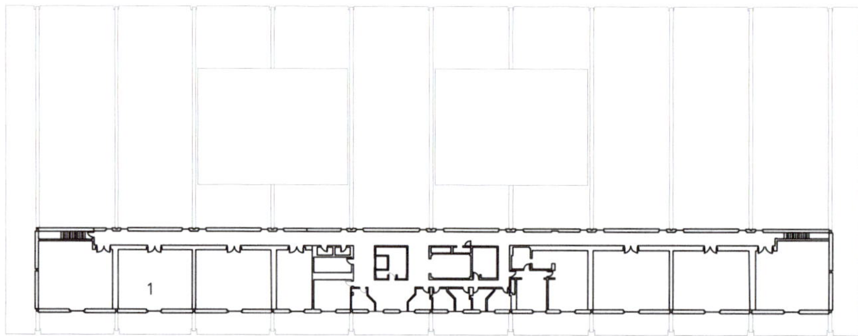

Second floor plan

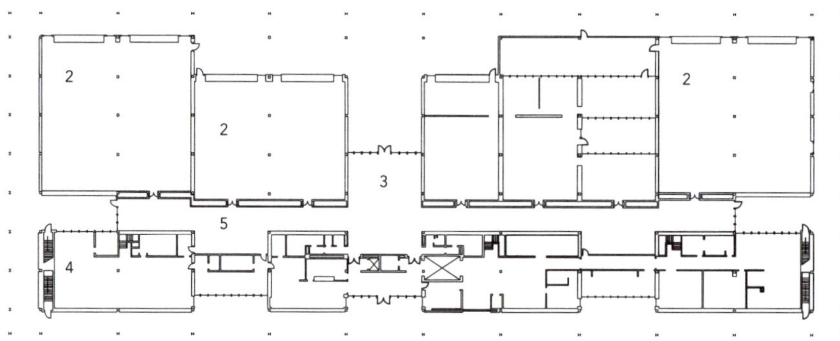

Ground floor plan

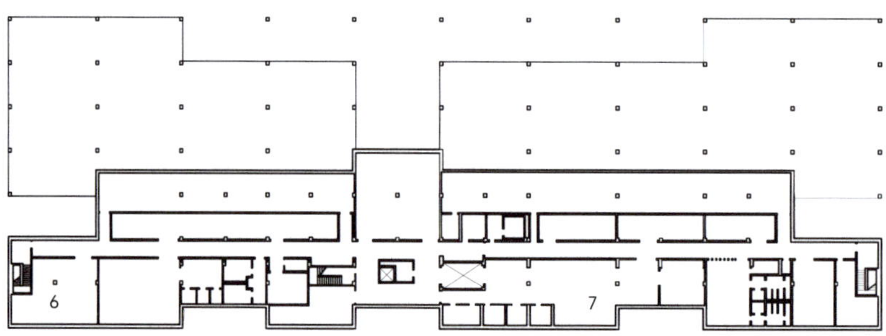

Basement floor plan

1 Storage
2 Gallery
3 Lobby
4 Office bar
5 Promenade bar
6 Laboratory
7 Shop

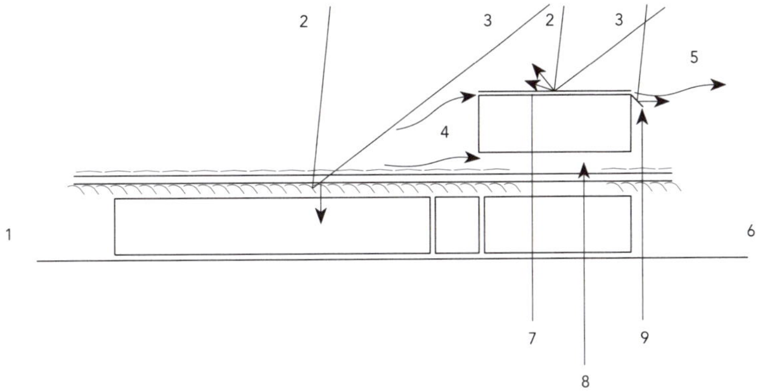

Environmental responses
1 North
2 Summer sun
3 Winter sun
4 Wind
5 Natural ventilation
6 South
7 Reflective roof
8 Mechanical zone
9 Sun screen

An interior view of one of the gallery spaces within the museum, brilliantly capturing the natural daylighting that changes the environment of the building

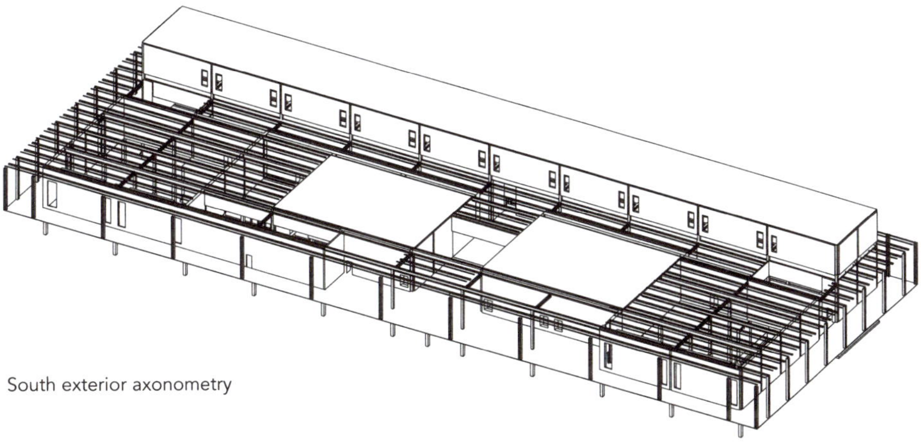

South exterior axonometry

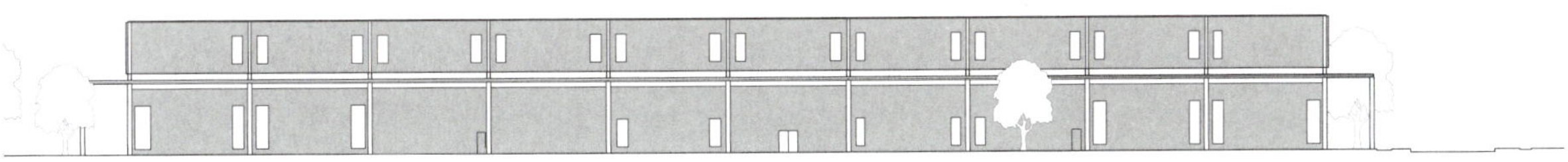

North elevation

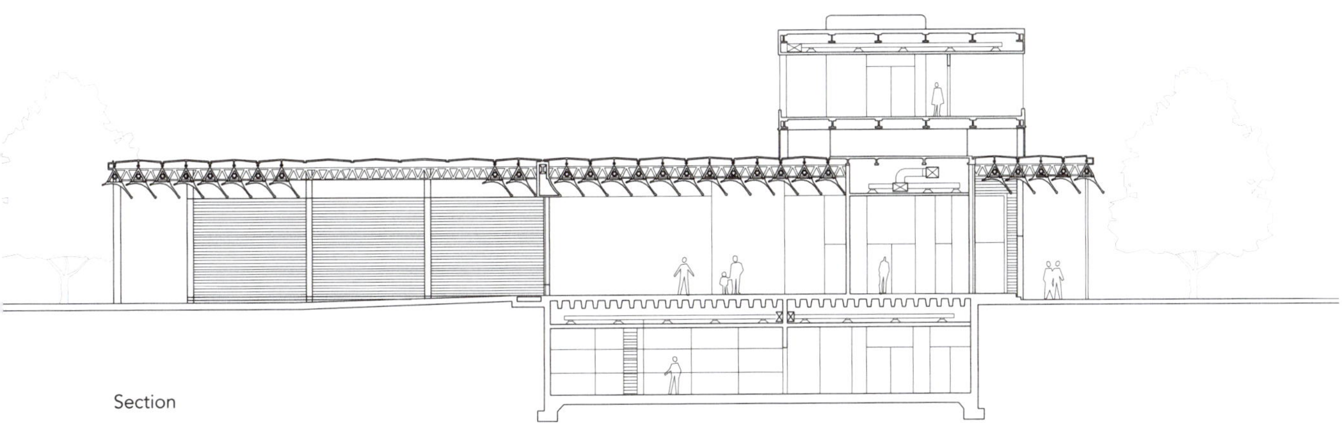

Section

The ferro-cement consisting of mortar is applied by spraying on multiple layers onto mesh reinforcement. Extreme accuracy in the arrangement of the steel mesh reinforcement was necessary to ensure structural integrity, especially at the edges measuring only 3.2 centimeters (1.25 inches) in thickness. The down-facing surface was cast against the mold and has a smooth finish; the upper face has a hand-tooled finish. The curved smooth surfaces reflect and diffuse sunlight from the underside of its neighboring eave. The structure is uncommon because of the placement of the ductile iron on top in the compression area and the ferro-cement below in the tension area; typically in composite structure it is the opposite.[3, 4]

Southeast facade of the building showing the roof extending and arcade over the sidewalk

The Menil Collection was designed for rotating exhibits from the prehistoric to the present day. The sky-lit galleries are illuminated by changing natural light that brings life to the artworks. This fixed daylight system allows the light intensity to fluctuate with the sky conditions and changes how the artwork is experienced based on the time of day as well as the season. In many ways, the building itself is a piece of interactive art where, while beautiful in its own right, certain elements emphasize and enhance the art it contains.

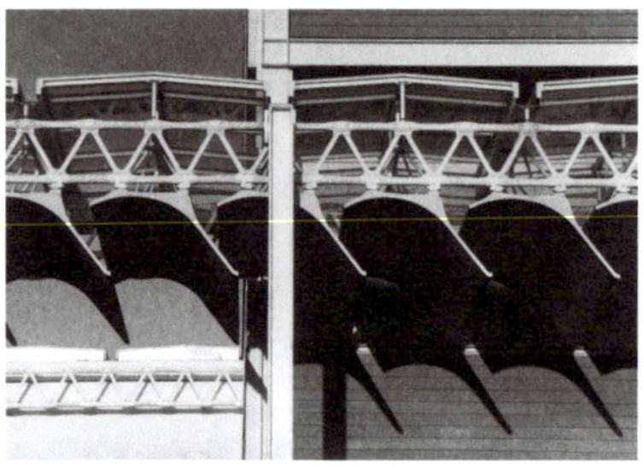

Facade detail

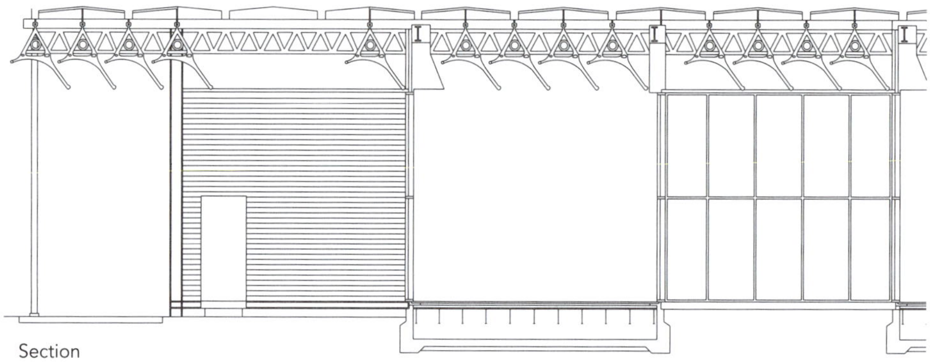

Section

Museum entrance with roof structure acting as a shading device

3 Mary K. Hurd, "Overhead and Underfoot: Concrete is Beautiful," *Concrete Construction*, May 1989 (5), pp. 456–457.

4 See also: Kenneth James Wyatt and Richard Hough, *Principles of Structure*, University of New South Wales Press, Sydney 2003.

Floating floor
The second floor of The Menil Collection is primarily used for preservation studios and offices. This floor appears to be "floating" above the museum roof.

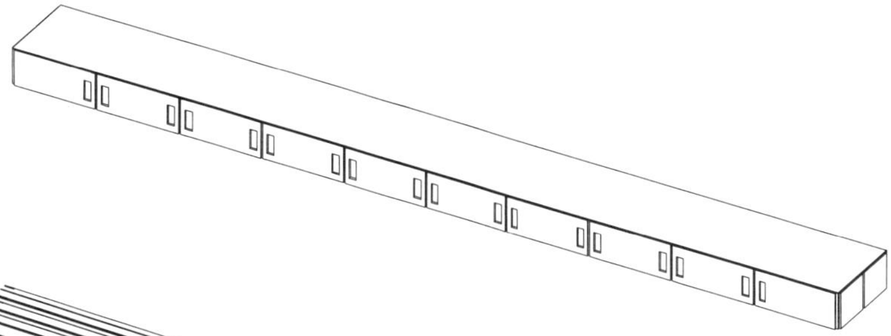

Roof
The roof is a complex series of layers designed to filter and diffuse sunlight. Pitched glass panels are supported by the structural composite beam consisting of iron trusses the ferro-cement leaves. A few spaces within the structure have flat concrete slab roofs to accommodate other needs of the program.

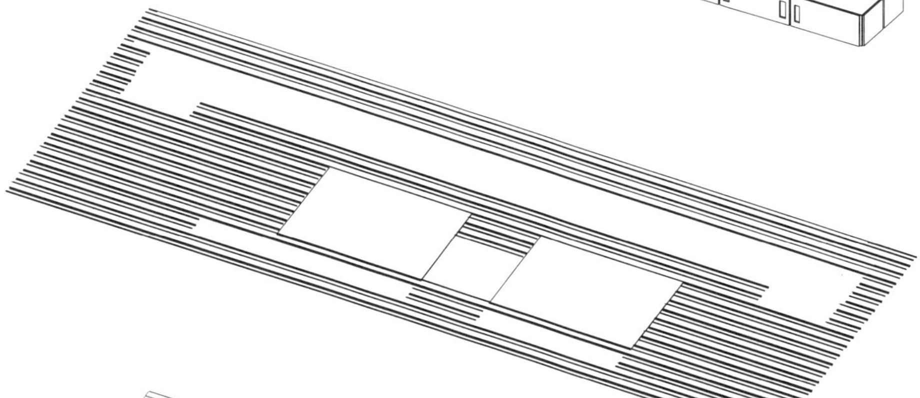

Shading fins
The prefabricated fixed ferro-cement shading leaves block the direct sunlight and diffuse and reflect the natural light into the gallery space below.

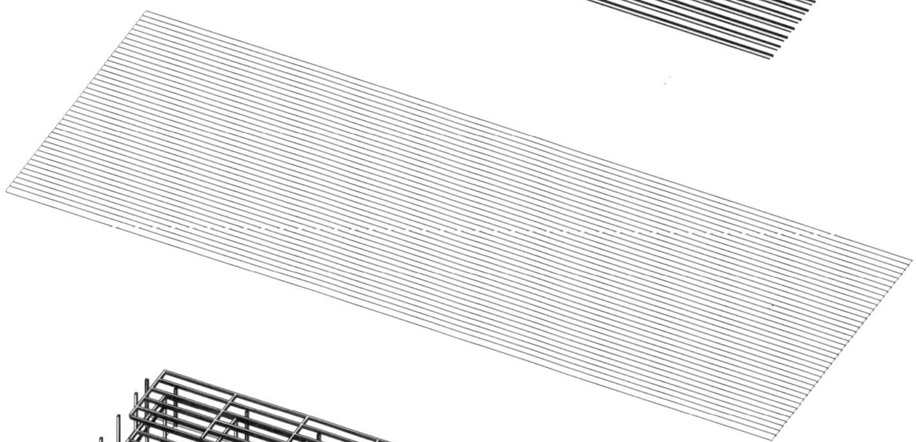

Steel structure
The primary structure is composed of steel columns, beams and trusses creating bays that are 12.2 meters (40 feet) wide and 6.1 meters (20 feet) deep. A row of steel columns around the perimeter of the building allows the roof to continue over the sidewalk.

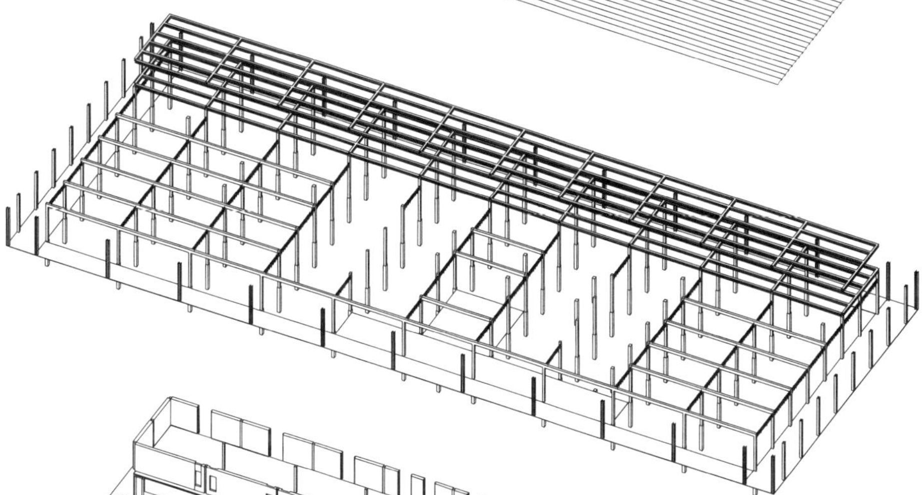

Walls
A series of non-loadbearing walls enclose and divide the gallery spaces. The exterior walls are covered in gray cypress siding that allows The Menil Collection to blend harmoniously into its residential context.

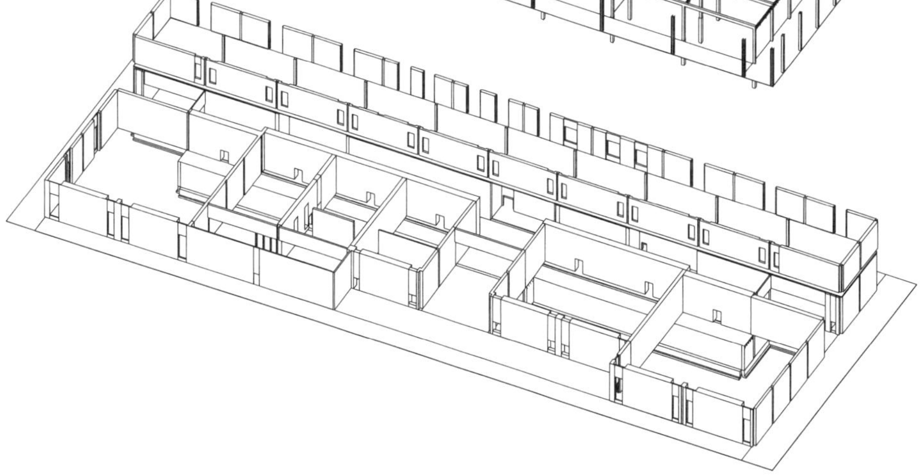

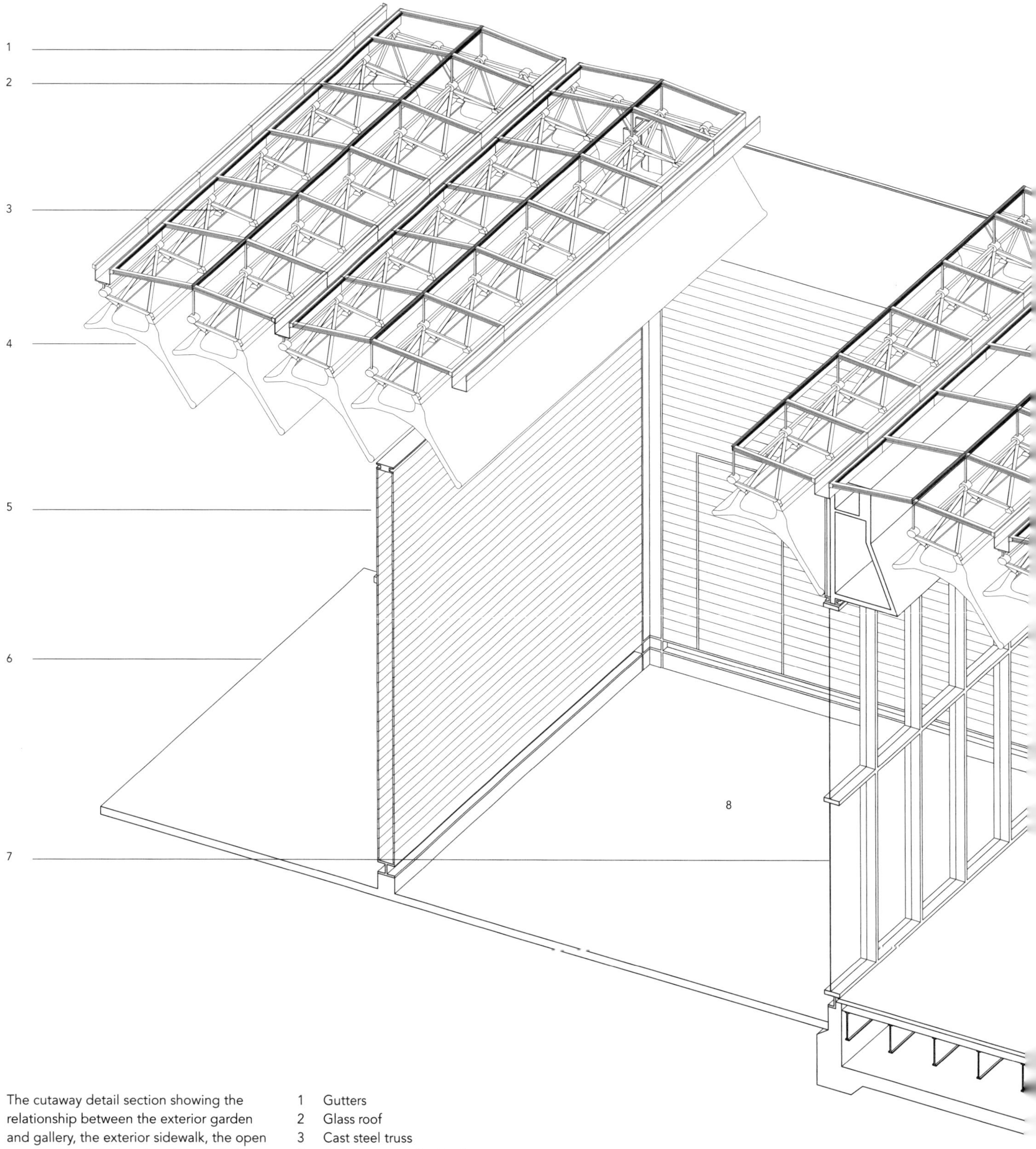

The cutaway detail section showing the relationship between the exterior garden and gallery, the exterior sidewalk, the open courtyard and the interior of the building beyond

1 Gutters
2 Glass roof
3 Cast steel truss
4 Light concrete shading leave
5 15 cm (6") cypress T&G weatherboards
6 Sidewalk
7 Curtain wall
8 Courtyard
9 Oak flooring
10 10 cm (4") concrete slab
11 Steel beam
12 Concrete footing and slab
13 Gallery space
14 Interior garden

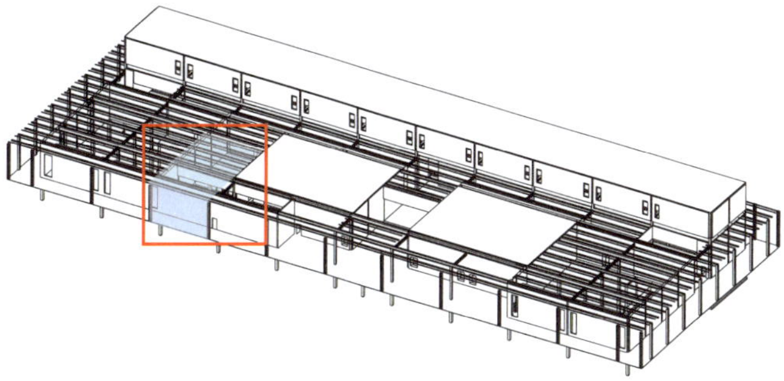

Axon key

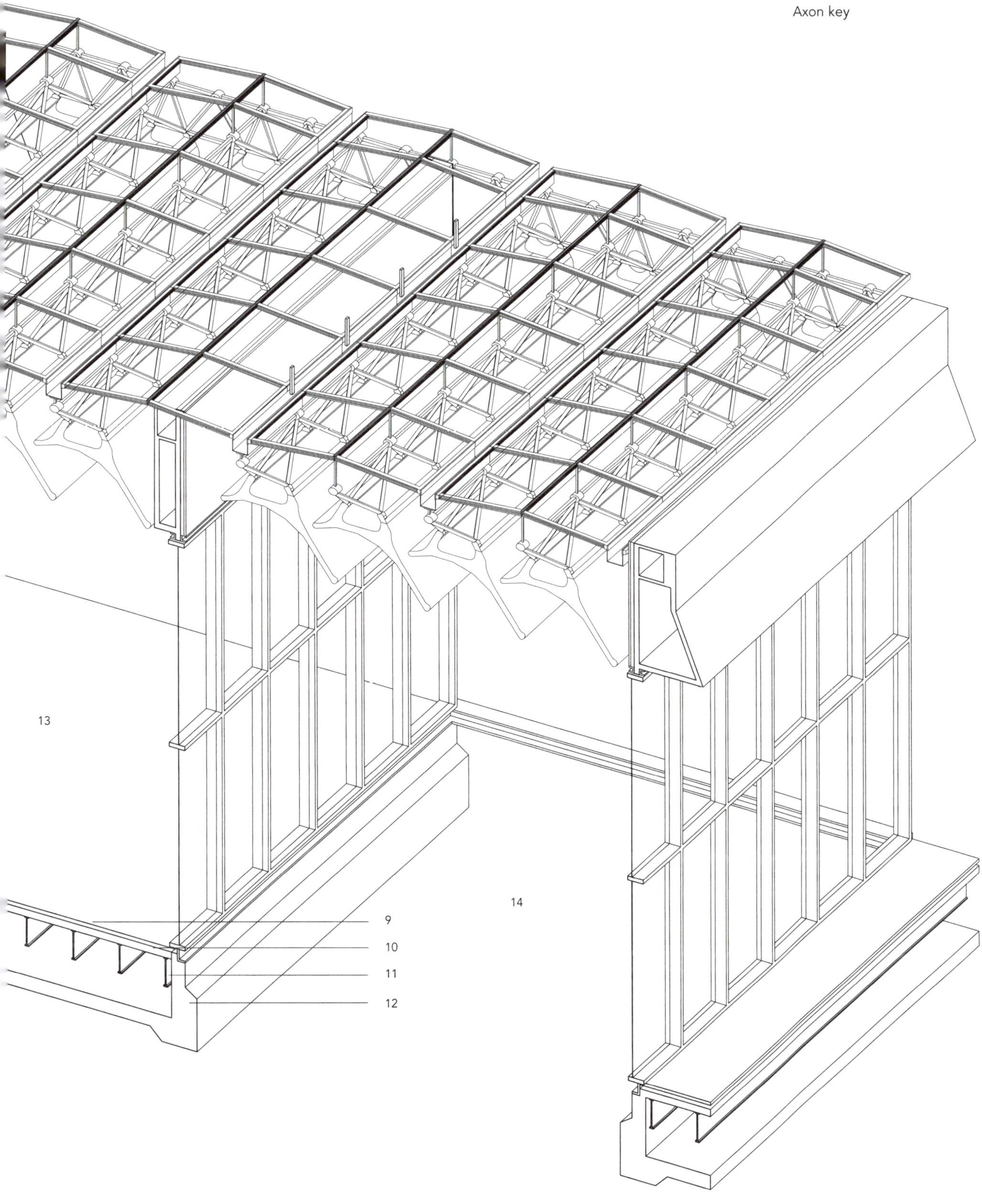

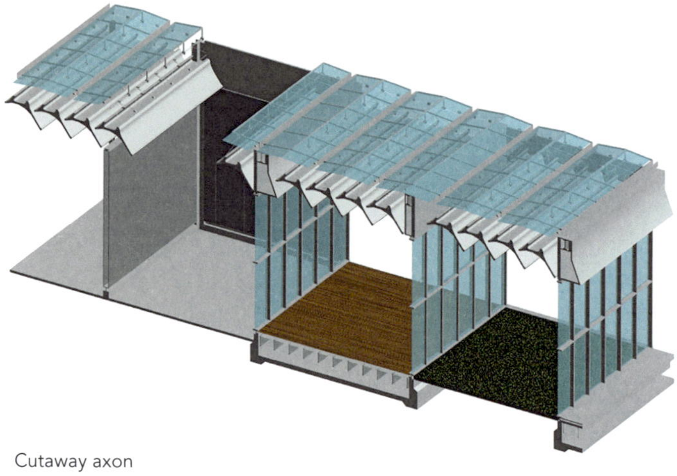

Cutaway axon

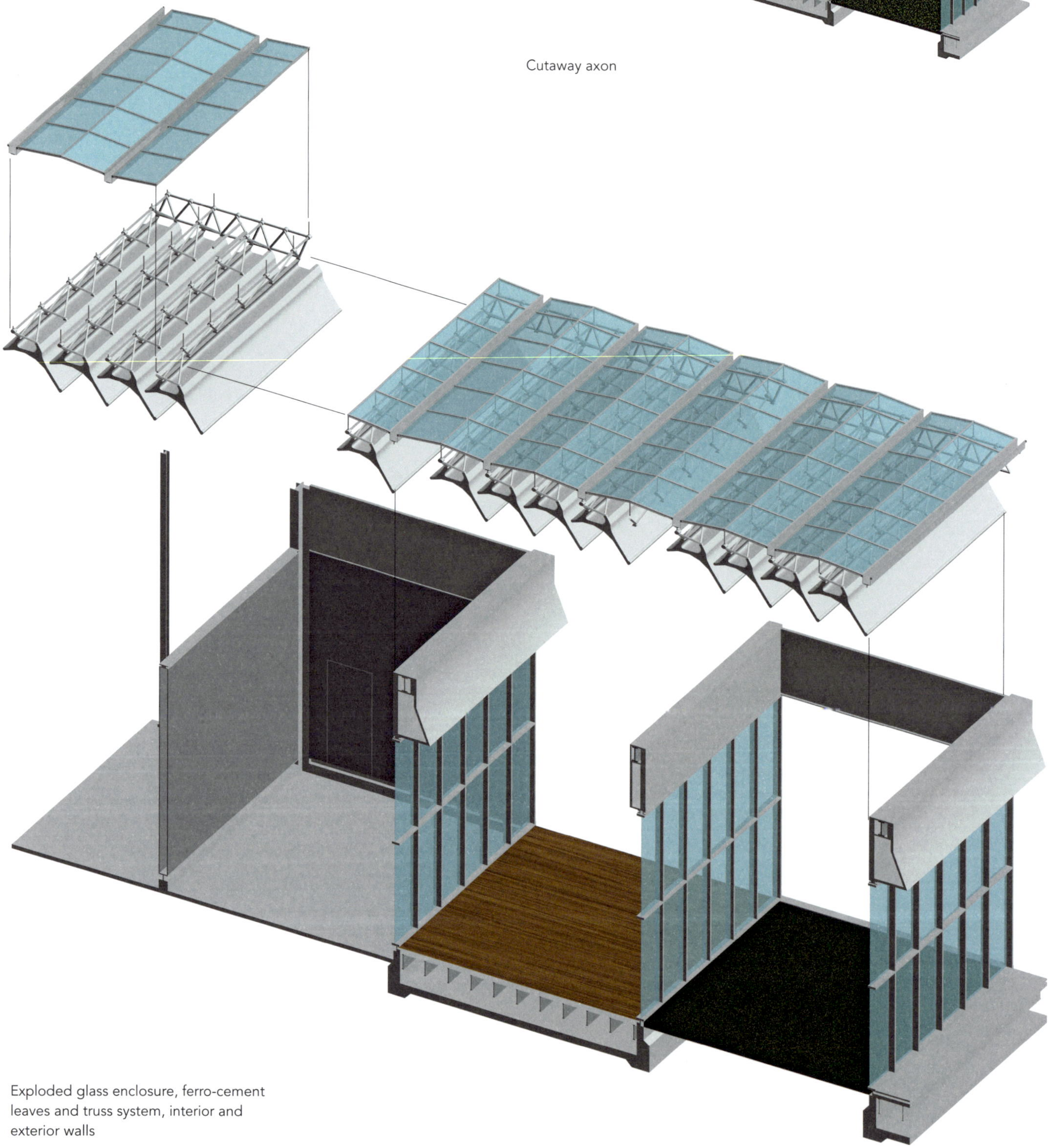

Exploded glass enclosure, ferro-cement leaves and truss system, interior and exterior walls

Shading system
Covered by a glass roof and supported by steel trusses, the cast ferro-cement leaves or baffles reflect and defuse both natural and concealed artificial lighting in the gallery spaces to protect the fragile artifacts and artworks. The ferro-cement leaves were first prototyped and tested in the Renzo Piano Building Workshop to achieve specific light qualities.

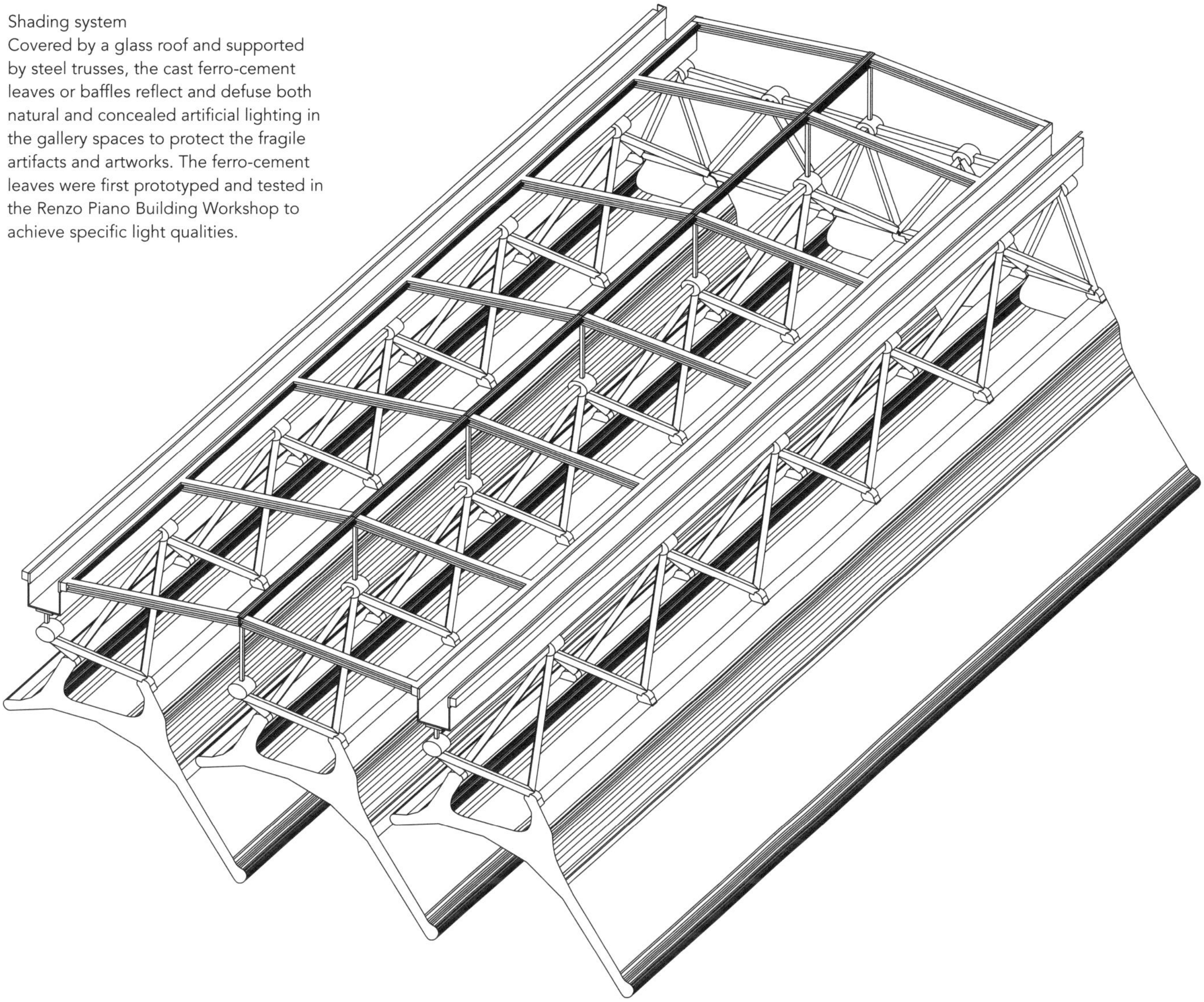

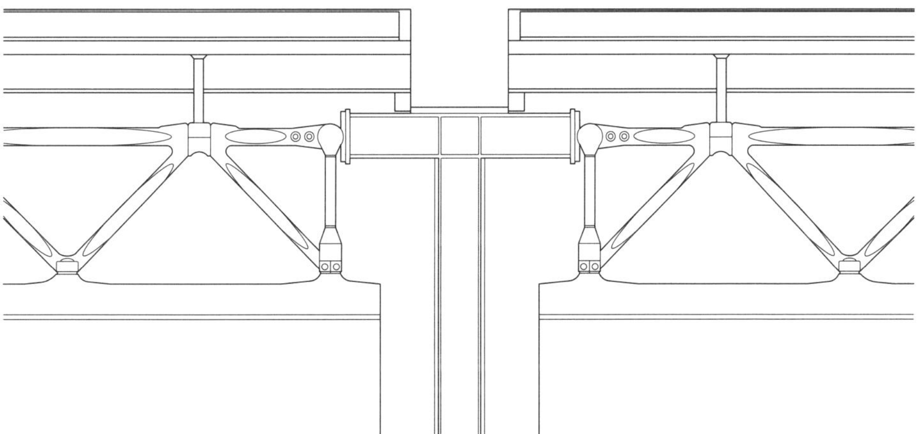

Detail shows structural connection of ferro-cement leaves to column and glass enclosure.

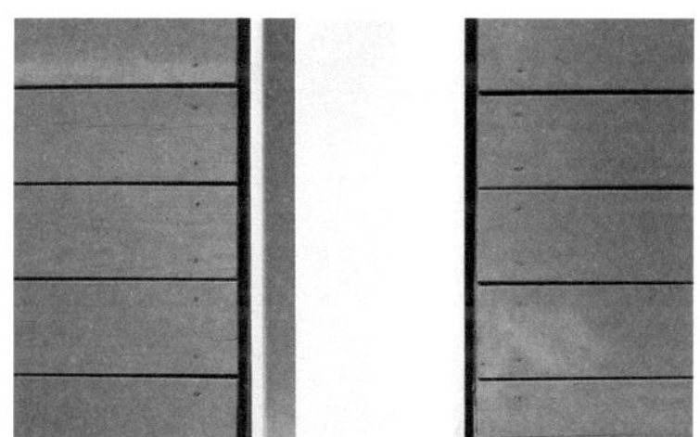

Detail of lower column connection

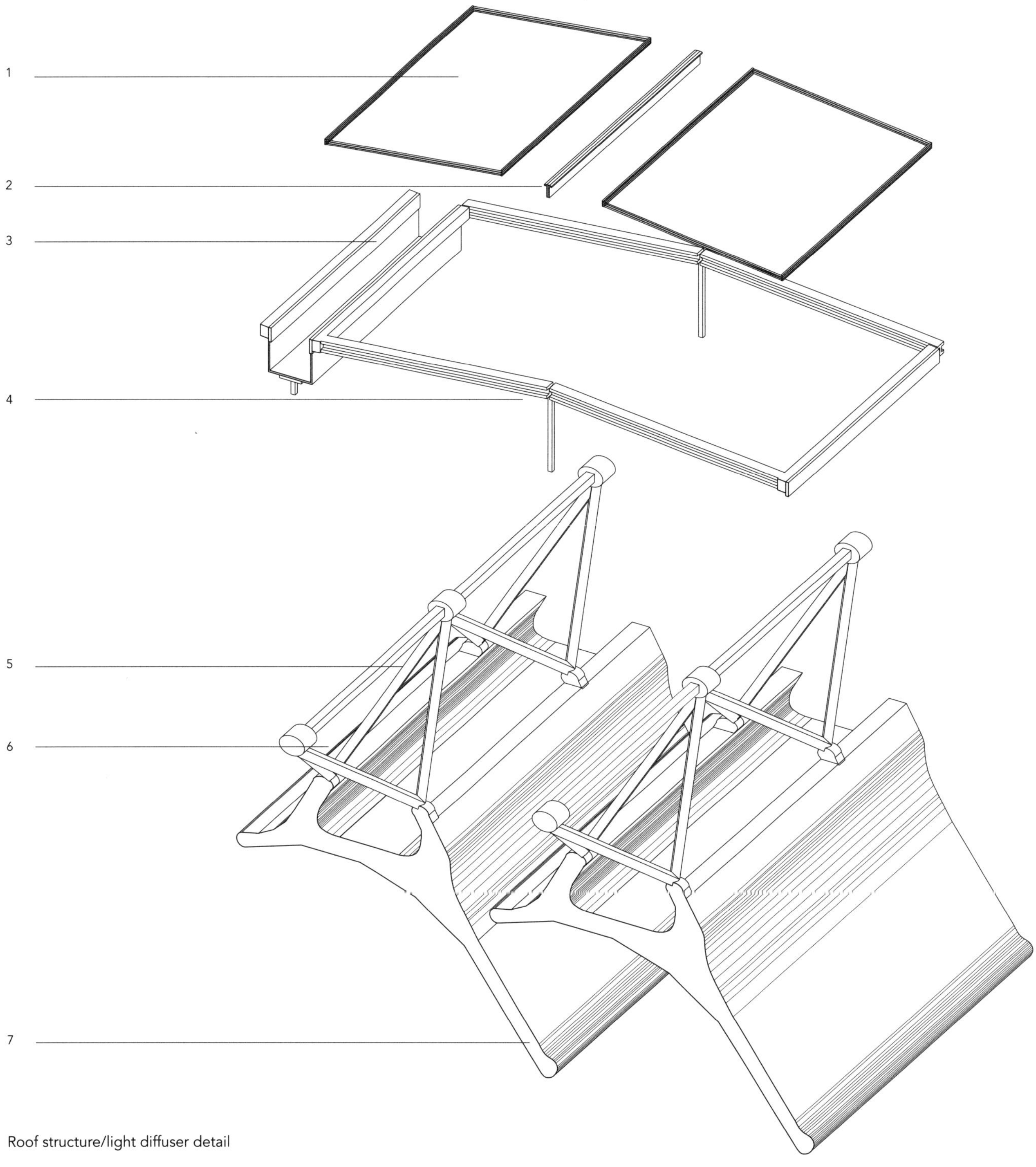

Roof structure/light diffuser detail

1 Glass enclosure
2 Steel divider
3 Gutter
4 Steel frame for glass
5 Ductile iron girder truss
6 Fastener
7 Ductile iron and ferro-cement leaf structure

Roof structure from one of the interior gallery spaces

Geographical context within Switzerland

Beyeler Foundation 1991–1997

Riehen, Basel, Switzerland

The Beyeler Foundation was founded in 1982 by the art collectors and gallery owners Ernst and Hildy Beyeler. The Beyeler Foundation was opened on October 18, 1997. Its permanent collection includes 400 classical modernist paintings and is considered one of the finest in the world. The Beyeler Foundation is located in the small town of Riehen close to Basel, Switzerland, near the border of Germany and the foothills of the Black Forest. The museum is situated in the Berower Park with its late-Baroque Villa Berower, and surrounded by old trees, a water lily pond, vineyards and views of pristine farmland with its fields and pastures. Sensitively integrated into this cultural scenery, it is a sophisticated expression, uniting nature, art and architecture harmonically.[1]

The design concept for the museum embodies simplicity and complexity at the same time. The 120-meter (395-foot) pavilion is spatially defined by four long parallel walls, each 108 meters (354 feet) long and 6.1 meters (20 feet) high, spanning from the north to the south. The walls, stone faced in volcanic rock (porphyry) from Patagonia, create a harmonious unity between building and landscape and create interior spaces with intimate character. The gallery spaces are grouped in spaces between walls 7.5 meters (25 feet) apart and open up to the landscape of rolling hills and the River Wiese at the north end and to a water lily pond reflecting the sky to the south.

The concept of natural light-filled galleries led to the development of the lightweight crystalline roof canopy measuring 28.3 by 127 meters (93 by 417 feet), which contrasts with the solid stone walls. The steel structure of the complex multilayer glass roof protrudes over the walls while shading the facades from the sun. The brise-soleil, made of white fritted glass panels, floats elegantly above the glass roof. The brise-soleil prevents direct sun from penetrating into the galleries but allows diffused light for subtle changes in light that create a lively atmosphere. Below the glass is the 1.4-meter (4.6-foot) high "loft thermal buffer zone," an air chamber to counter the effects of outdoor temperature changes. Located in this zone between the glass roof and the gallery ceiling are computer-motorized aluminum louvers that control illumination levels in the individual galleries. The louvers and electric lights are concealed by a laminated-glass ceiling and a grid of perforated metal panels combined with paper that diffuses light once more.

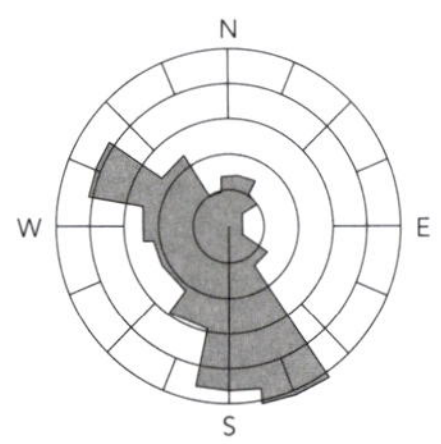

Wind rose: January

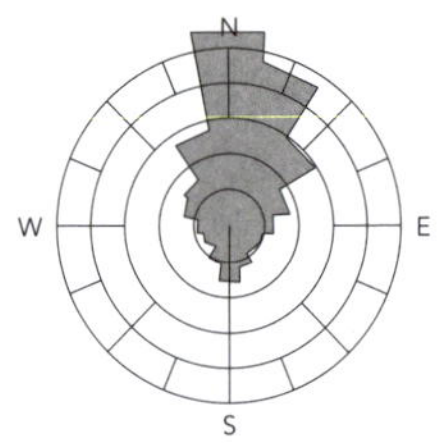

Wind rose: July

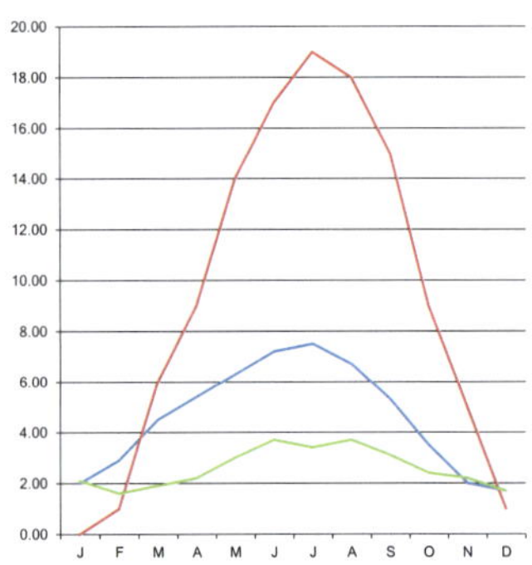

Sunlight hours/day
Temperature (°C)
Average rainfall/month (in)

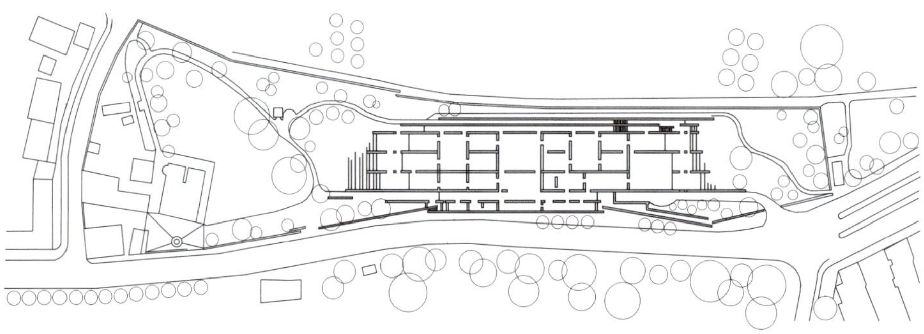

Site plan

1 Fondation Beyeler (ed.), *Renzo Piano – Fondation Beyeler, Ein Haus für die Kunst*, Birkhäuser, Basel 2001.

Ground floor plan

1 Gallery spaces
2 Lobby
3 Circulation
4 Entry

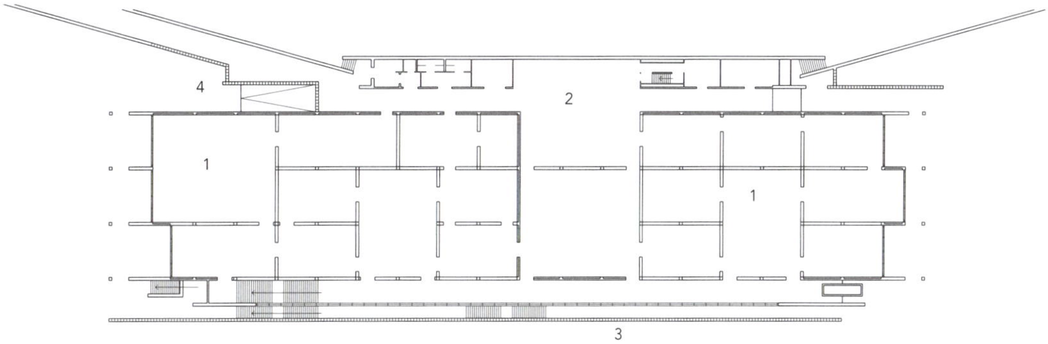

Basement floor plan

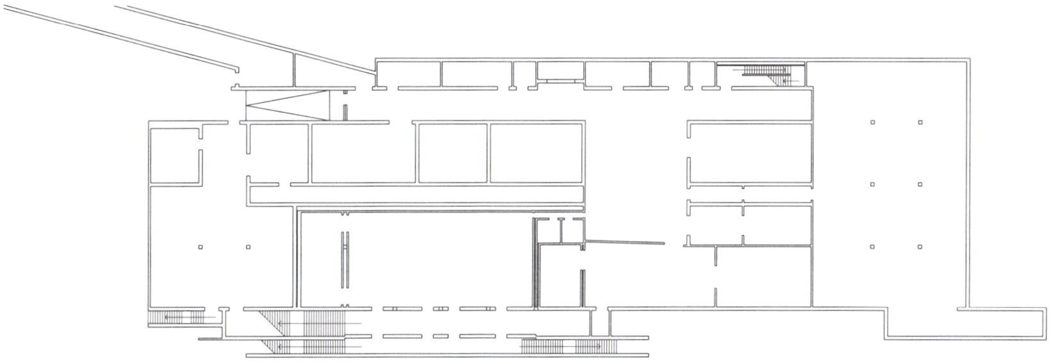

Gallery spaces and facade as seen from the exterior, interacting with pond reflections

Ernst Beyeler envisioned a calm and naturally lit atmosphere for his art collection: "… it might turn out well, if the sunshine lasts …"[2] His exhibit concept of "natural light for the art"[3] is contrary to the general practice of keeping sunlight off delicate works of art as much as possible. Renzo Piano and the RPBW team's design concept was to create a daylit gallery with a multilayer lightweight glass canopy that would modulate the effects of the sky and the sun[4] and maximize the number of hours during which the collection could be viewed by daylight. At the same time, the exposure of works of art to daylight in terms of time illuminance levels and spectral content needed to be controlled. After studying the lighting conditions in Basel, Ove Arup & Partners lighting engineers recommended target daylight illuminance values for the gallery spaces. The lighting strategy had to ensure illuminance levels within predetermined limits, therefore the multilayer roof design includes an active shading system to control interior light levels, especially in bright sky conditions.

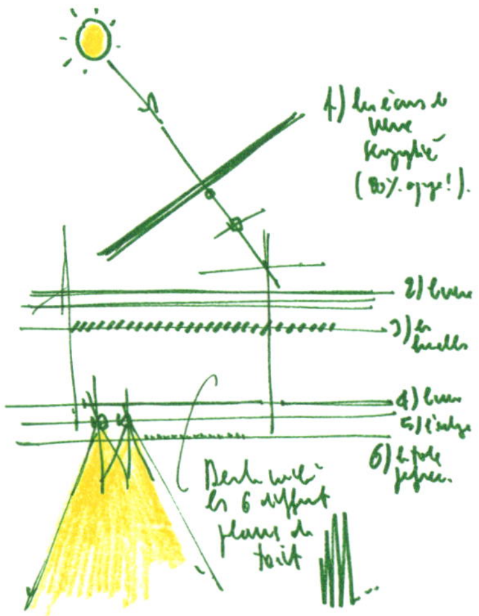

Renzo Piano sketch

The electric general lighting system located in the loft thermal buffer zones provides diffused light and is enhanced by small low-voltage spotlights placed on stems attached to the ceiling panel. The spotlights add highlighting and directional light essential for three-dimensional reception of objects and sculpture. To maintain ideal lighting levels throughout the day and during the museum's opening hours the electric lighting is designed to complement the daylighting strategy by gradually compensating for the fading daylight.

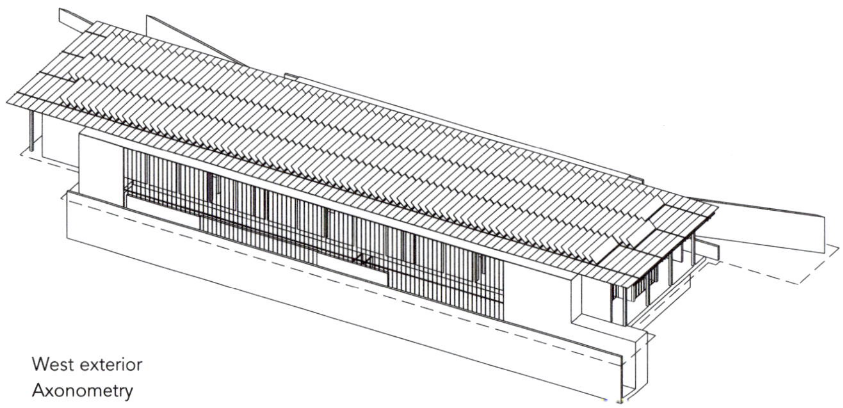

West exterior
Axonometry

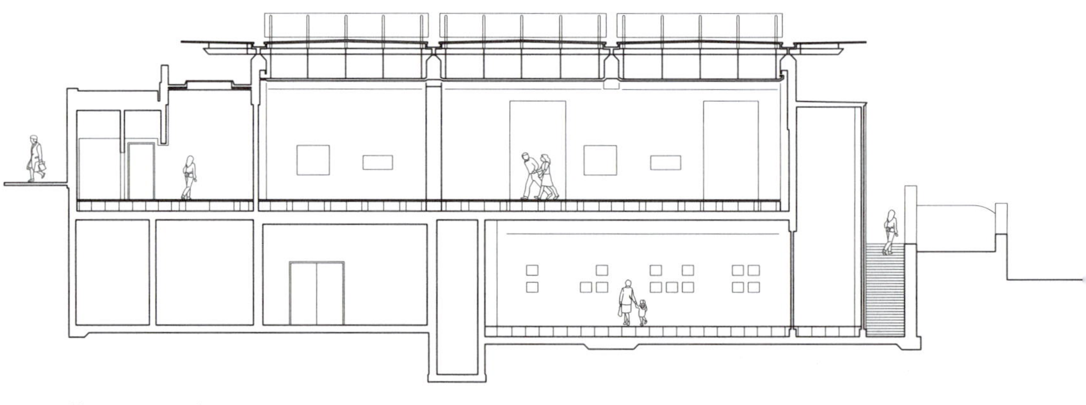

Transverse section

2 Ernst Beyeler, quoted in: Theodora Vischer (ed.), *It Might Turn Out Well, if the Sunshine Lasts. The Collection*, Hatje Cantz, Ostfildern 2017.
3 Ibid.
4 Dean Hawkes and Wayne Forster, *Energy Efficient Buildings: Architecture, Engineering, and Environment*, W. W. Norton, New York 2002.

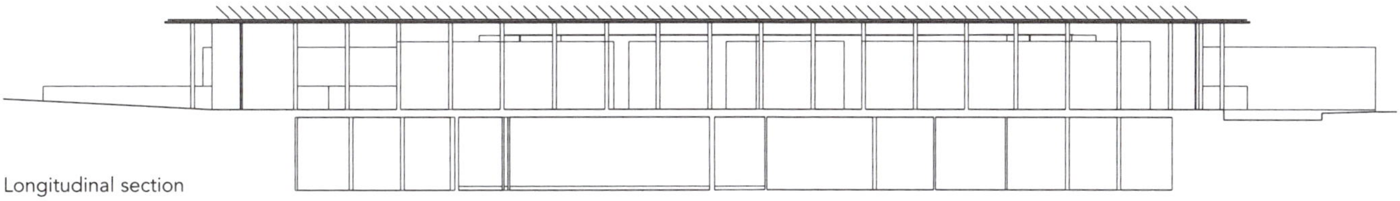

Longitudinal section

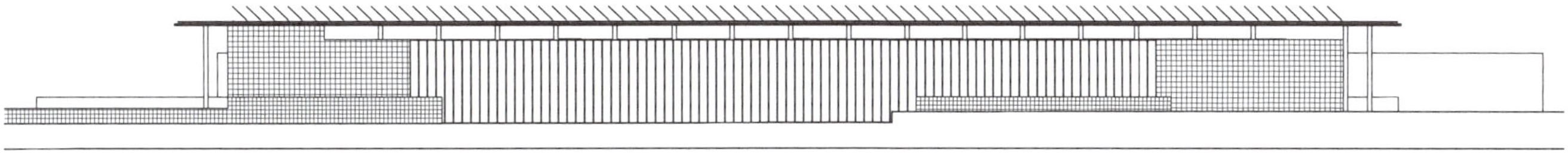

West elevation

Aerial view of the Beyeler Foundation's western facade situated in its local, natural and residential surroundings

Roof
The multilayer glass roof consists of exterior inclined glass shading, a double pane glass roof, internal automated aluminum louvers, a glass ceiling and an opaque screen.

Structure
The glass roof is supported by a steel structure resting on concrete columns.

Partition walls
The freestanding walls define the gallery spaces and allow the light ceiling to float freely above.

Glass facades
On the south and north side of the museum, the large glass facades spanning between the natural stone-clad walls and extend the gallery spaces visually into the landscape. The west facade opens the museum's promenade and circulation to the pristine farmland and rolling hills of the Black Forest.

Walls
The concrete columns of the structure are concealed in the walls resulting in long bearing walls. The four long parallel walls define the gallery spaces; wide openings allow visitors to move in between galleries.

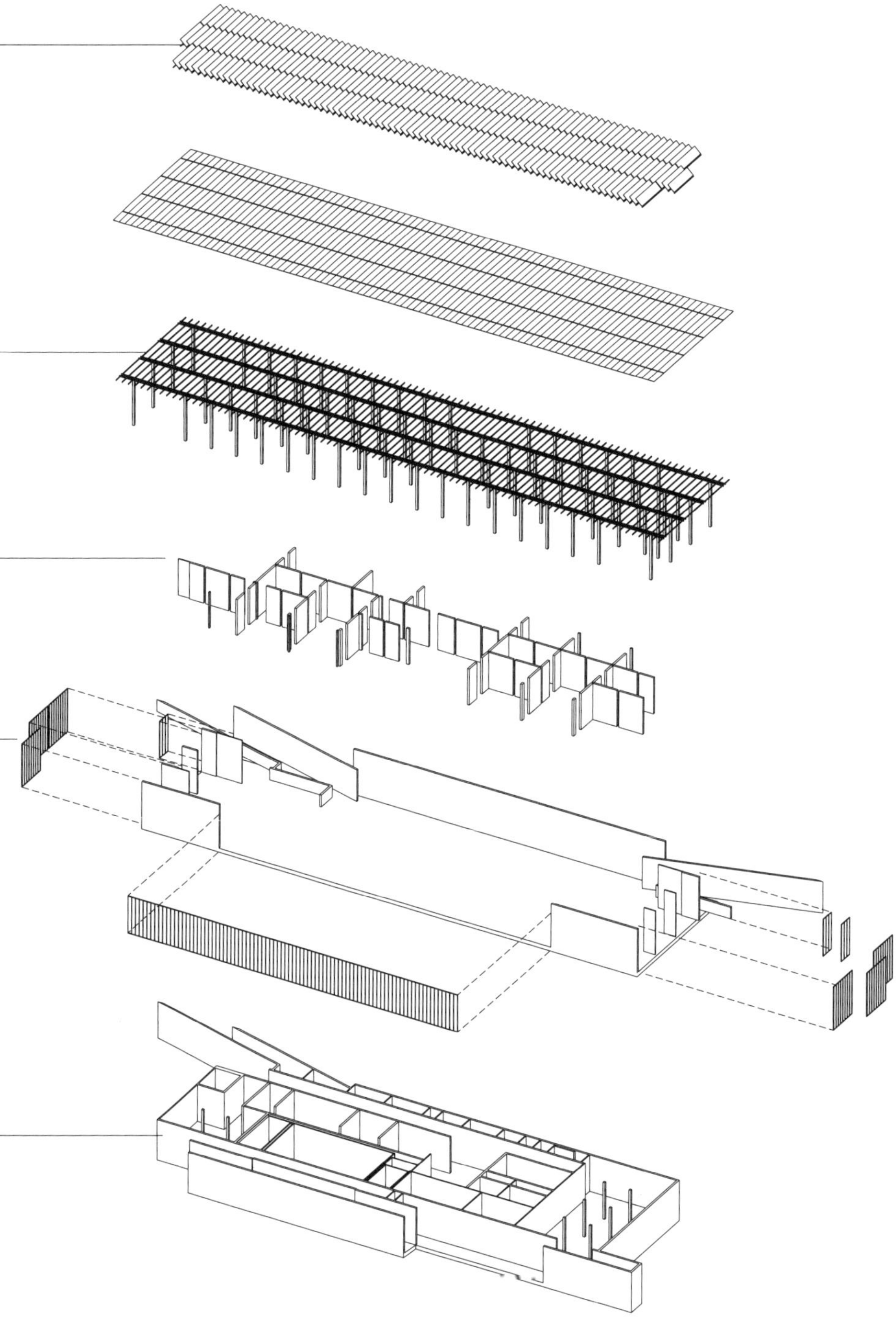

Longitudinal building section
Axonometry

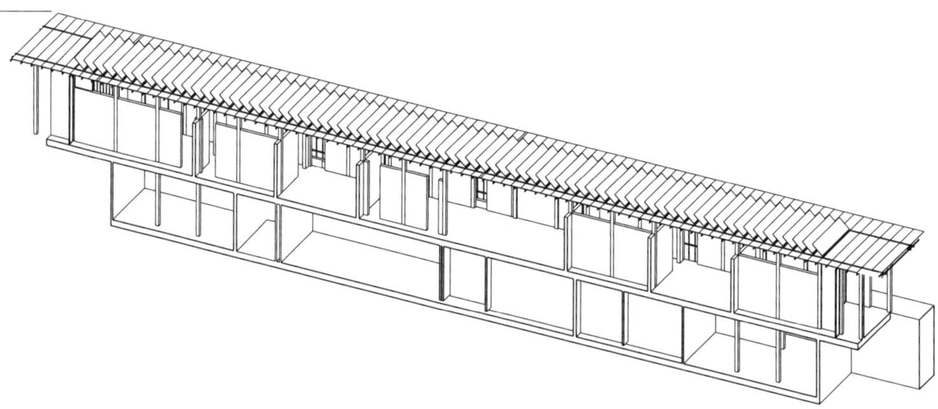

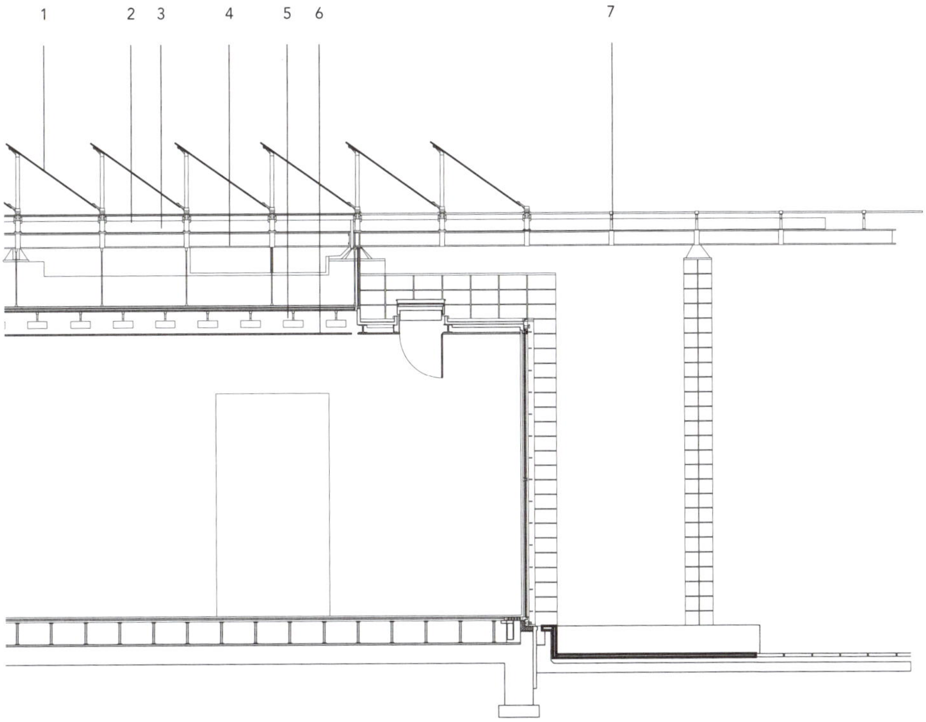

1 Brise-soleil, fritted glass sunshading, 12 mm (0.47")
2 Glass roof double glazing with ultraviolet filter
3 Airspace as buffer (thermal)
4 Laminated glass ceiling with movable shading louvers
5 Suspended lighting
6 Suspended ceiling grill
7 Steel profile

Section through west facade
The section detail shows the inclined shading panels above the glass roof and a horizontal shading screen located directly underneath the steel profile (7). The loft space within the roof also serves as an effective thermal buffer.

View of west-facing facade overlooking the farmland. The museum created a harmonious merging of building and landscape.

View of the south-facing facade, the interior walls extend into the garden and expand the gallery space visually into the landscape. The walls, clad with volcanic rock (porphyry) from Patagonia, blend harmoniously into the landscape. The refined detailed roof overhang shades the glass facades.

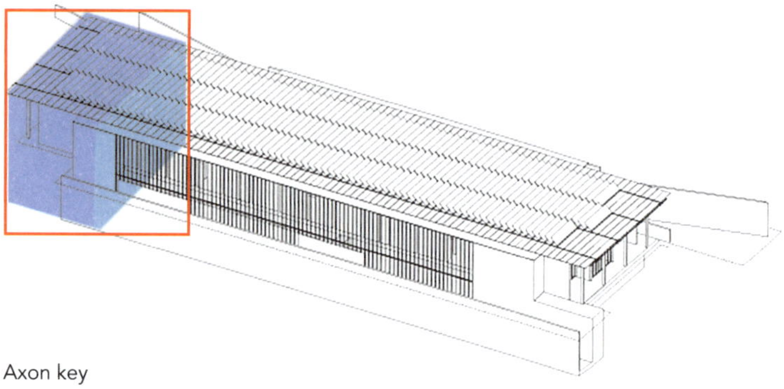

Axon key

The roof overhang on north and south elevations has horizontal white fritted glass screens to shade the facade.

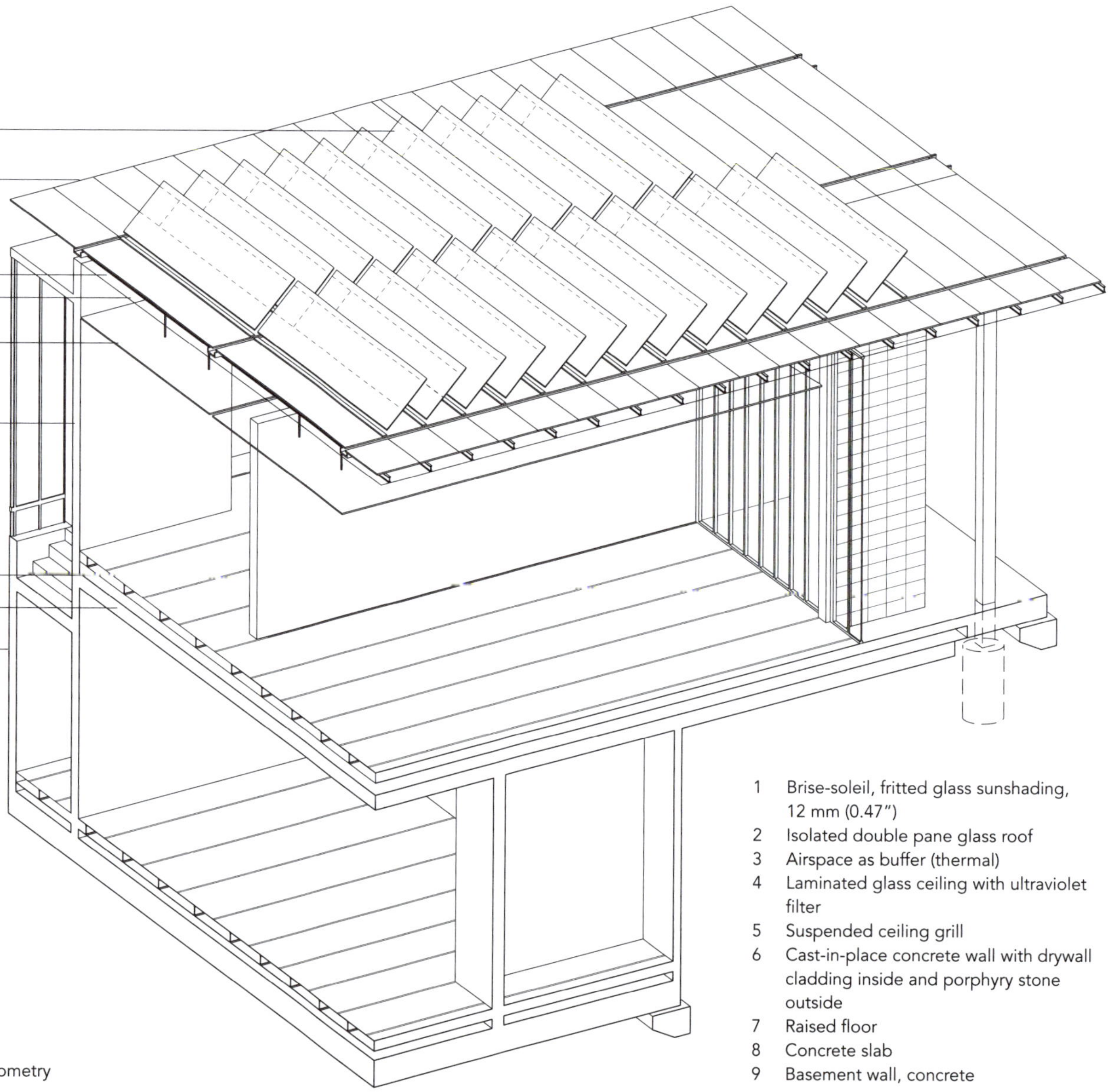

1 Brise-soleil, fritted glass sunshading, 12 mm (0.47")
2 Isolated double pane glass roof
3 Airspace as buffer (thermal)
4 Laminated glass ceiling with ultraviolet filter
5 Suspended ceiling grill
6 Cast-in-place concrete wall with drywall cladding inside and porphyry stone outside
7 Raised floor
8 Concrete slab
9 Basement wall, concrete

Interior detail
Sectional axonometry

Sheets of solid glass, double-fritted solid white, are held an angle above the glass roof to shade it from direct sun.

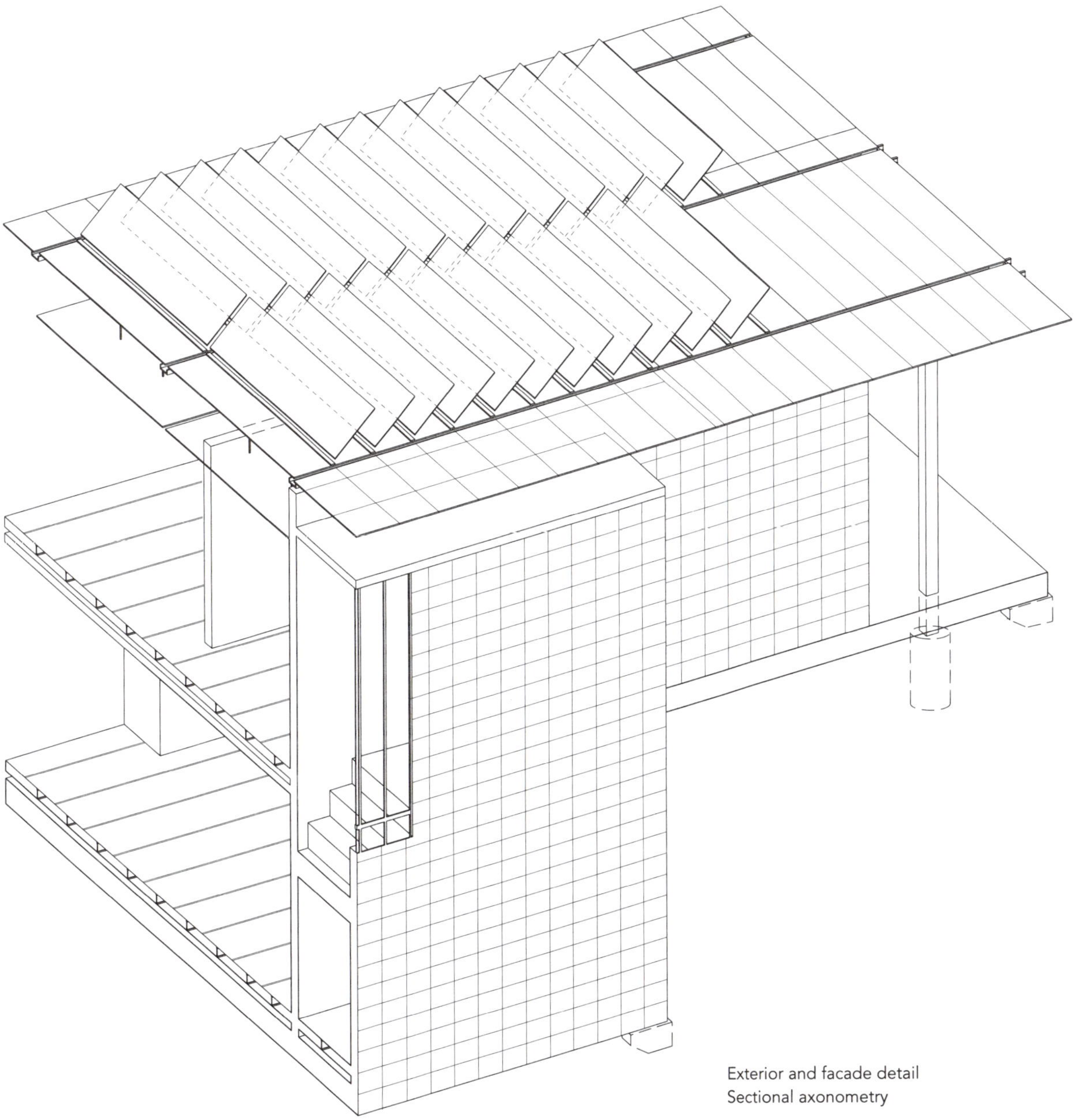

Exterior and facade detail
Sectional axonometry

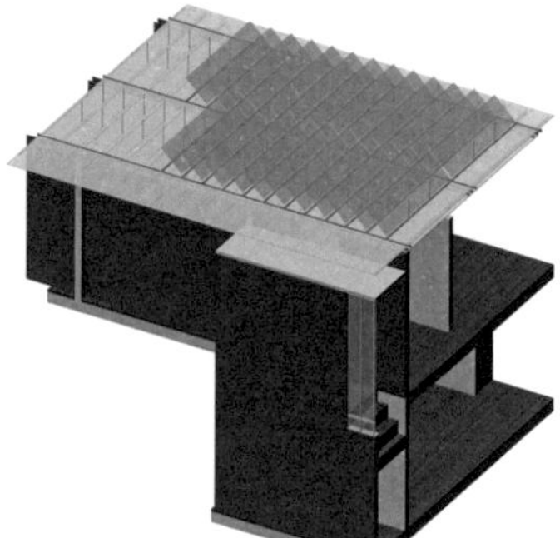

Rendered exploded axon of exterior corner section

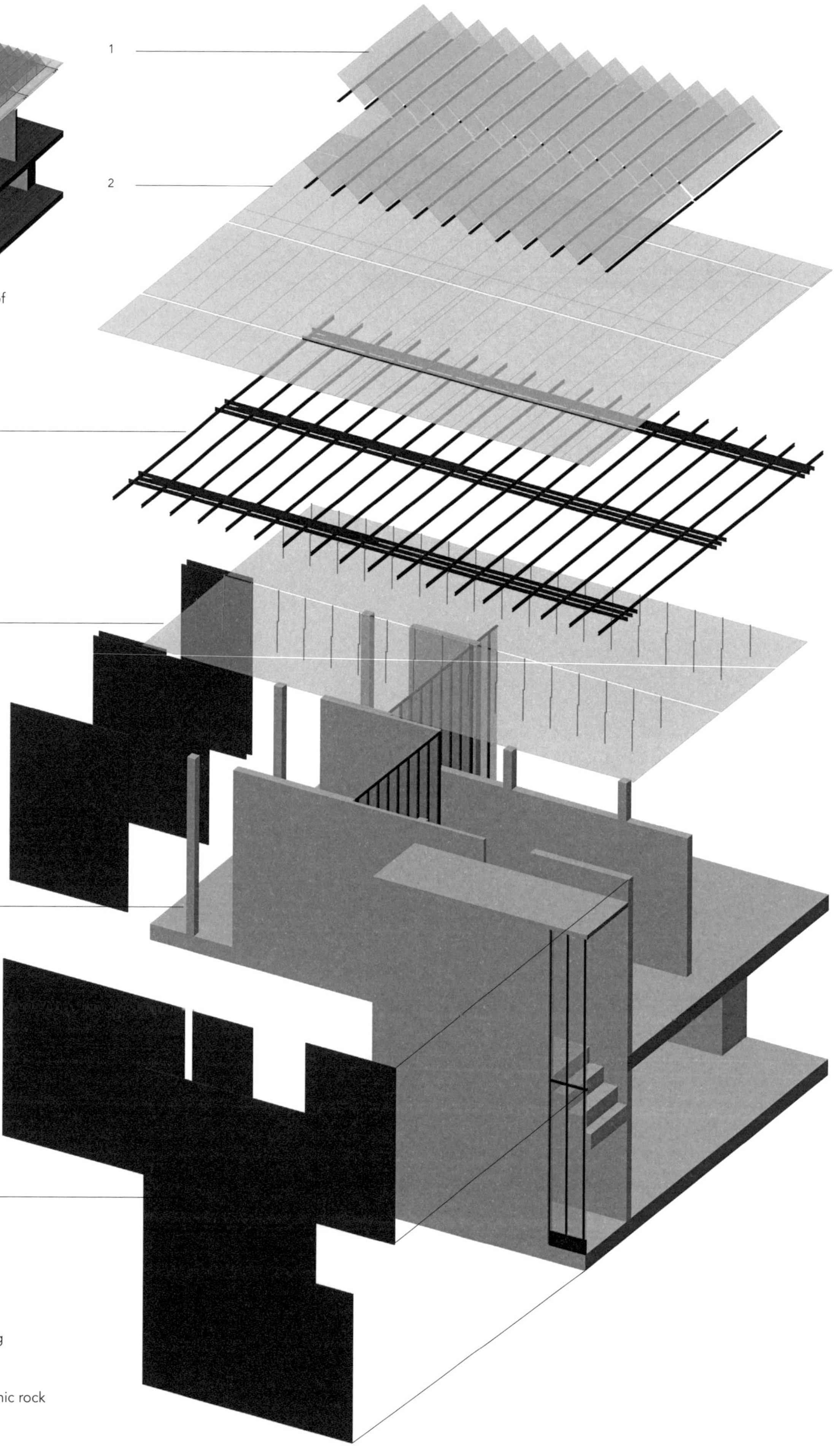

1 Inclined glass fins
2 Glass roof
3 Steel structure
4 Suspended glass ceiling
5 Concrete columns and loadbearing walls
6 Facade cladding, volcanic rock (porphyry)

Exploded axon roof detail

1 Inclined glass panel with white fritting
2 Steel tube and cast aluminum mounting
3 Stainless steel point fixing
4 Glass roof panel
5 Sheet steel gutter, insulated
6 Beam grid of steel I-sections

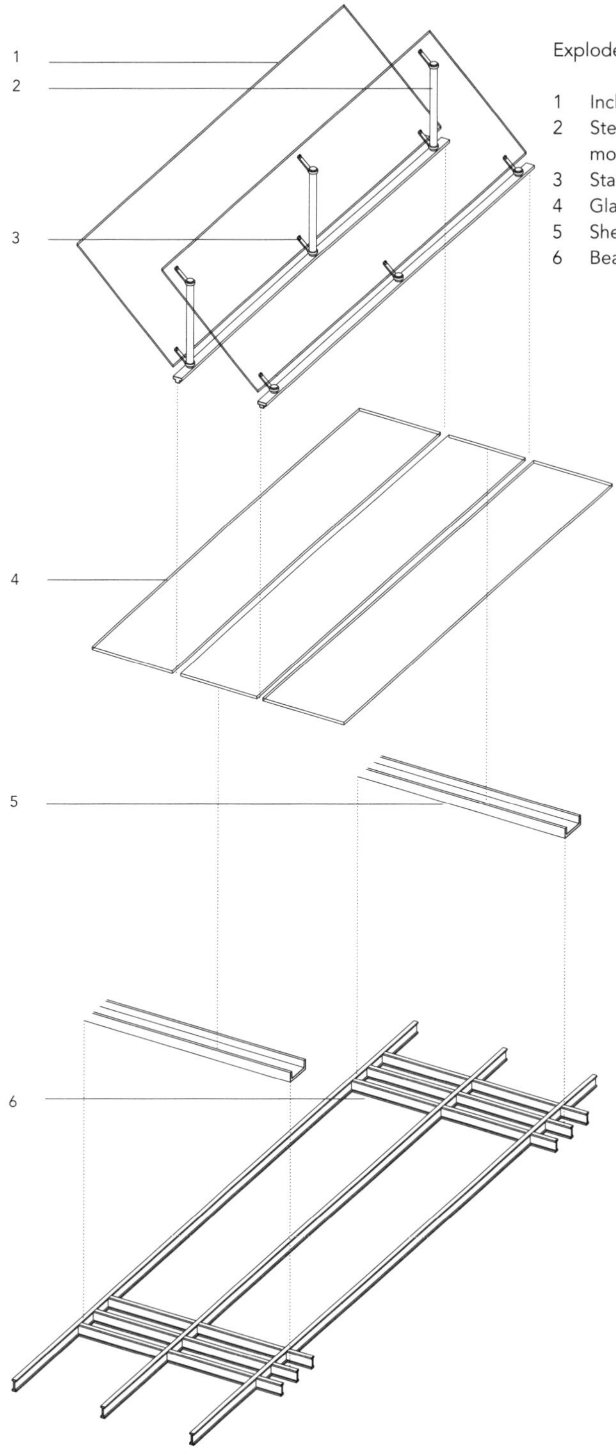

Roof section detail
Detail drawing of the structural stems and fasteners holding the sun-shading glass panels

1 Stainless steel point fixing
2 Sunshading, toughened safety glass, panel white enamel finish to underside, 12 mm (0.47")
3 Cast aluminum mounting
4 Steel tube, 60 mm (2.4") diameter
5 Glass roof, double glazing, safety glass with alarm sensor

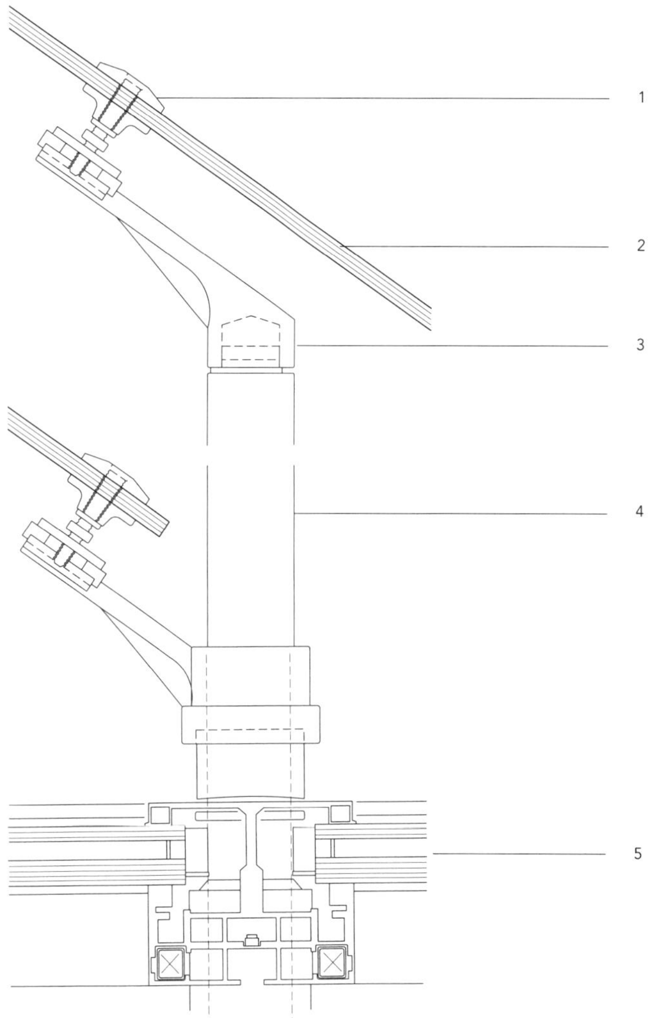

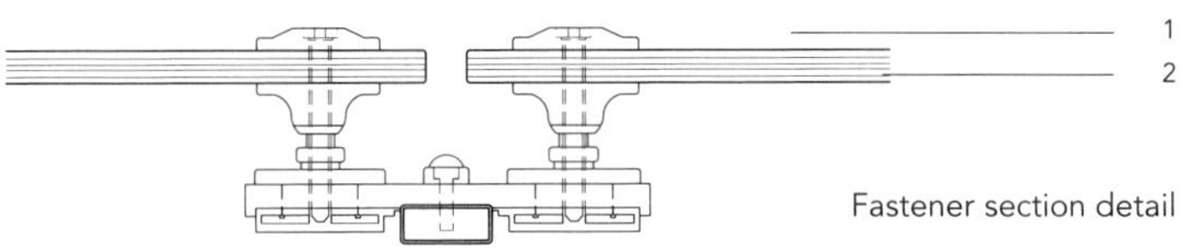

Fastener section detail

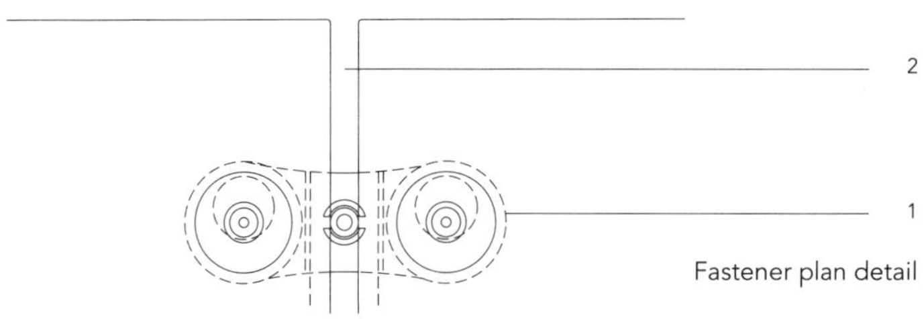

Fastener plan detail

Fastener details

1 Stainless steel joint connection
2 Sun-shading glass panel, 12 mm (0.47")

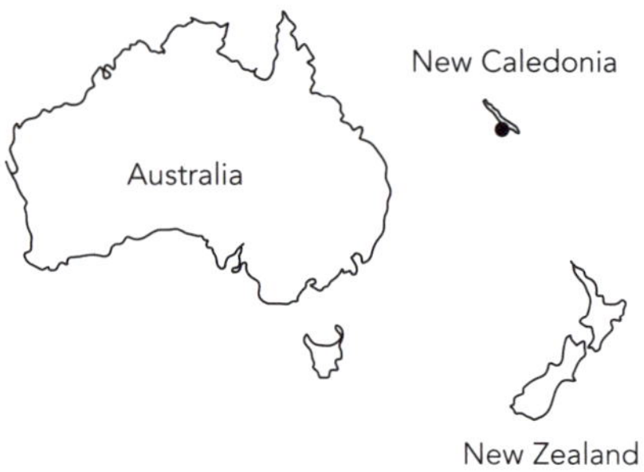

Geographical context within New Caledonia/France

Jean-Marie Tjibaou Cultural Center 1991–1998

Nouméa, New Caledonia

The Jean-Marie Tjibaou Cultural Center is located to the east of the capital Nouméa, on the island of New Caledonia, a French overseas territory in the South Pacific. The cultural center was named after the French-Kanak politician and leader of the Kanak independence movement Jean-Marie Tjibaou,[1] who had the vision to display the linguistic and artistic heritage of the Kanak people in a cultural center. The center is devoted to and celebrates the vernacular Kanak culture, the indigenous culture of New Caledonia.

The architecture of the center was inspired by the Kanak people's profound connections with nature. This is represented by the landscape and the architectural concept. The center itself is designed similarly to the traditional Kanak villages. The communities are made up of a series of huts that distinguish the different functions and hierarchies of the tribes and contain a central alley along which the huts are arranged.

The 7,000-square meter (75,350-square foot) cultural center consists of exhibition spaces, a multimedia library, the cafeteria, as well as conference and lecture rooms. The building is made up of three "villages" comprised of ten huts or "Great Houses." They vary in size measuring between 55–140 square meters (590–1500 square feet) in area and 20–28 meters (66–92 feet) in height, and there is a horizontal structure with the museum programs. The "Great Houses" are organized and linked by a long, gently curving enclosed walkway, the "alley." The "villages" are arranged in a progression from the most public program in the first "village" to the quieter atmosphere of the east "village," representing the connection between the natural landscape and the built structures in the Kanak traditions.

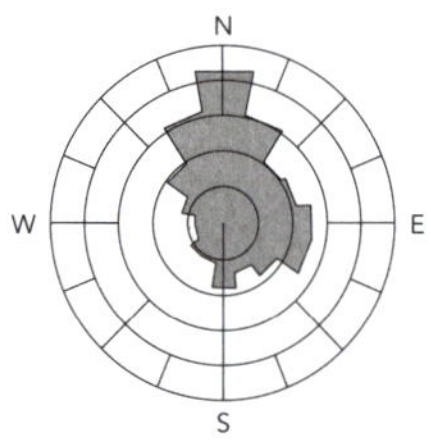

Wind rose: January

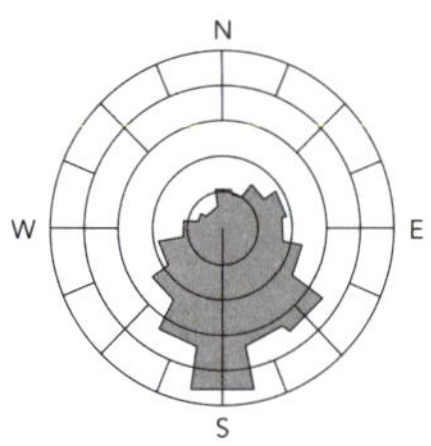

Wind rose: July

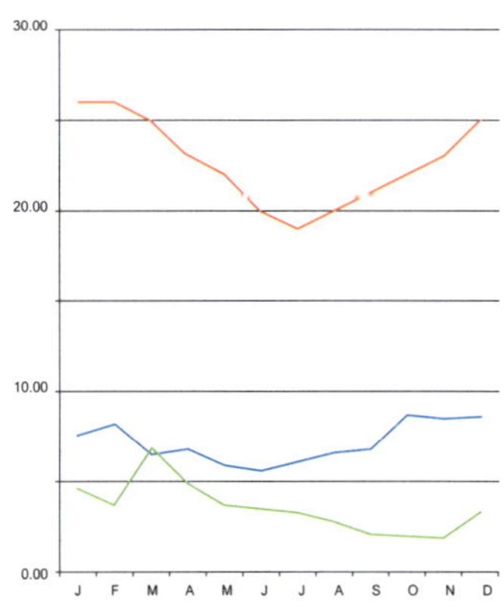

- Sunlight hours/day
- Temperature (°C)
- Average rainfall/month (in)

Site plan

1 January 30, 1936 to May 4, 1989 (assassinated)

Coastal view of the Great Houses and the cultural center

Aerial view of the cultural center

The project blends the Kanaks' traditional building technique using wood and stone with modern technologies and materials such as glass, aluminum and steel. For the vertical structural components of the houses, modern laminated wood technology and Iroko wood was used. The passive ventilation system of the huts uses the monsoon winds coming in from the sea and eliminates the need for mechanical air-conditioning.

The facade consists of two layers: the inner layer is the building envelope, with insulated prefabricated facade panels and glass windows, and the outer layer is the shading screen with slatted wood and louvers. The adjustable louvers of the external facade layer were designed to regulate the airflow and shade the windows from the sun. Full-scale mock-ups of the facade system were tested in a wind tunnel to ensure the desired environmental performance. The vertical extension of the outer facade shades the roof from the direct sun and helps to control the temperature in the interior spaces. The Jean-Marie Tjibaou Cultural Center's exhibitions are rotated throughout the year; this allows for higher illuminance values in the exhibition spaces as normally acceptable for light-sensitive artwork due to the shorter annual exposure time.

View of the cultural center overlooking the narrow Tina peninsula and the Pacific Ocean

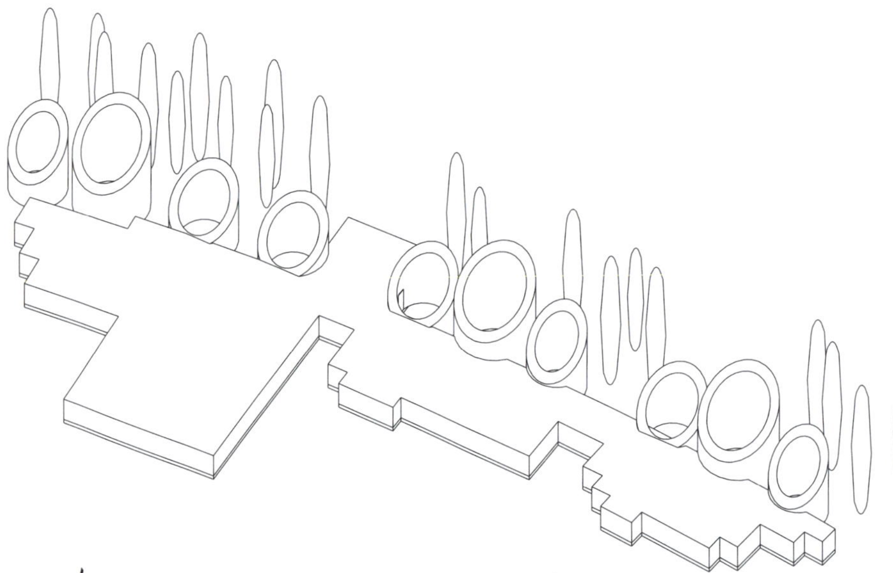

Massing model
Axonometry

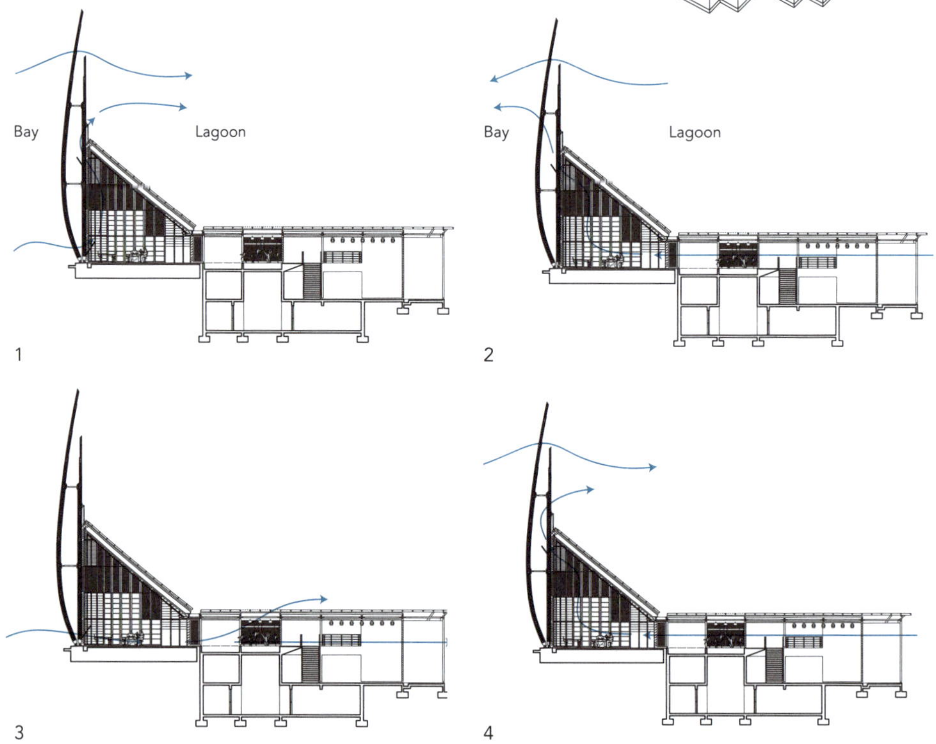

Wind/ventilation diagrams
The building's natural ventilation concept utilizes two wind forces to push or pull hot air out of the top of the double envelope: the Venturi effect and the stack effect. The shape of the facade creates a Venturi effect, which pulls hot, stale air up through the space between the two facade layers and out of the building. In light wind, the building uses the stack effect by opening the series of horizontal louvers at the base and top of the interior facade to allow air to rise and escape the interior space. The louvers automatically open and close in tandem and are controlled by an integrated computer system that constantly adjusts to the wind speed.

1 Wind from the bay generates ventilation through the thermal chimney of the double-skin structure.
2 Wind from the lagoon generates negative pressure through the thermal chimney.
3 Cross-ventilation scheme; all windows are open.
4 Still air or light wind; passive ventilation creates a stack effect through thermal chimney.

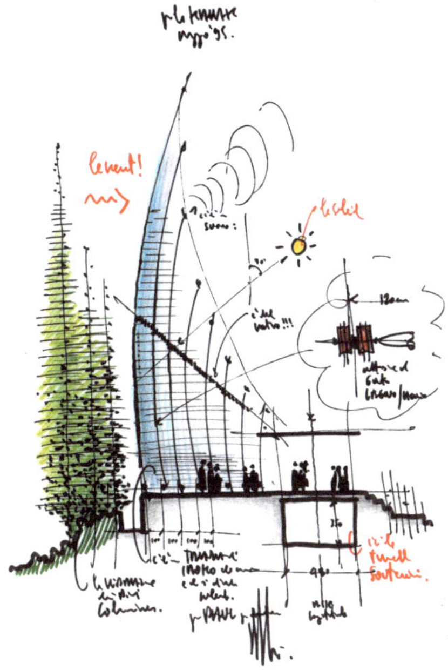

Renzo Piano sketch

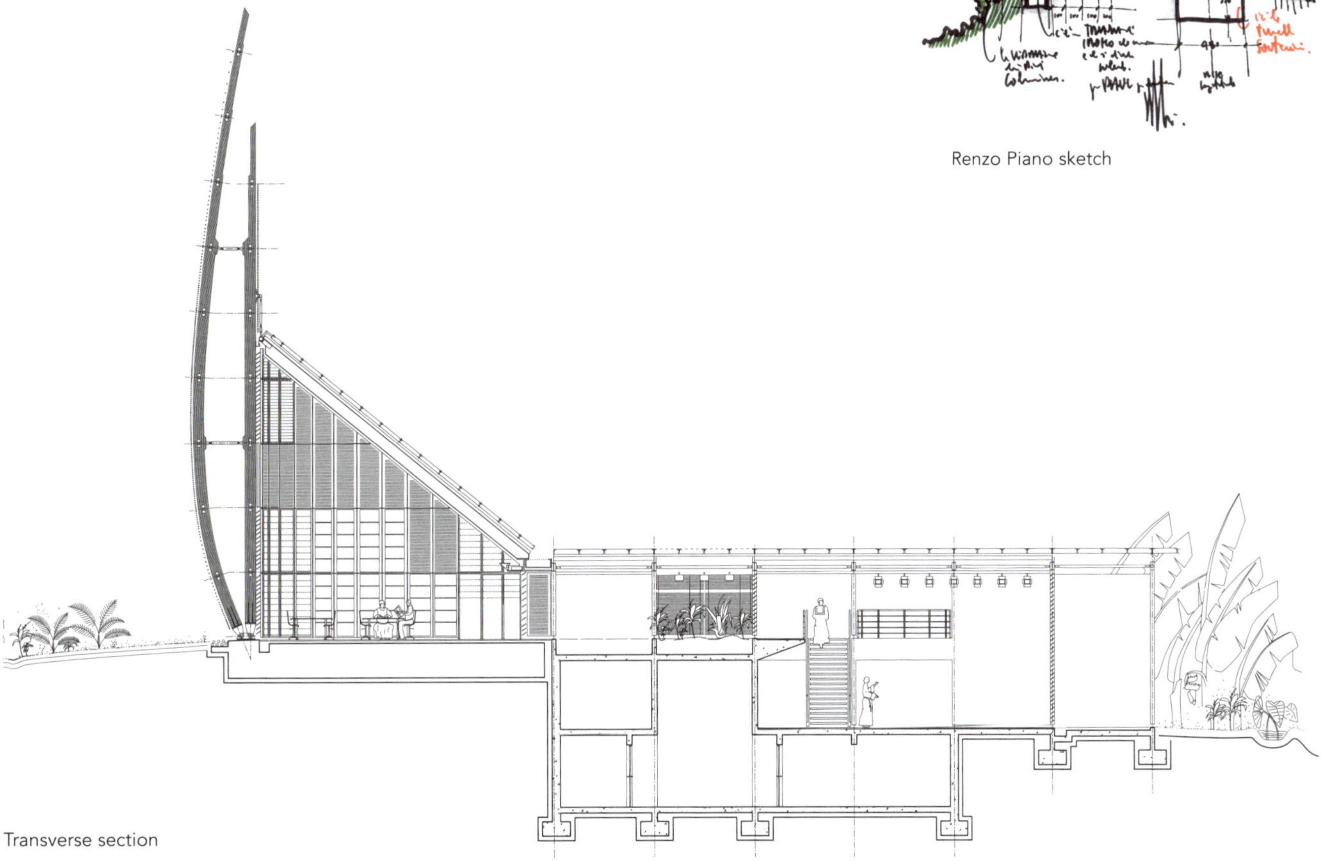

Transverse section

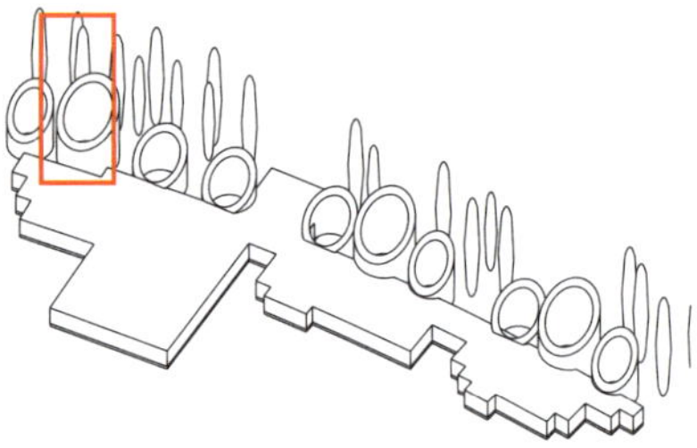

Axon key

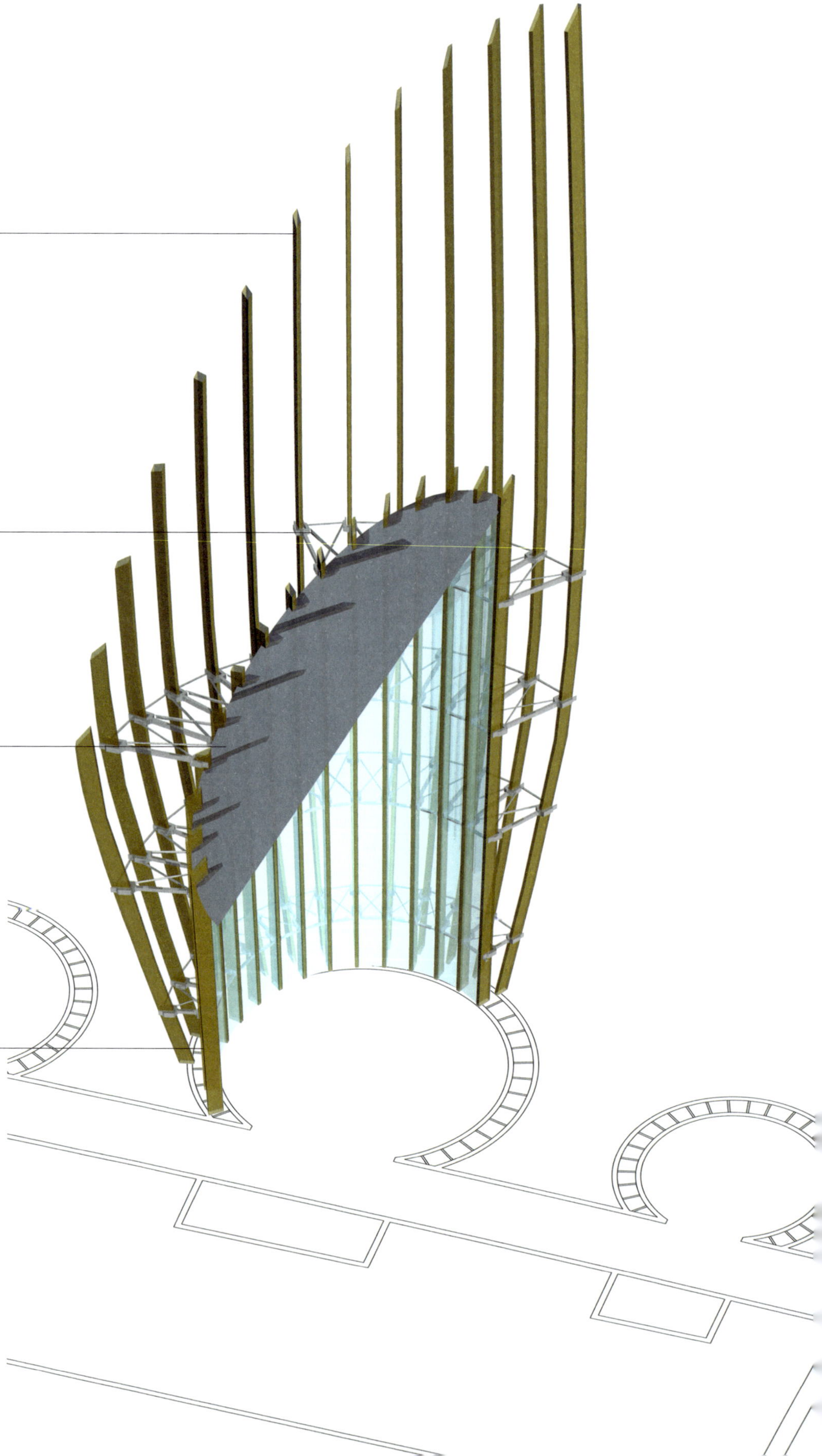

Facade
A double-skin system, supported by curved outer ribs each linked to a straight vertical rib, allows the curved exterior batten wall to shade the vertical interior wall. The verticality of the cases shade the roof from the direct sun helping to control the temperature in the interior spaces.

Structure
Galvanized steel connectors brace the glue-laminated Iroko timber to form three-dimensional circular trusses strong enough to withstand hurricane winds

Roof
The roof structure consists of a double layer system with a cavity between the outer and inner layer to control temperature. The high reflectivity of the outer aluminum roof bounces a large amount of incoming solar radiation. The cavity underneath allows the residual heat to be naturally ventilated off.

Walls
The structure and facade was developed as a kit-of-parts system and the majority of the materials were prefabricated in France and then shipped to the site. The double-skin facade consists of two layers, the inner layer with insulated prefabricated facade panels and glass windows and the outer layer of slatted wood and louvers.

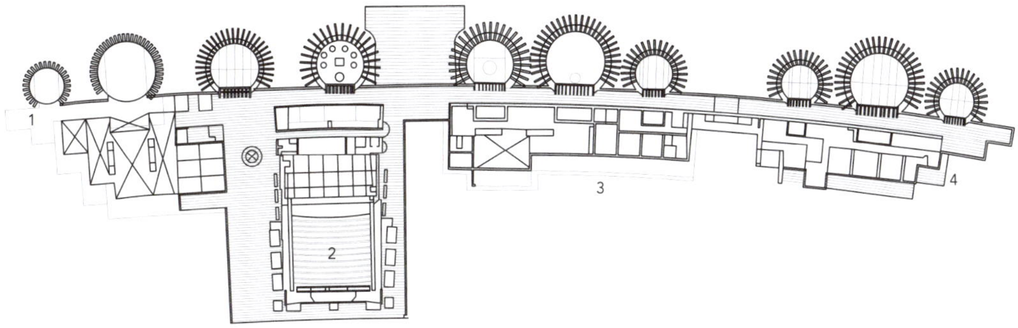

1 Covered pedestrian walkway, the "alley"
2 Auditorium
3 Offices
4 Workshop spaces

Ground floor plan

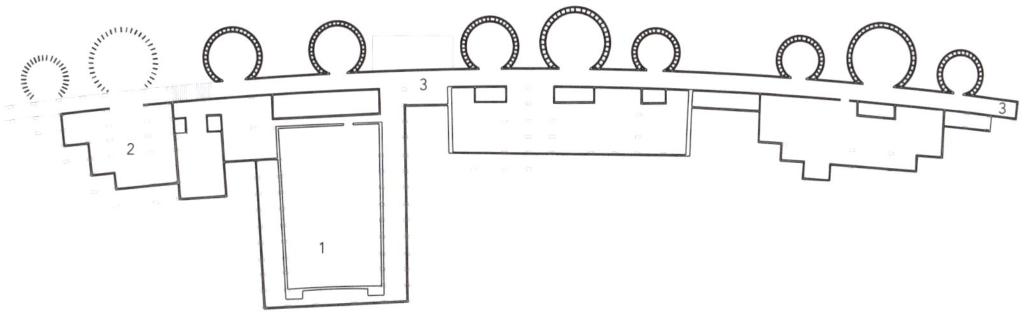

Lower level plan
Cultural huts line up along a circulation walkway along the northern edge of the building.

1 Auditorium
2 Exhibition spaces
3 Pedestrian walkway

View of timber ribs and aluminum roof

View of the cultural center's huts

Interior view of library and reading hut

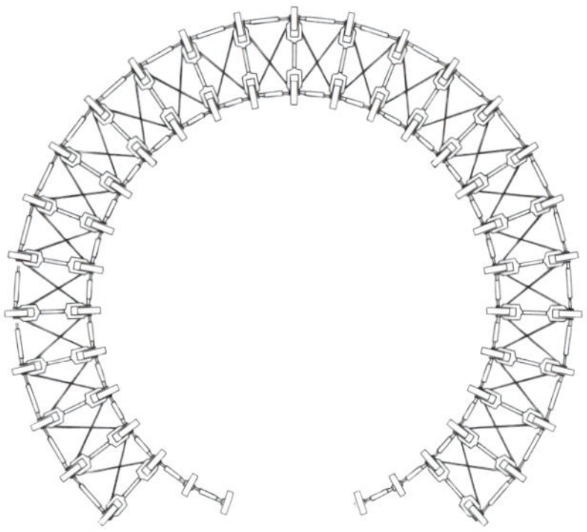

Plan layout of the galvanized steel structure connected to the laminated timber rib structure system

Connection between steel structure and laminated timber rib structure

Exterior corner detail

1 Aluminum and steel roof
2 Galvanized steel structure
3 Laminated timber rib structure
4 Wooden louvers (not shown)

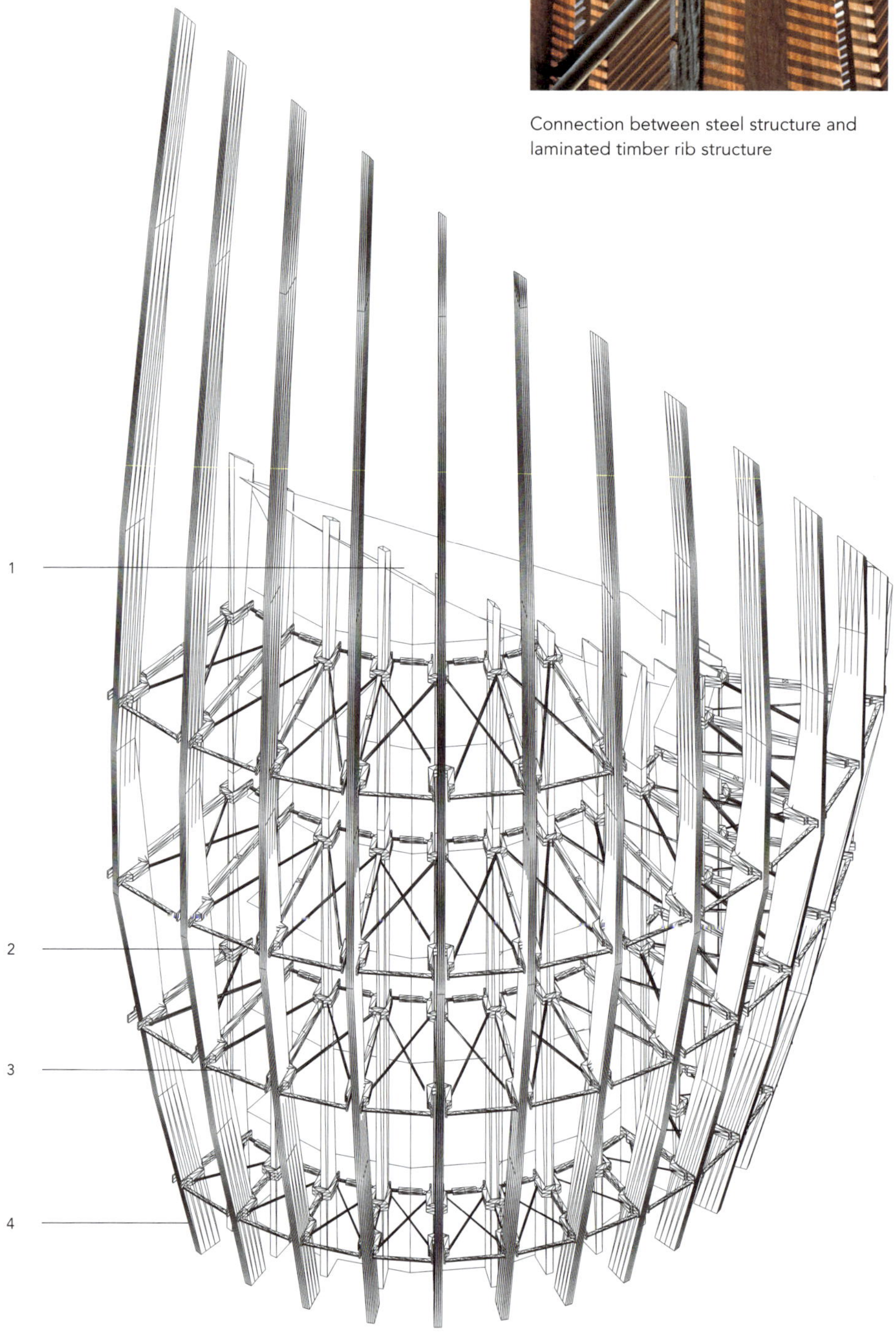

Facade system

Connection between steel structure, laminated timber rib structure and wooden louvers

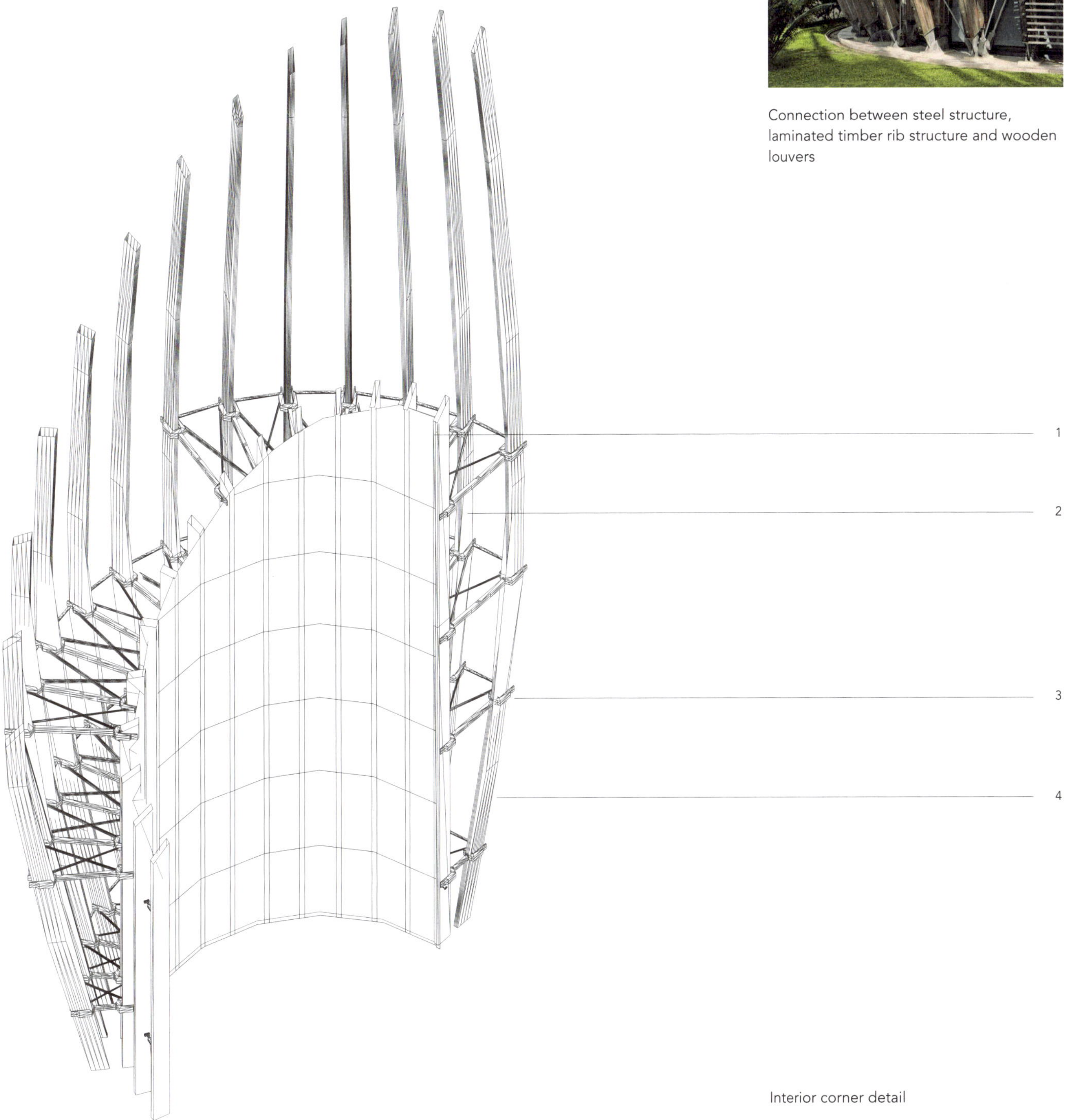

Interior corner detail

1 Facade panels
2 Vertical facade structure
3 Galvanized steel structure
4 Laminated timber rib structure

Construction process of roof structure

View of timber structure

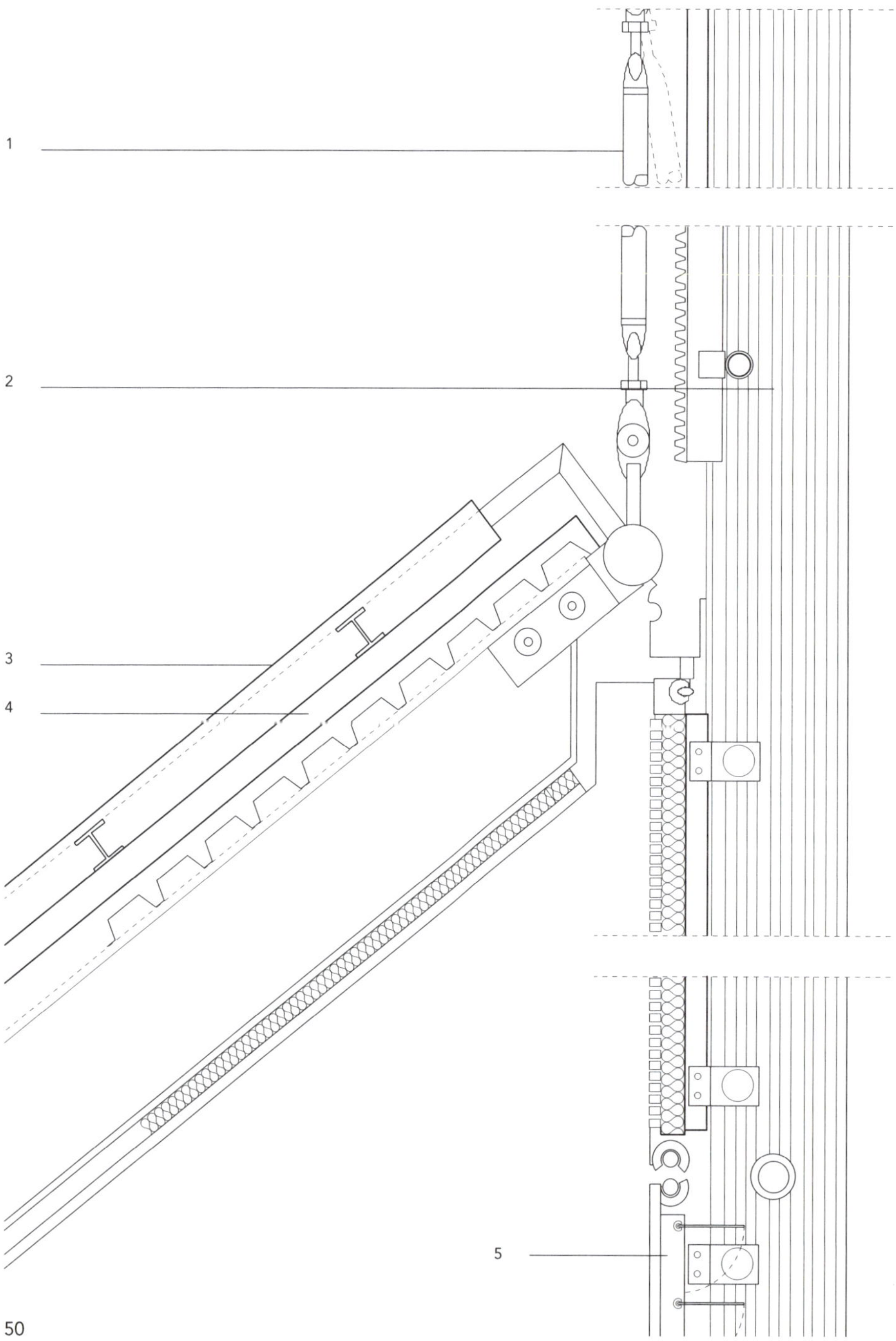

Detail of the connection between the timber ribs and the aluminum roof

1 Galvanized steel structure
2 Glue-laminated structure, Iroko wood
3 Aluminum and steel roof
4 Air circulation/ventilation space
5 Glass louvers

Setting the timber ribs

Galvanized steel connector and timber ribs

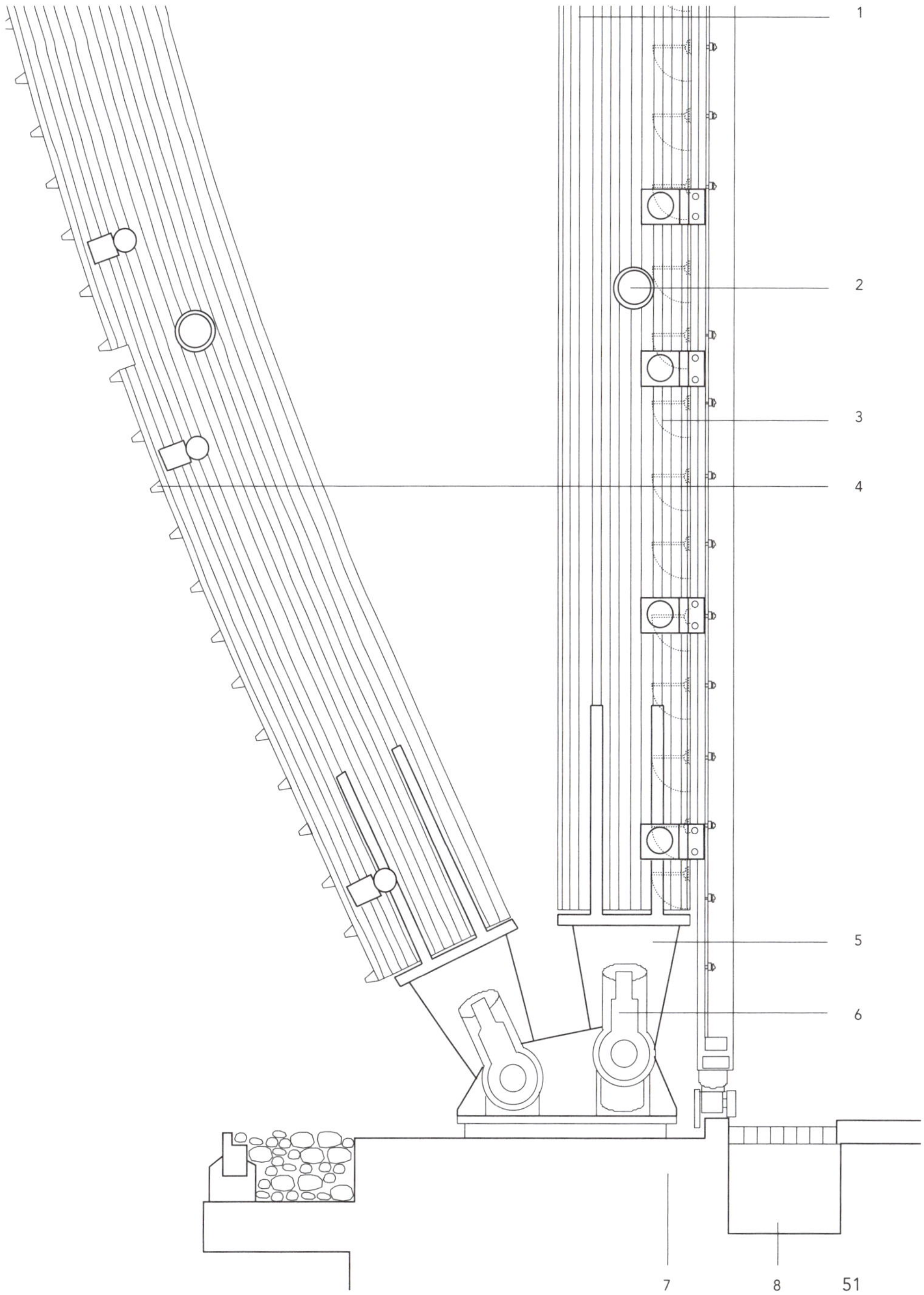

Detail of the connections of the double-skinned timber rib facade. Louvers on the curved and vertical ribs allow the passage of air while blocking out excessive sunlight.

1 Laminated timber ribs
2 Galvanized steel structure
3 Adjustable glass louvers
4 Sunshade on outer facade
5 Galvanized steel anchor with pin connection
6 Anchor for steel cross bracing
7 Foundation
8 Floor-channel for technical installations

Cy Twombly Pavilion
1992–1995

Houston, Texas, USA

Geographical context within the USA

In 1992, Dominique de Menil commissioned RPBW to build the second gallery building for The Menil Collection. The independent pavilion is dedicated to the artist Cy Twombly and is located adjacent to the main museum building on The Menil Collection campus. This gallery stands among the bungalows of the "museum village" and has a grand appearance with its solid walls in gray-colored concrete and its light roof, described by Renzo Piano as "a butterfly alighting on a firm surface." At the same time, the 864-square meter (9,300-square foot) building is modest in scale. Its nine galleries are arranged in a square ground plan.

Similar to the main Menil building, the Cy Twombly Pavilion is naturally lit through a sloped glass roof and roofing composed of four layers: diffusing louvers, glass envelopes, adjustable and motorized louvers and a translucent cloth ceiling. In contrast to the heavy-weighted stone walls, the roof with its shading canopy seems to float over the entire building.

The exceptional light quality and desirable illuminance levels within the gallery spaces were addressed using a sophisticated layered roof and ceiling system. A sensor-operated internal louver system controls daylight to the desired illuminance levels. The canvas sailcloth ceiling accentuates and diffuses the intense Texas sun while softly illuminating the galleries with their plaster walls and white oak floors. The ever-changing natural light that illuminates Twombly's artwork makes it appear different depending on the time of day and sky condition. The Cy Twombly Pavilion brilliantly captures this incredible synthesis of art, architecture and light.

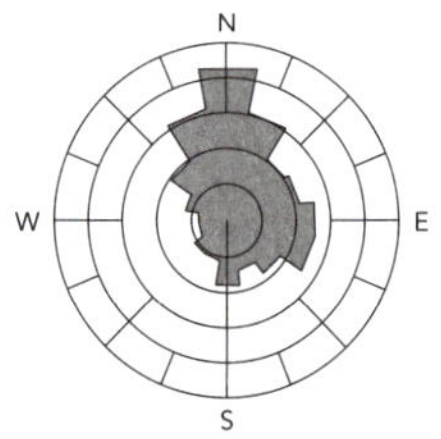

Wind rose: January

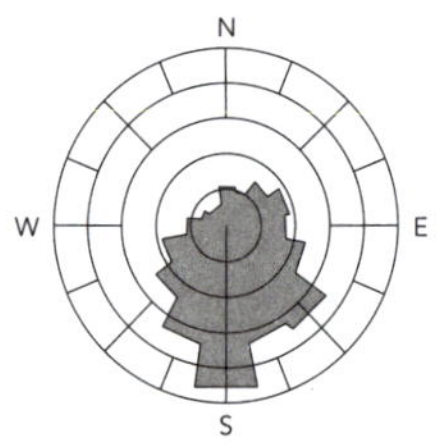

Wind rose: July

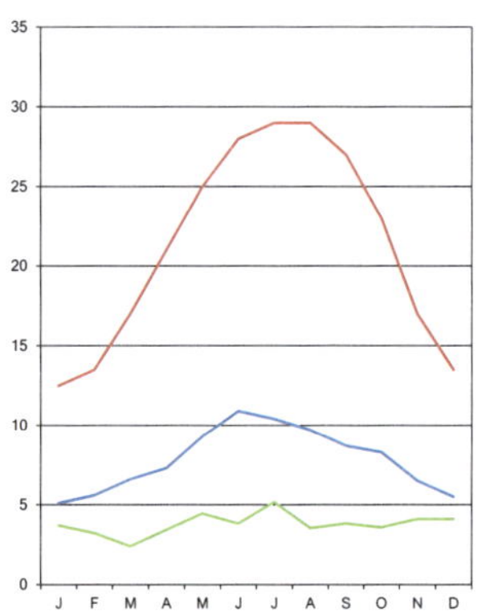

Sunlight hours/day
Temperature (°C)
Average rainfall/month (in)

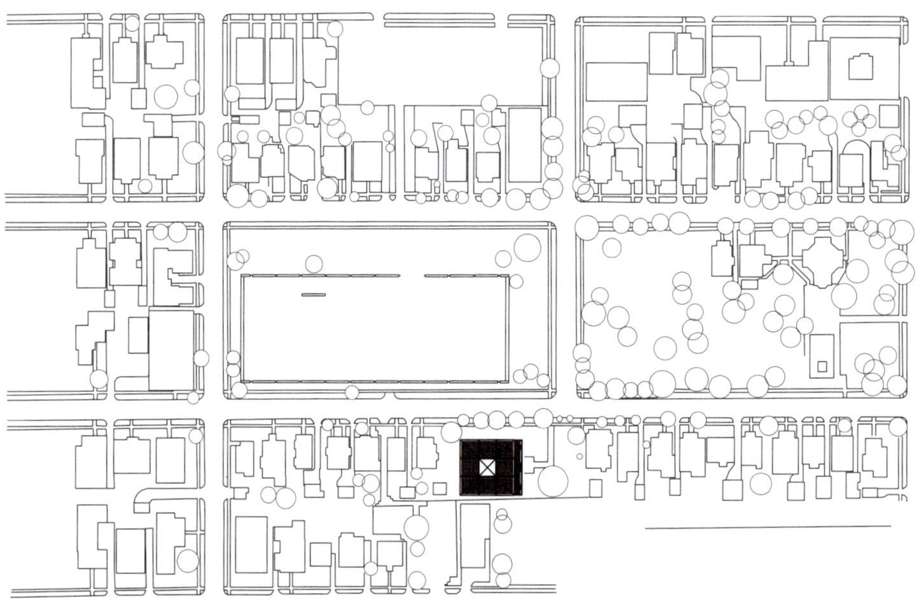

Site plan

Main entrance on east side

Interior gallery space facing the entry and showing the fabric ceilings

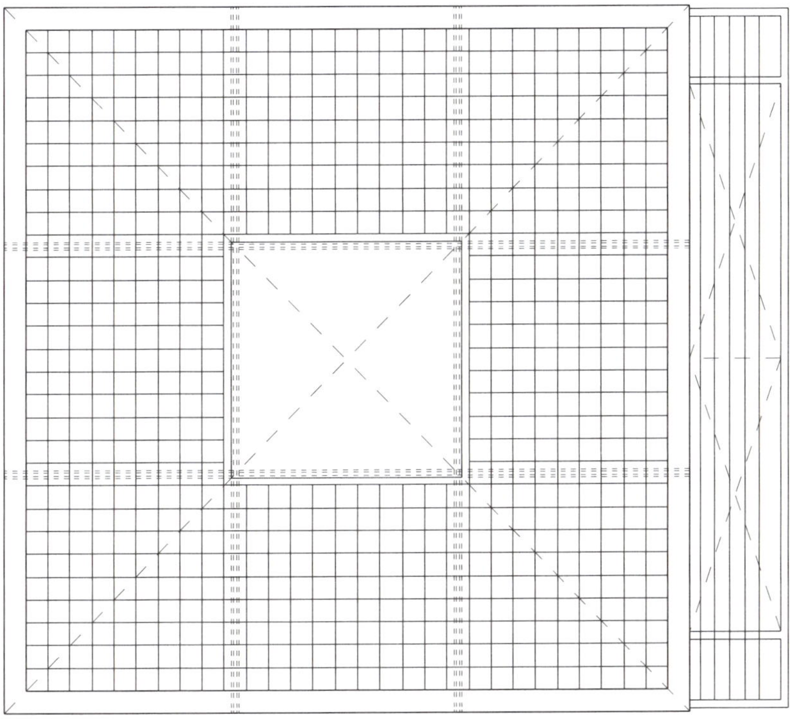

Roof plan

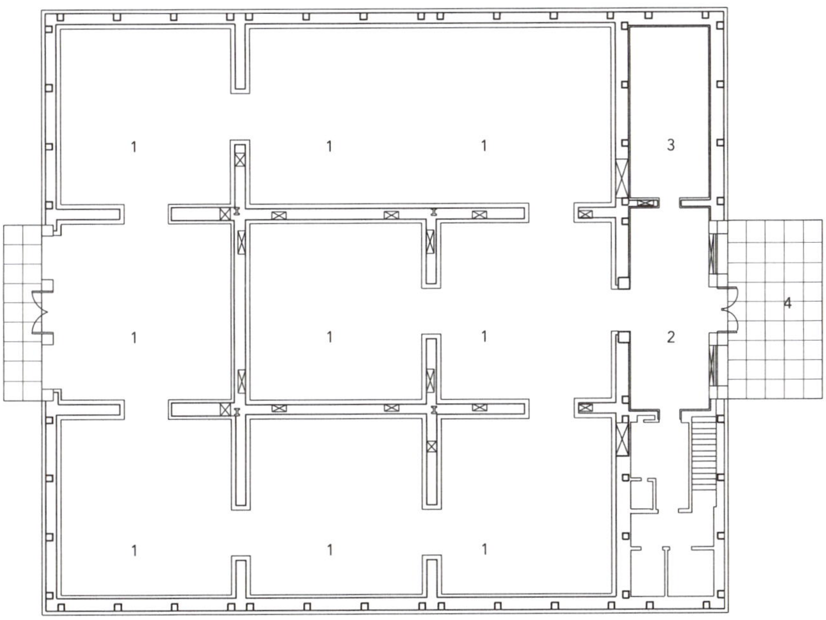

Ground floor plan

1 Gallery spaces
2 Lobby
3 Archives
4 Entrance

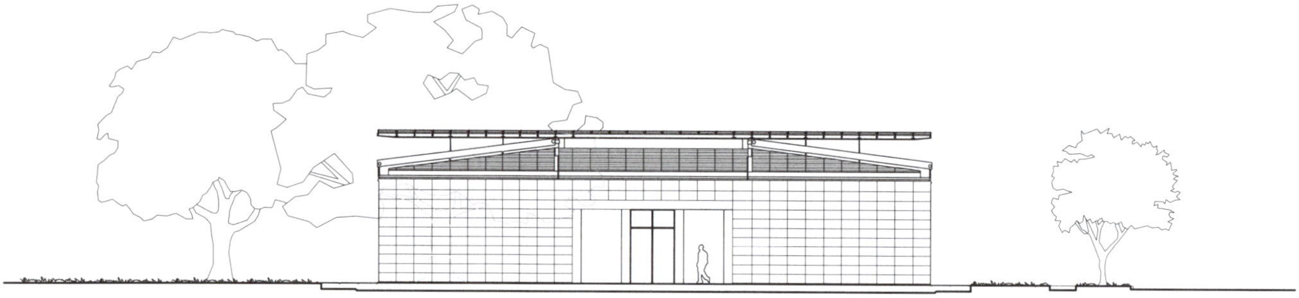

East elevation

Entrance to the Cy Twombly Pavilion in relationship to The Menil Collection

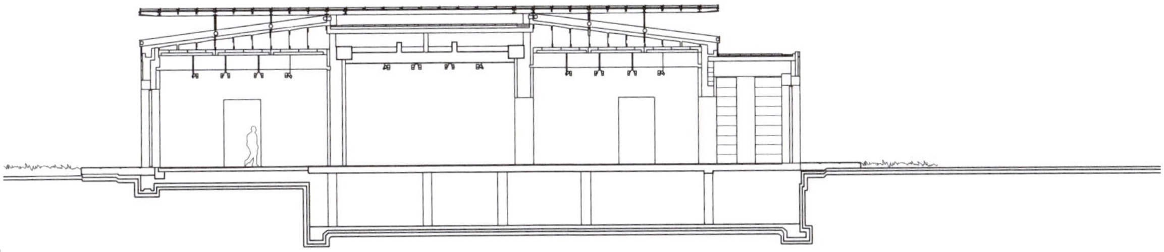

Section through gallery

Exploded axon of the roof and shading elements

The roof is a complex series of layers designed to control and diffuse sunlight to protect the artwork.

Section rendering

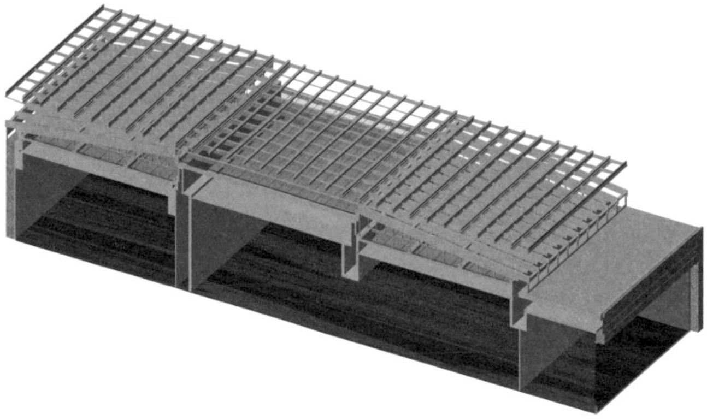

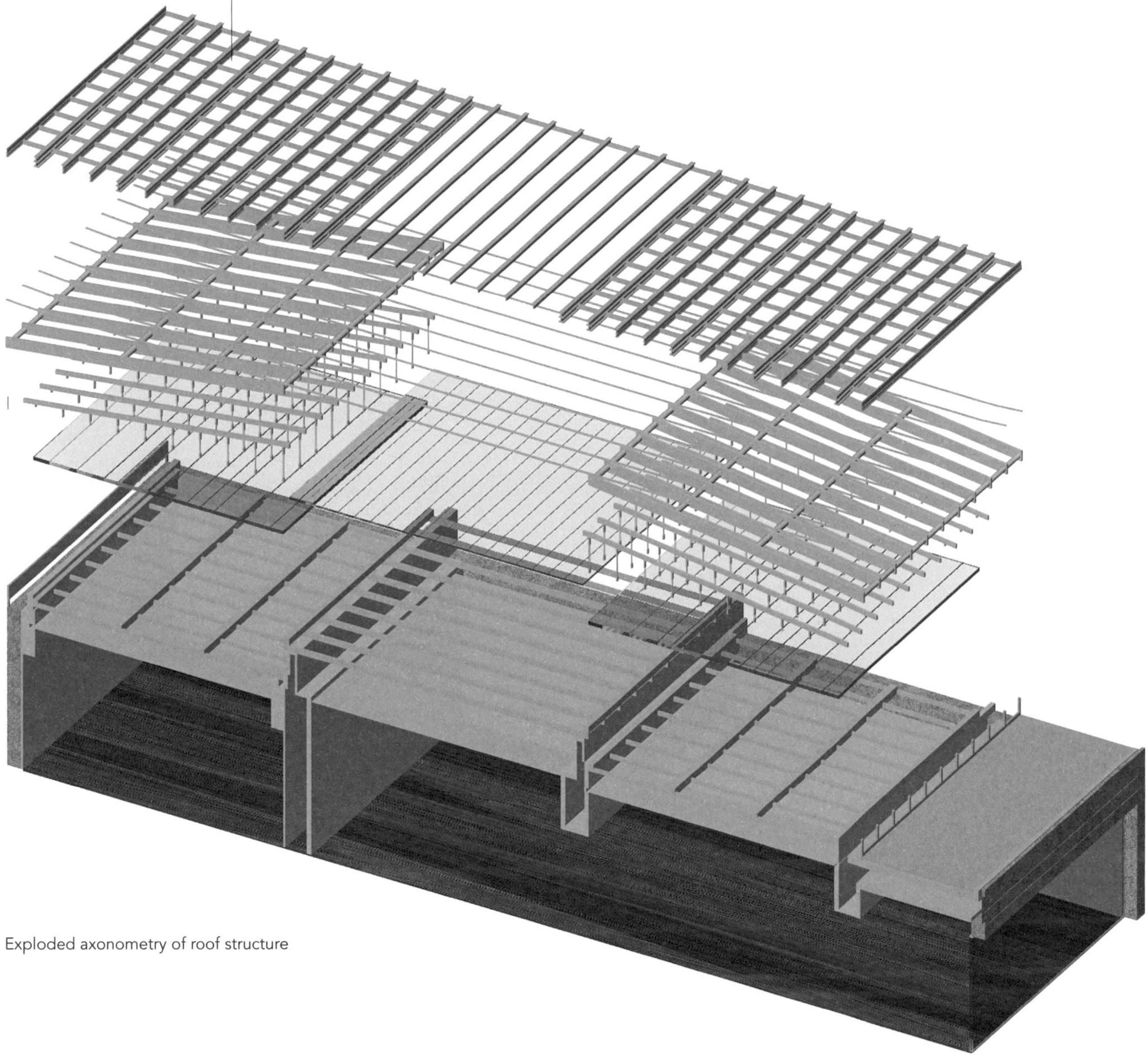

Exploded axonometry of roof structure

Fixed external louvers, computer-controlled internal louvers and translucent fabrics diffuse and control natural daylighting levels. Fixed electric spotlights highlight artwork within the galleries.

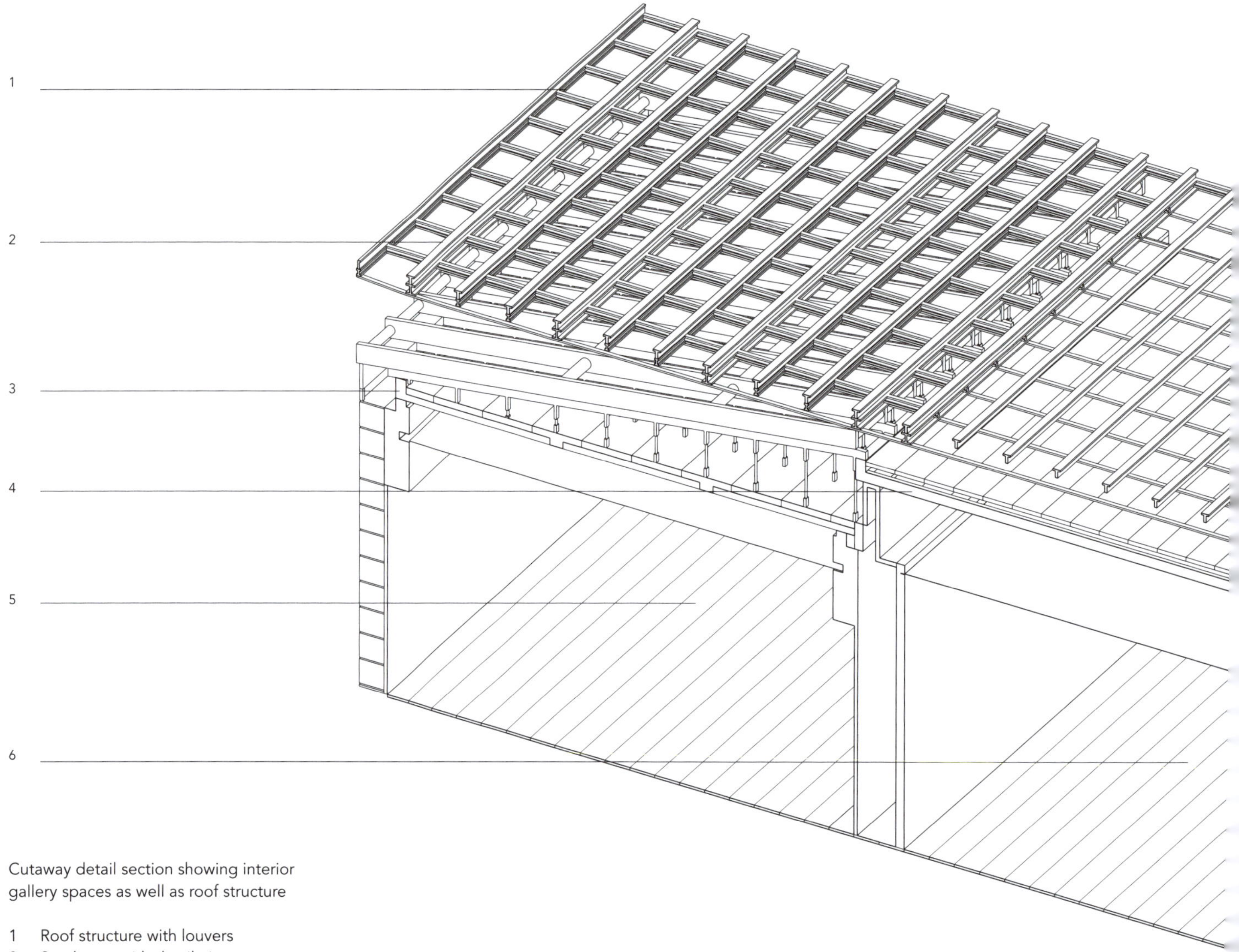

Cutaway detail section showing interior gallery spaces as well as roof structure

1 Roof structure with louvers
2 Steel truss with ductile iron support members
3 Exterior wall stone siding
4 Flat roof structure
5 Wood flooring
6 Gallery space
7 Lobby

The steel roof edge condition

The steel roof structure during construction

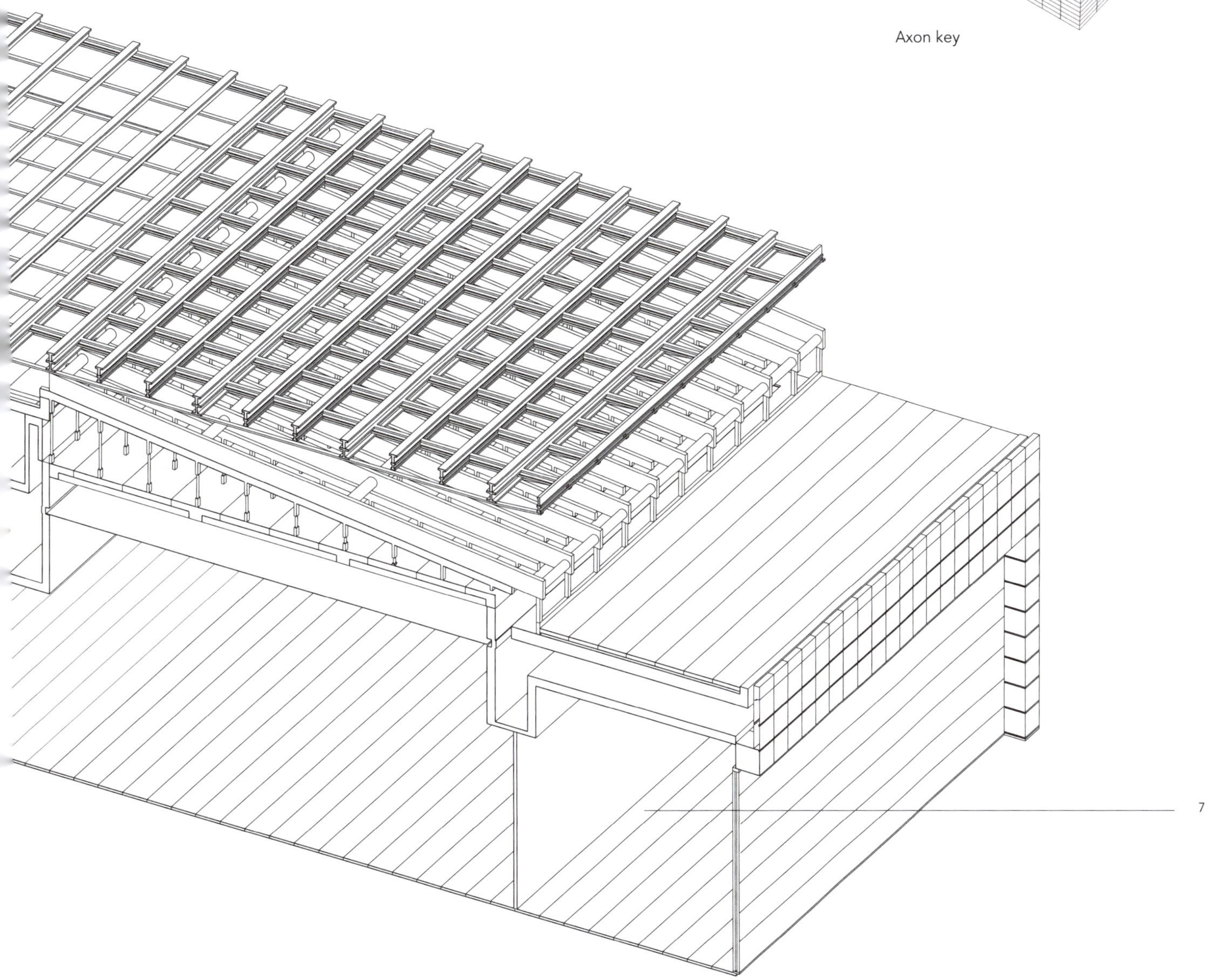

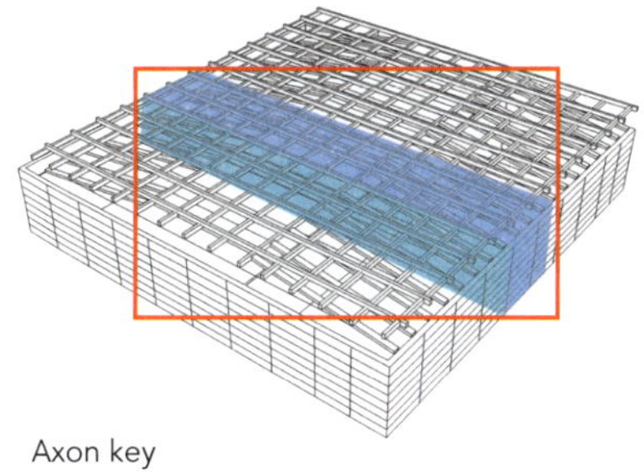

Axon key

Detail of adjustable louvers

Horizontal adjustable louvers fill the steel grid below the double-glazed roof. The motorized blinds have sensors that automatically adjust the louvers above each room independently. This helps maintain the ambience of the diffused light within the exhibition space, thus allowing any relief in the works to be read clearly.

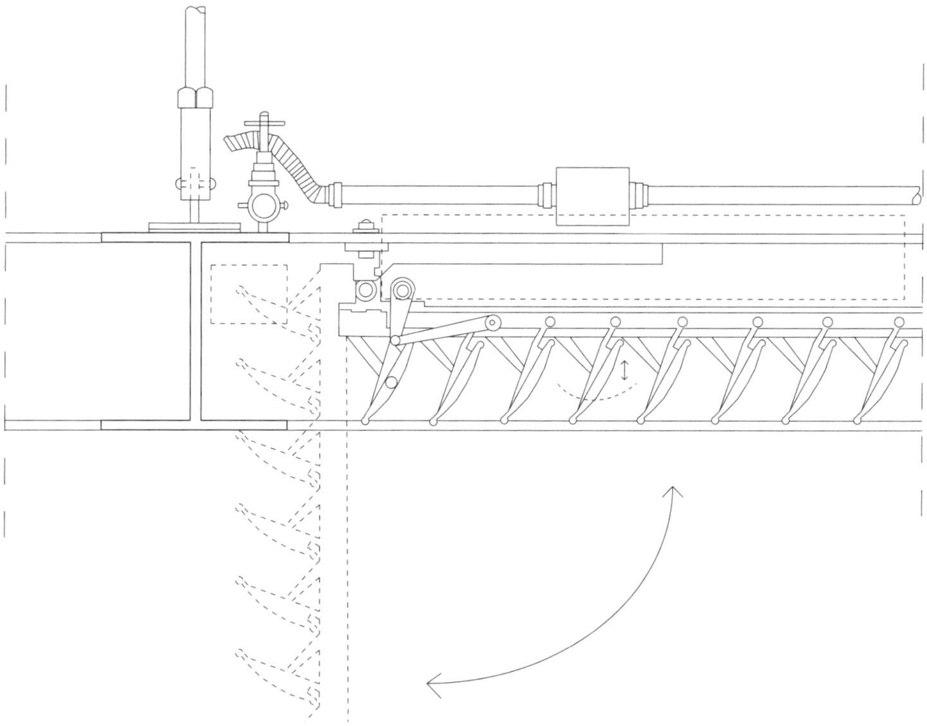

Section through the gallery space

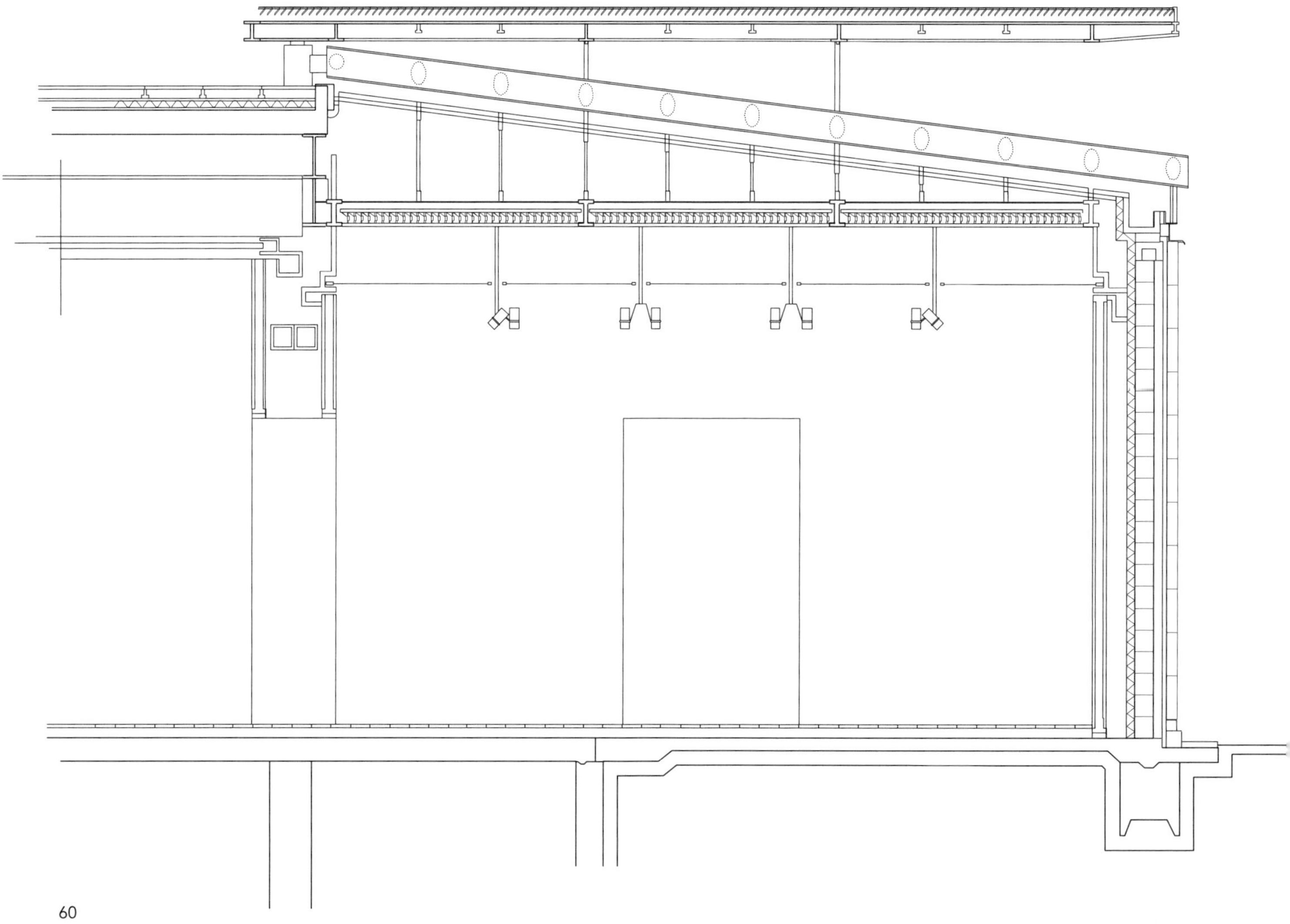

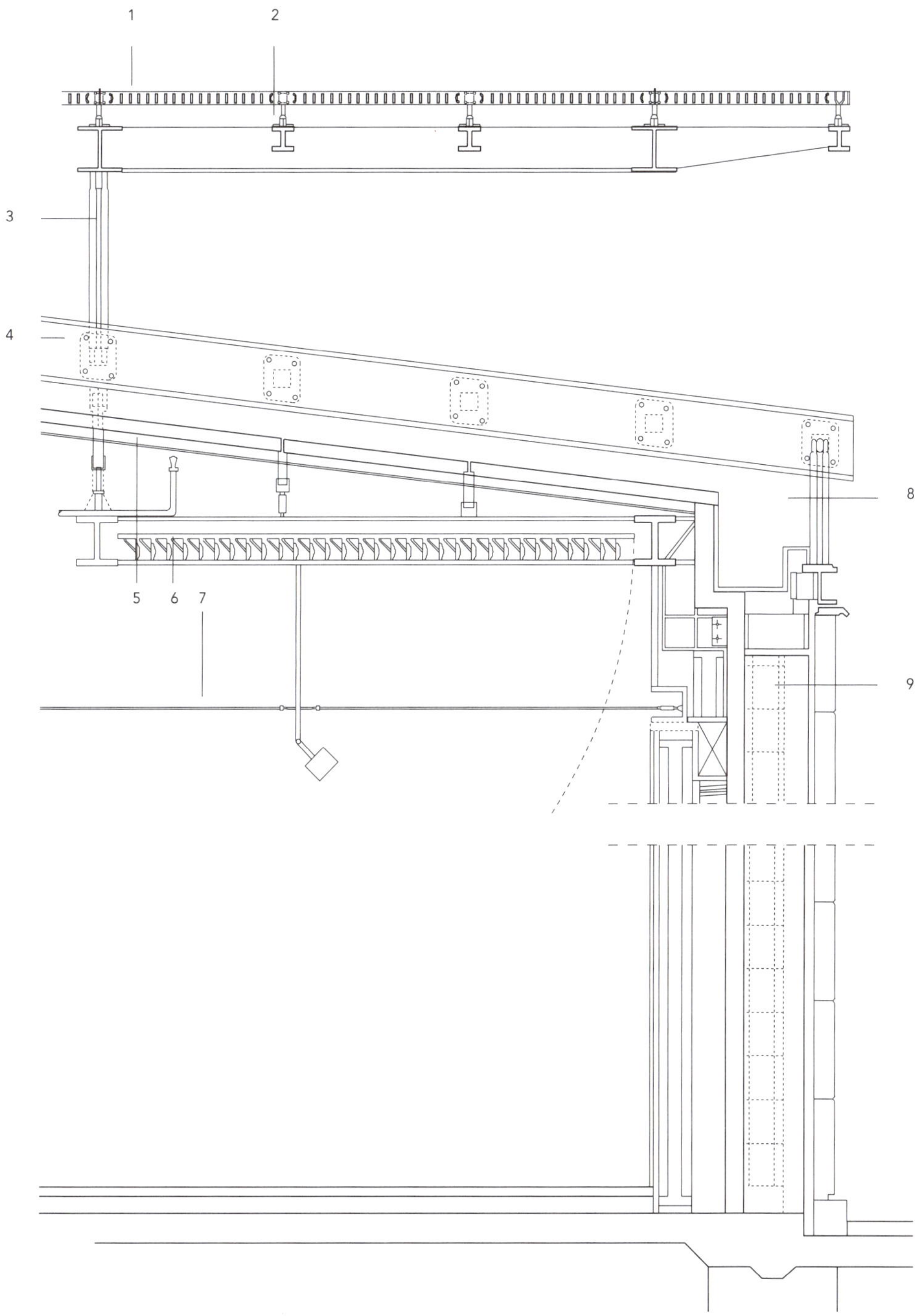

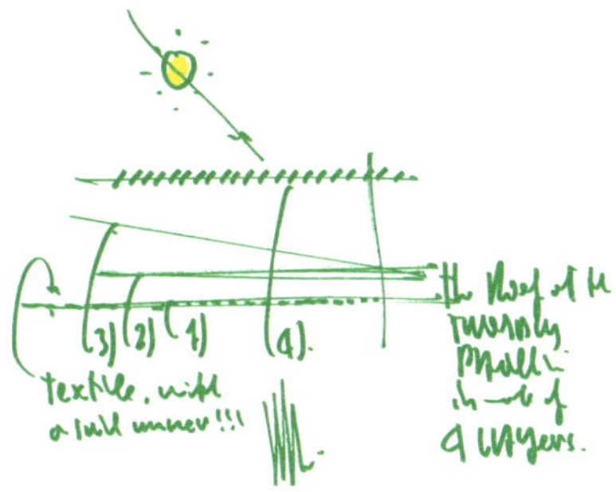

Renzo Piano sketch

Roof and wall section detail through gallery space

1 Non-adjustable sunshade louvers
2 Steel canopy
3 Ductile iron support member
4 Double-member steel beam supports skylight system
5 Glass skylight
6 Light-activated motorized louver system
7 Textile ceiling, translucent
8 Gutter
9 Wall system

Interior view of gallery space

Corner of building showing cladding and roof structure

Nasher Sculpture Center
1999–2003

Dallas, Texas, USA

Geographical context within the USA

The Nasher Sculpture Center is situated in the downtown Dallas Art District and is nestled in the city's skyline. It is one of the few institutions in the world devoted to the exhibition, study and preservation of modern sculpture. It represents Ray Nasher's vision to create an outdoor "roofless" museum that would serve as a peaceful retreat for reflection of art and nature, as well as house his collection of 20th-century sculpture. The goal was to design a museum and garden of lasting significance that will sustain the legacy of the collection. He wanted it to be a "noble ruin" or archaeological find, reminiscent of the solidly grounded archaeological sites of ancient civilization and their continuity through time.

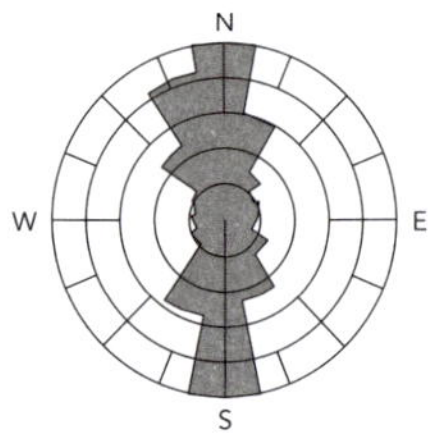

Wind rose: January

From early on in the design concept, the emphasis was on creating a quiet oasis amidst the busy activity of the urban center. The resulting design includes an indoor gallery with an area of nearly 5,000 square meters (55,000 square feet) and an outdoor sculpture garden. The gallery building features long walls faced with 5-centimeter (2-inch) wide slabs of Italian travertine that divide five equal-sized parallel pavilions. The pavilions' facades at each end are completely transparent and visually extend the interiors toward the outside, into the garden. The garden acts as an extension of the sculpture garden, and vice versa.

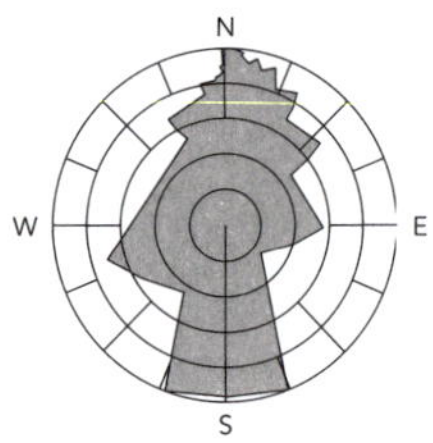

Wind rose: July

The museum consists of two levels with very different lighting conditions. The ground floor houses the exhibit of sculptures and less light-sensitive paintings as well as the cafeteria, the shop and the museum's administration. Located on the lower level is a smaller gallery for light-sensitive art, such as prints and drawings along with the preservation laboratories, research and teaching areas and the auditorium. The auditorium has access to an outdoor theater and the sculpture garden and can be opened by a mobile facade for both indoor and outdoor performances. The sculpture garden was

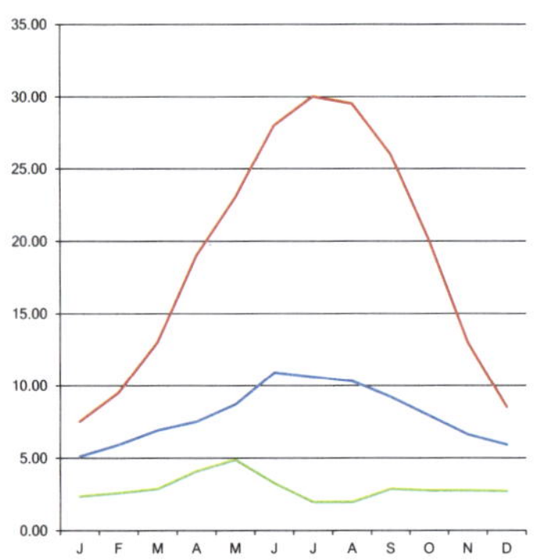

- Sunlight hours/day
- Temperature (°C)
- Average rainfall/month (in)

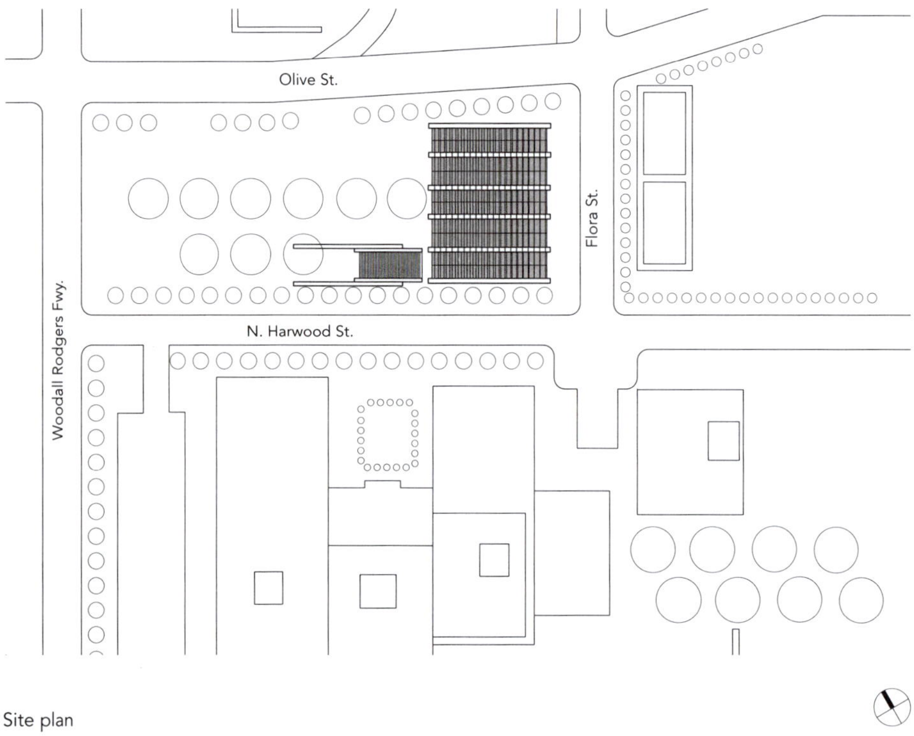

Site plan

The aerial view shows the facade of the Nasher Sculpture Center and garden within the Dallas Art District. The sculpture garden, surrounded by travertine-clad walls, provides a sanctuary of art and nature in the vibrant city center of Dallas.

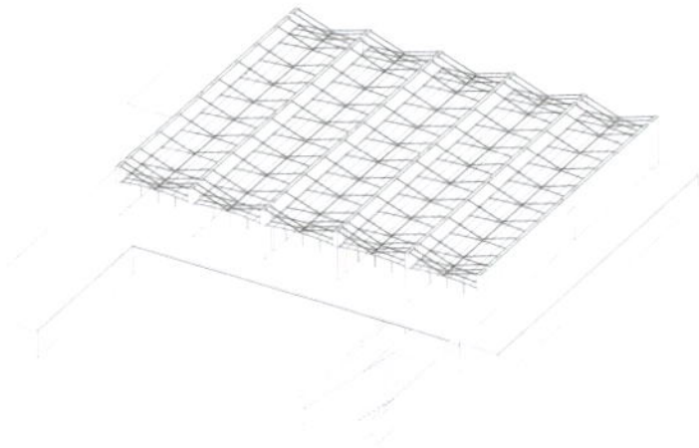

Garden exterior
Axonometry

designed by the landscape architect Peter Walker and is completely confined by travertine walls. It is situated just slightly below street level giving the impression of an archaeological site. On its 8,000 square meters (1.5 acres), the garden features sculptures and objects embedded in a landscaped park with cedars, oaks, Afghan pines, weeping willows and bamboo.

The exterior Italian travertine stone is rough and pitted, while the interior walls have been smoothed and honed to remove the weathered outer layers. This exposes the creamy surfaces beneath that serve as a neutral but lively background for the sculptures. The understated architectural palette endows the building with a lasting quality, ensuring that the timeless sculptures it contains will be appreciated for generations to come.

The view into the gallery space in evening light shows the transparency and openness of the space.

The museum's roof above the pavilions consists of five glass vaults supported by a small steel beam and suspended by stainless steel tie rods from the travertine-clad walls. The sun-shading system is made up of aluminum panels positioned above the glass roof. The combination of vaulted glass roofs with fixed die-cast aluminum shading panels provides lighting levels up to 2,000 lux and contrast values perfect for viewing sculptures.

In the summer of 2011, a 42-story residential tower was constructed close to the Nasher Sculpture Center. The tower's glass curtain wall reflects sunlight onto the Nasher building and its sculpture garden. This greatly compromised Renzo Piano's carefully designed skylights. Instead of bringing in only indirect north light, the tower reflects sunlight directly through the roof and enables it to hit the art, while generating destructive shading patterns and heating up the interior space.

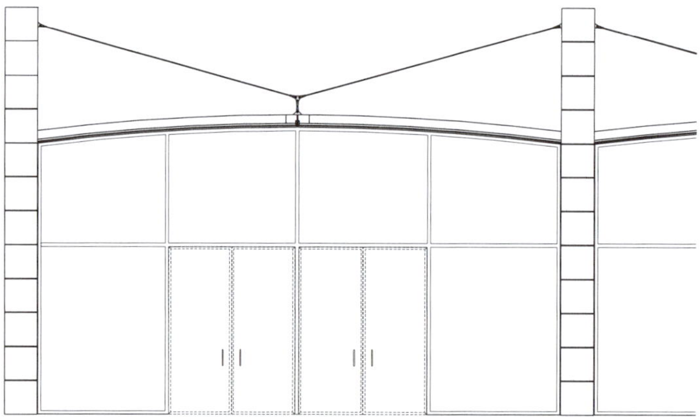

Elevation detail

Building section

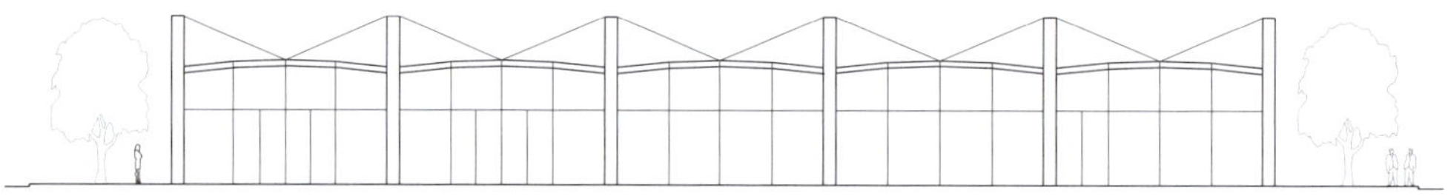

North elevation

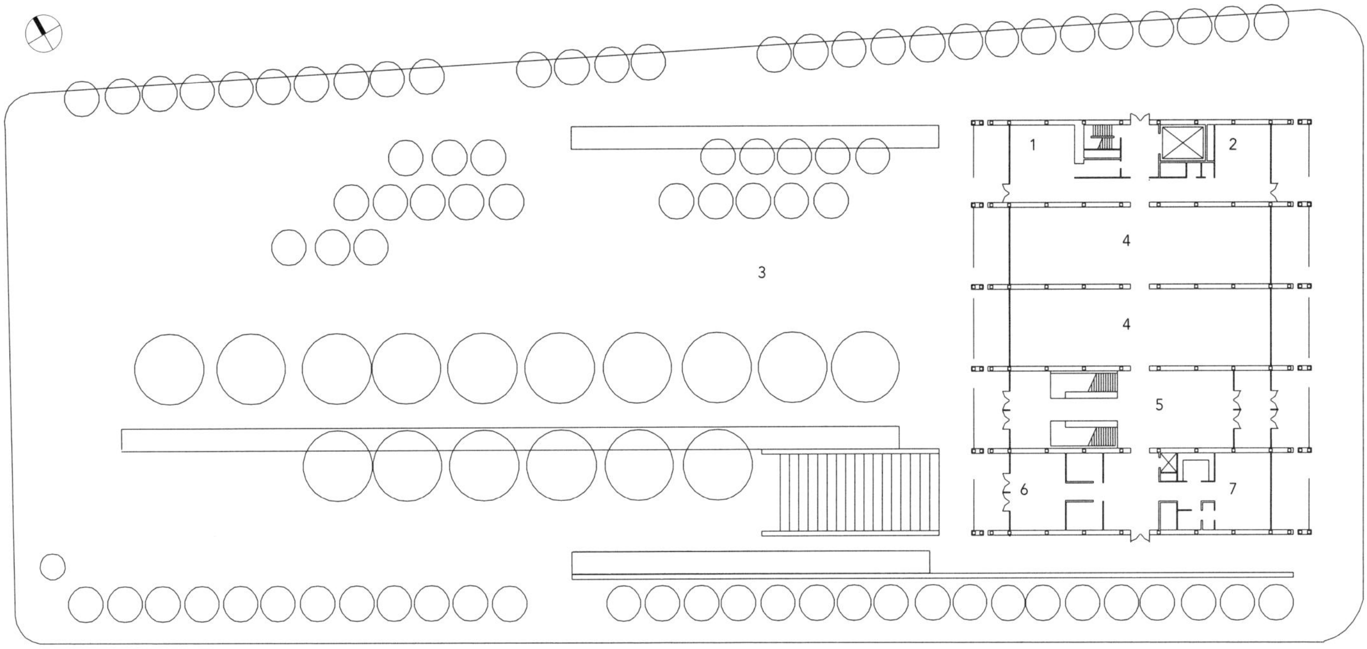

Ground floor plan

1 Restaurant
2 Security
3 Garden
4 Gallery space
5 Entrance lobby
6 Offices
7 Gift shop

Lower level floor plan

1 Loading dock area
2 Kitchen
3 Storage/mechanical
4 Administration
5 Gallery space
6 Outdoor seating
7 Auditorium

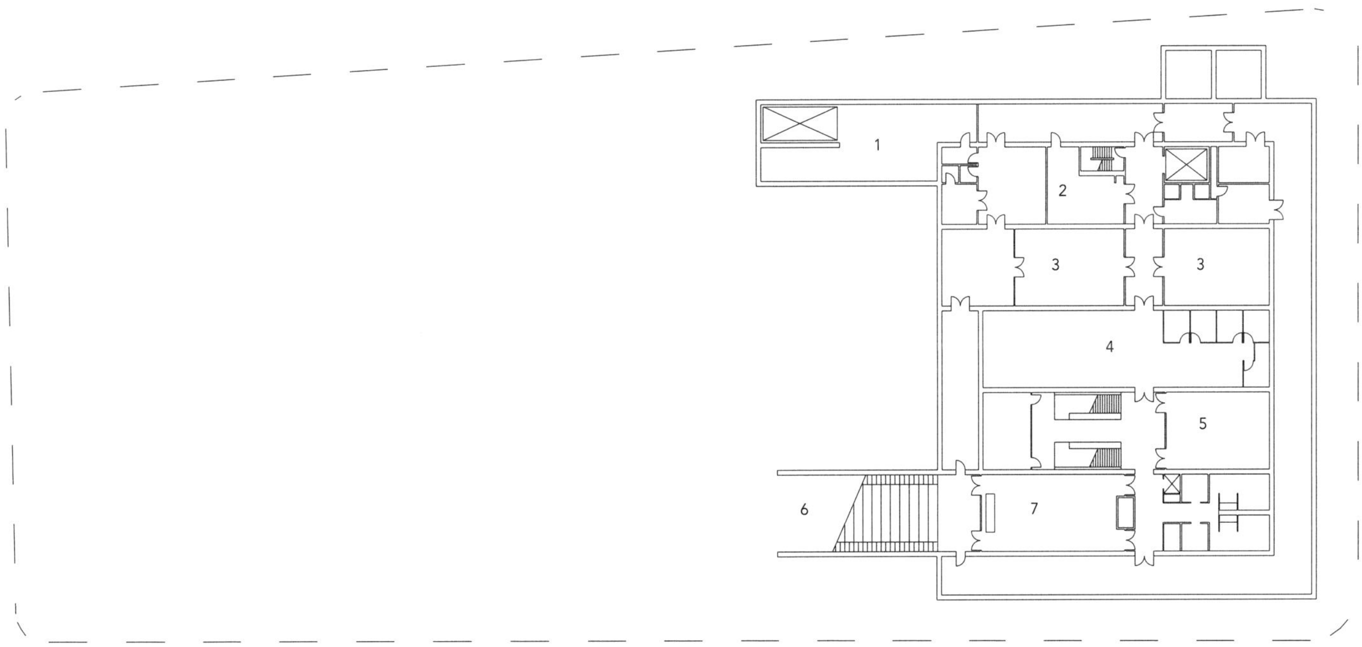

The material of the entrance hall, gallery and main circulation stair is accentuated by diffused light entering the space through the roof.

An exterior view of travertine-clad walls interacting with the canopy and roof structure

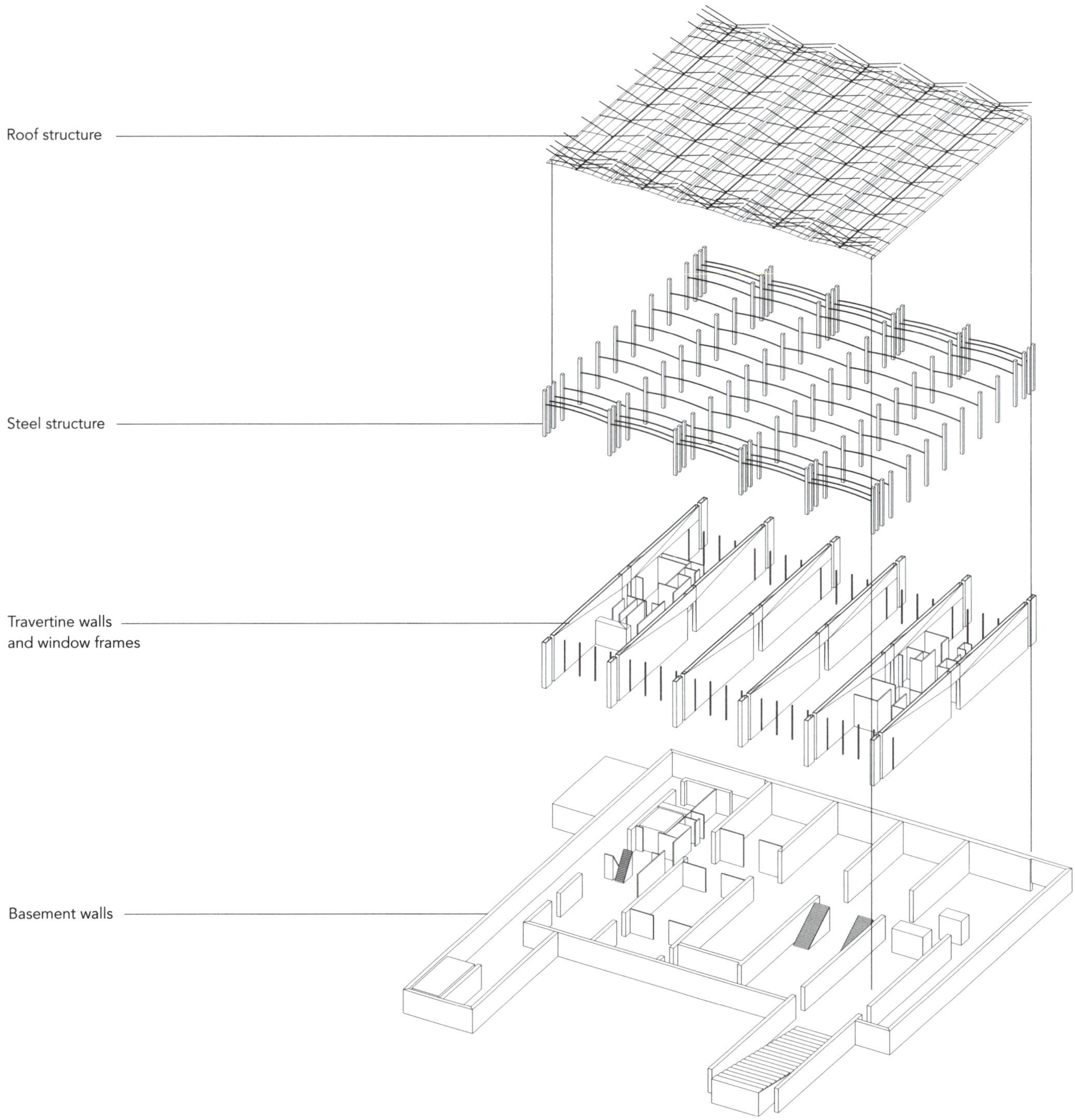

Construction process of the gallery space and roof structure

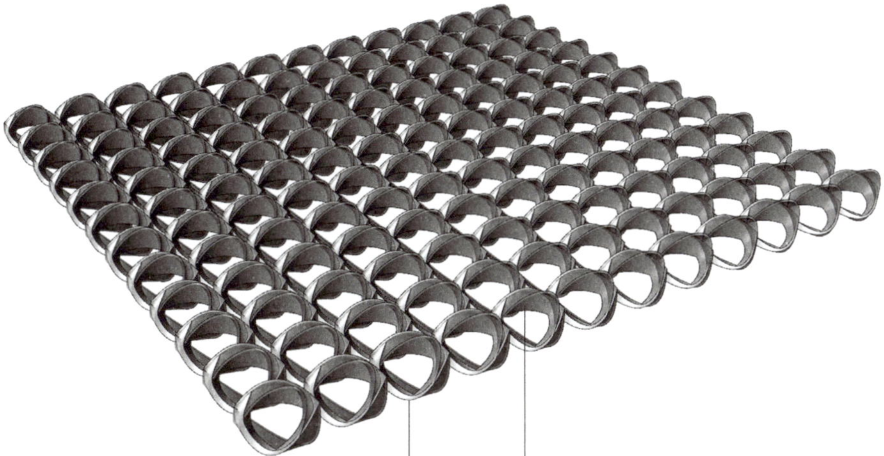

Zoomed-in view of a typical sun-shading panel that sits above the roof glazing. These north-oriented filters diffuse light into the spaces below. The shape and orientation of the filter blocks harsh, direct lighting, allowing primarily north light to enter.

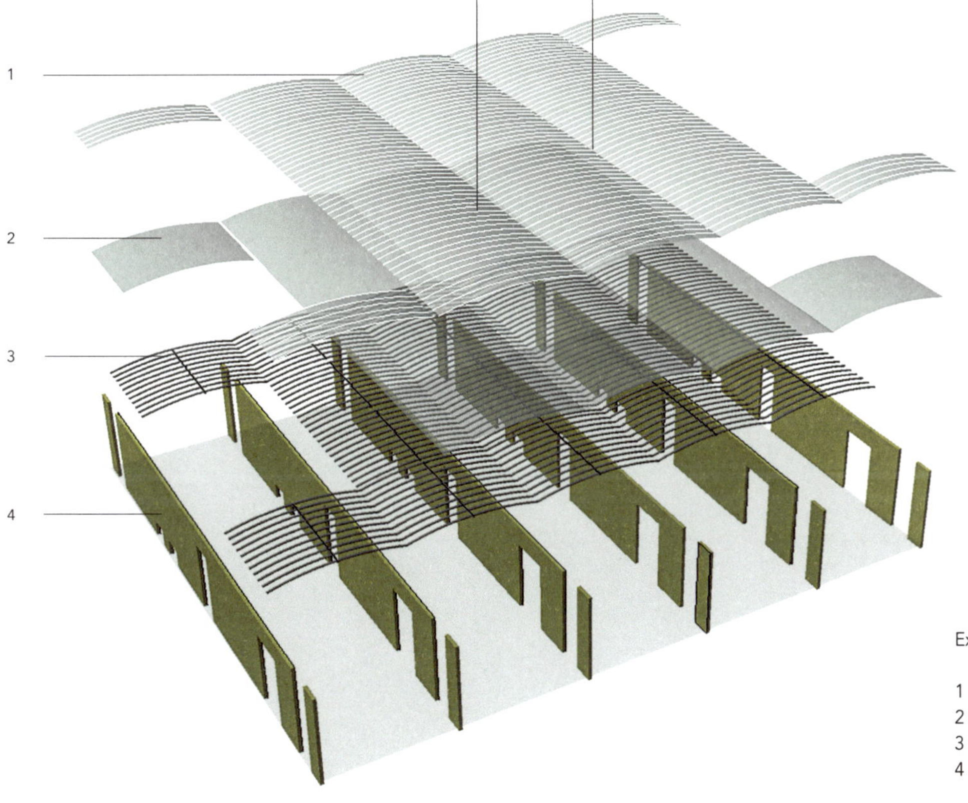

Exploded axon of layered roof form

1 Cast aluminum sun-shading panels
2 Extra-white glass panels
3 Pre-tensioned steel roof structure
4 Travertine-clad walls

The gallery seen from the sculpture garden. The roof extends over the facade and shades the outdoor space and gallery.

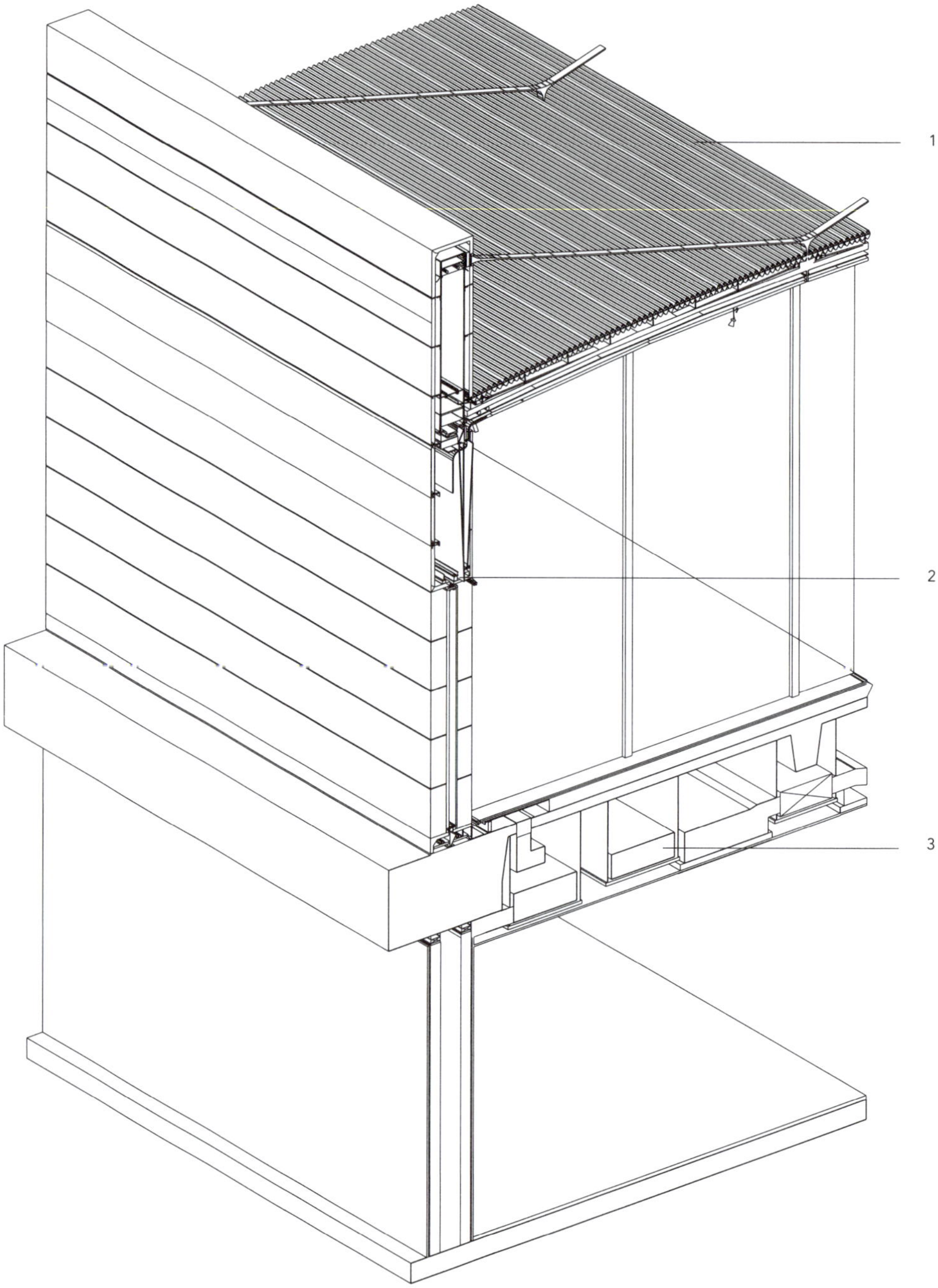

Exterior corner
Axonometric detail

1 Sun-shading panels
2 Galvanized steel beam in wall
3 Mechanical system

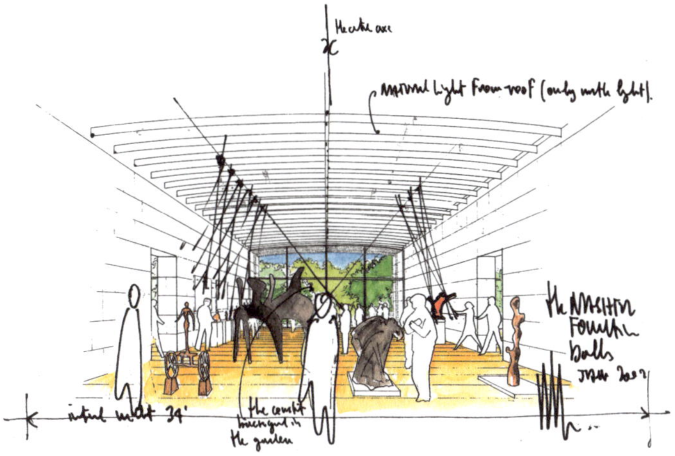

Renzo Piano sketch showing design intent of controlling daylight

The simple geometry of the sun-shading panel provides diffused light to the interior gallery spaces, eliminating sun glare and overexposure.

The interior wall and roof continues outside into the garden and street on either end of the building.

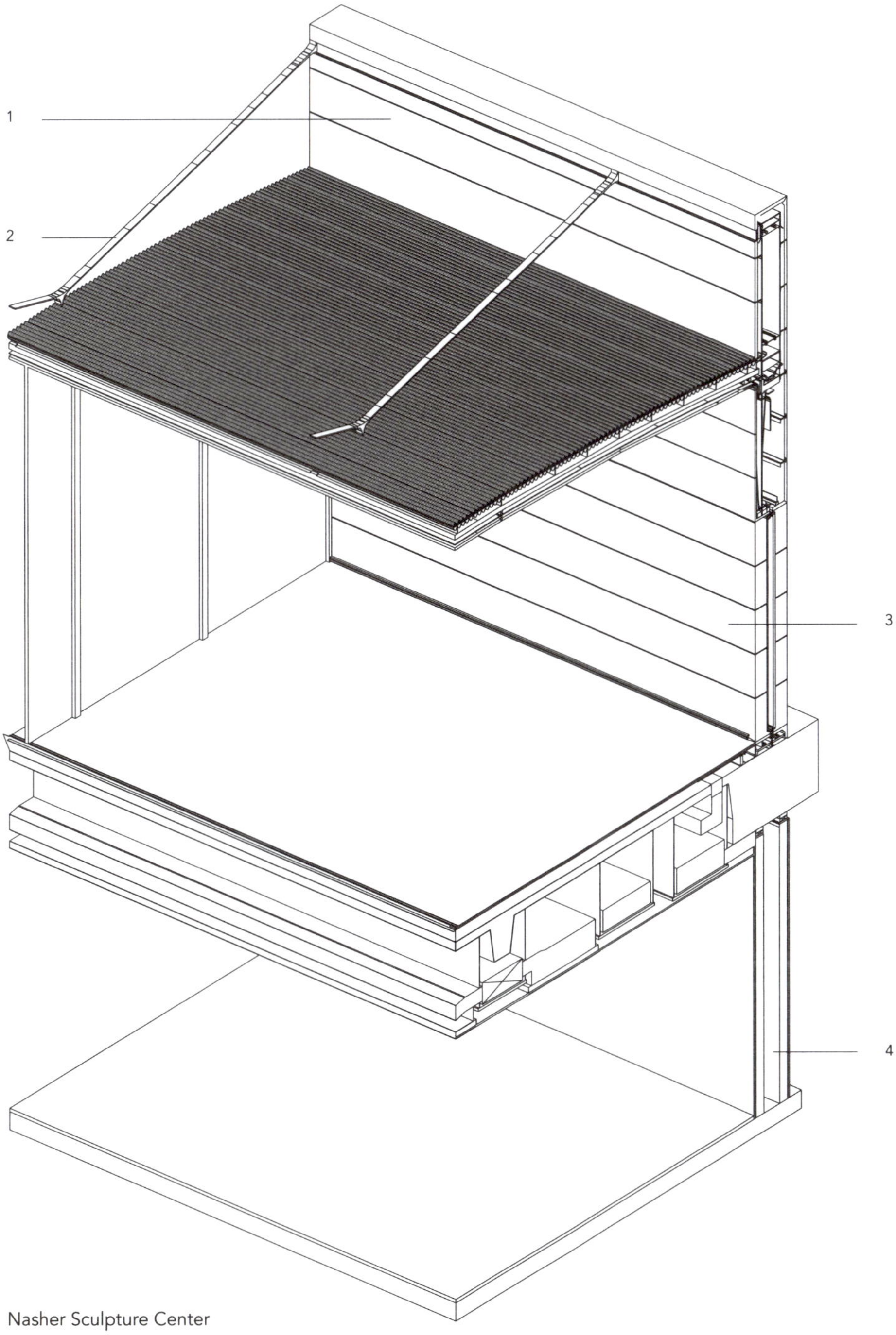

Interior of corner
Axonometric detail

1 Travertine panel (natural finish)
2 Stainless steel tension rod
3 Travertine panel (polished finish)
4 Concrete foundation wall

The continuation of materials, such as the travertine panels, from exterior to interior is emphasized by the simple, planar design of the gallery spaces.

A zoomed-in view of the sun-shading panels

The street view of the sculpture center shows the intimate relationship between public space, sidewalk and gallery.

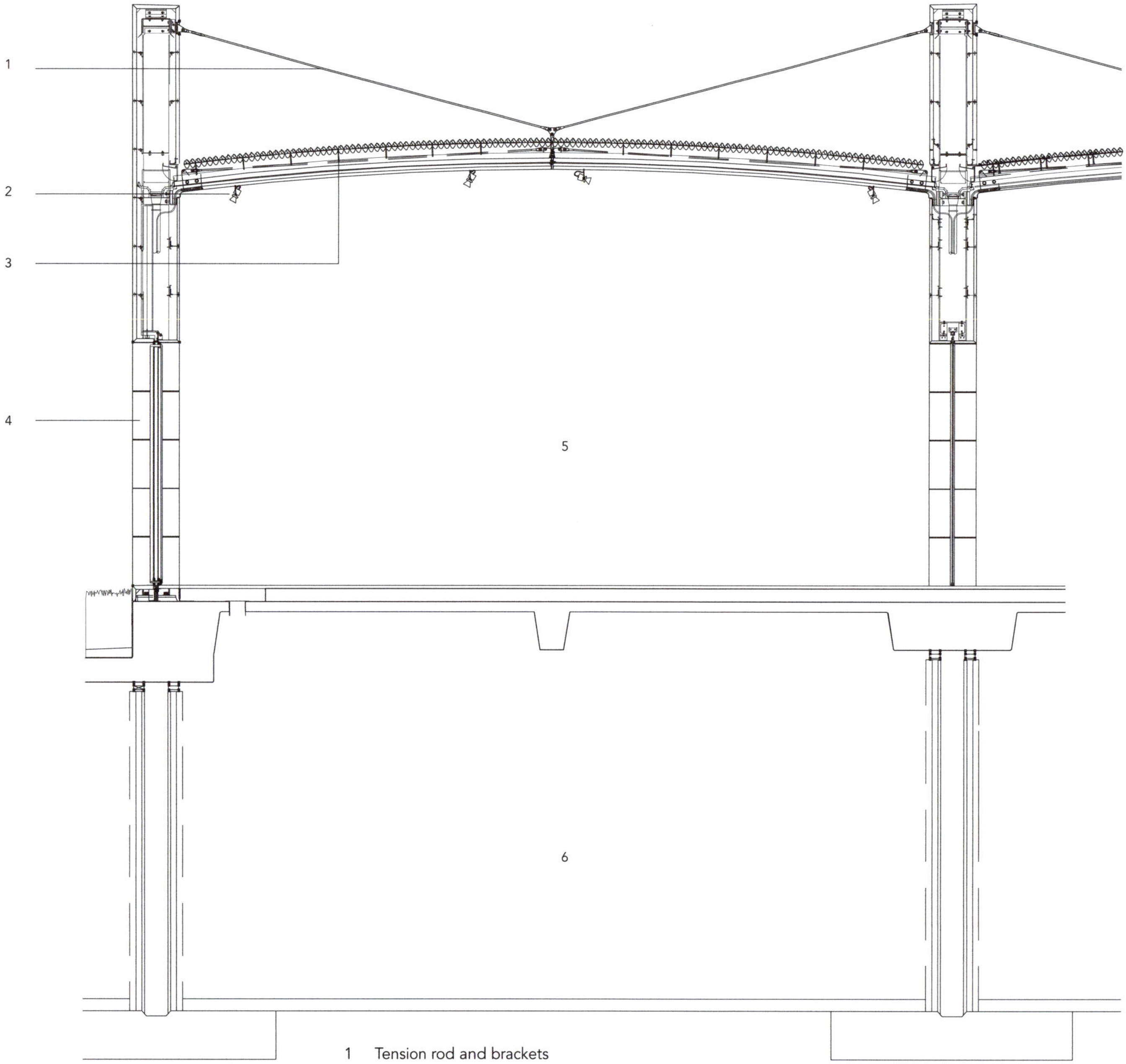

1 Tension rod and brackets
2 Electric spot lighting
3 Light filters and glass roof
4 Travertine panel
5 Ground floor
6 Basement

Partial section through basement and ground floors

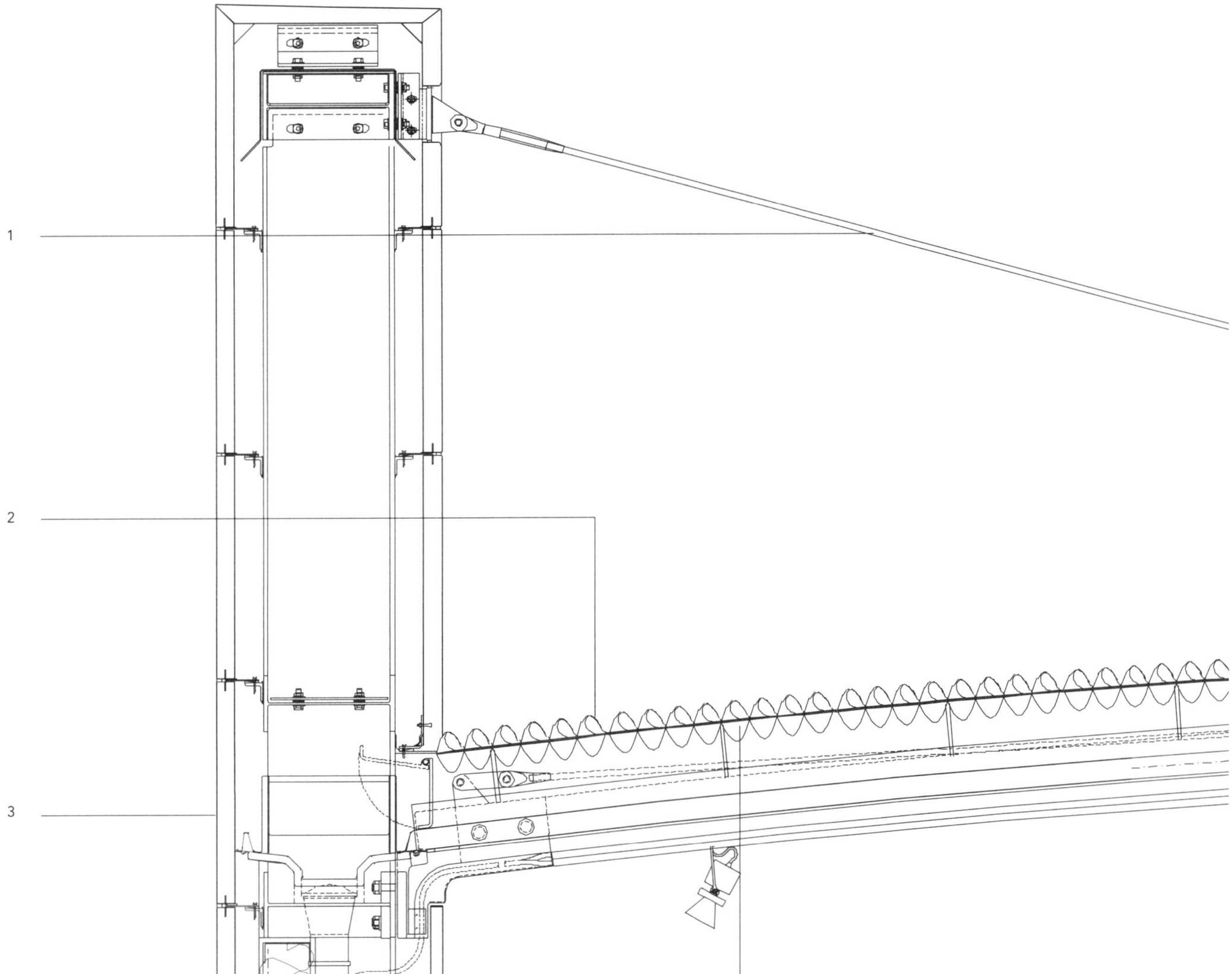

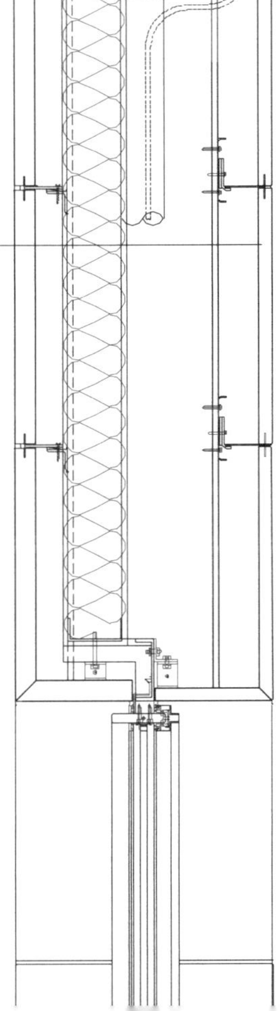

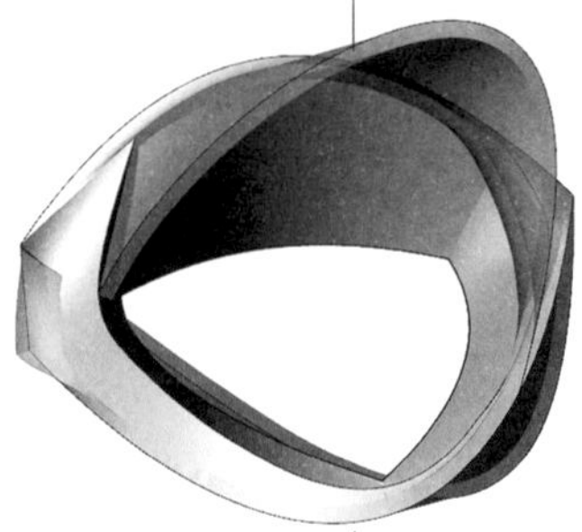

Plan

Detailed model of complex geometry and profile of an individual light scoop

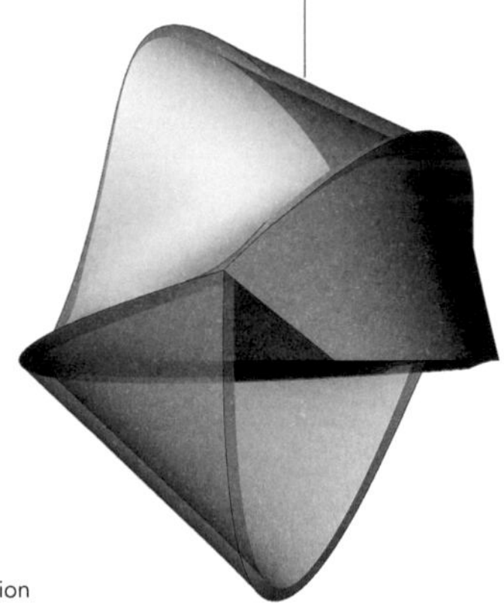

Elevation

Travertine wall and sun-shading device detail

1 Stainless steel tension rod
2 Sun-shading panels and glass roof
3 Exterior travertine panel (natural finish)
4 Interior travertine panel (polished finish)

The travertine-clad walls are constructed in structural steel. They anchor the tension rods, collect rainwater in hidden gutters and roof drains and house all pipes and cables for interior spaces.

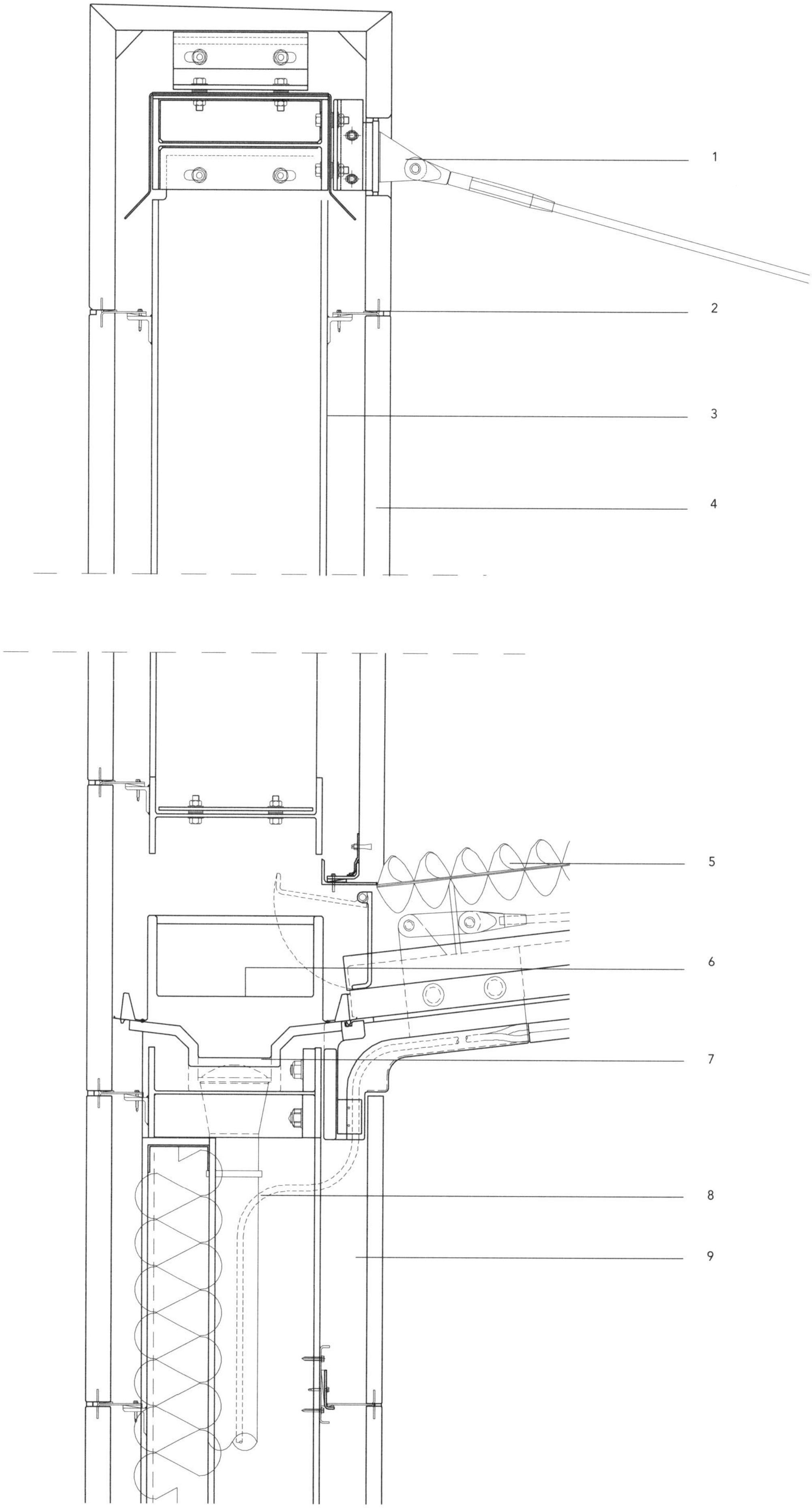

Wall and roof connection detail

1 Tension rod and bracket
2 Travertine panel bracket
3 Wide flange steel
4 Exterior travertine panel (natural finish)
5 Sun-shading panel
6 Gutter located within parapet
7 Roof drain and downspout
8 Spot lighting conduit
9 Interior travertine panel (polished finish)

Panel connection detail

1 Tension rods and cables, stainless steel
2 Pin joint, stainless steel
3 Stainless steel plate
4 Roof ridge beam cover strip
5 Sun-shading panels

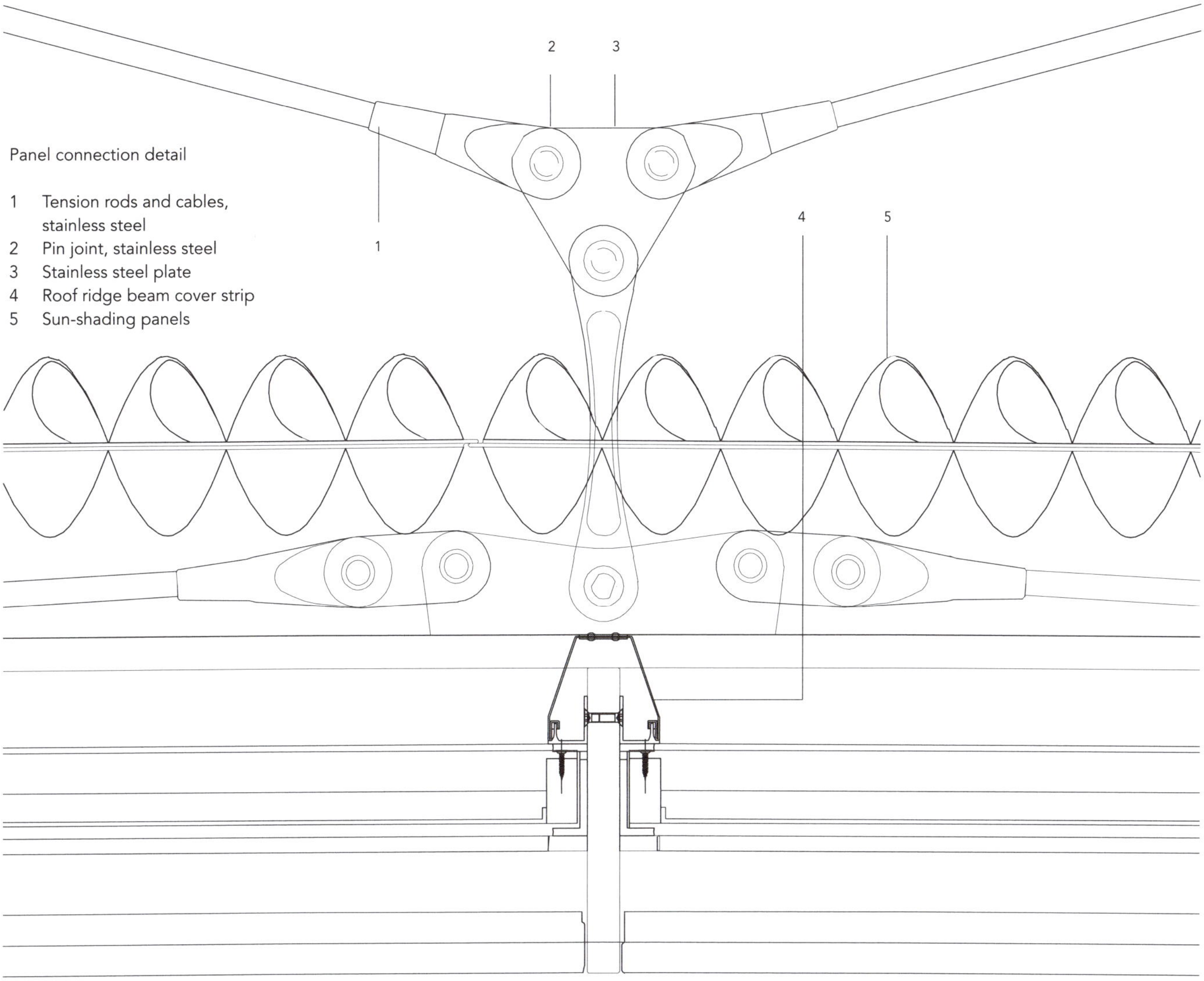

Connection between tension rods, steel beam and sun-shading panels

High Museum Expansion 1999–2005

Atlanta, Georgia, USA

Geographical context within the USA

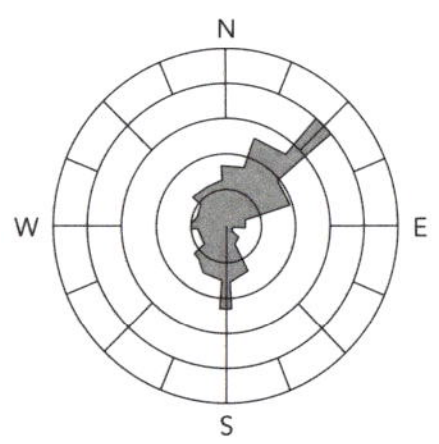

Wind rose: January

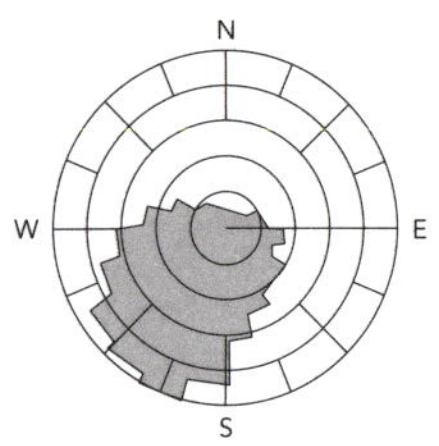

Wind rose: July

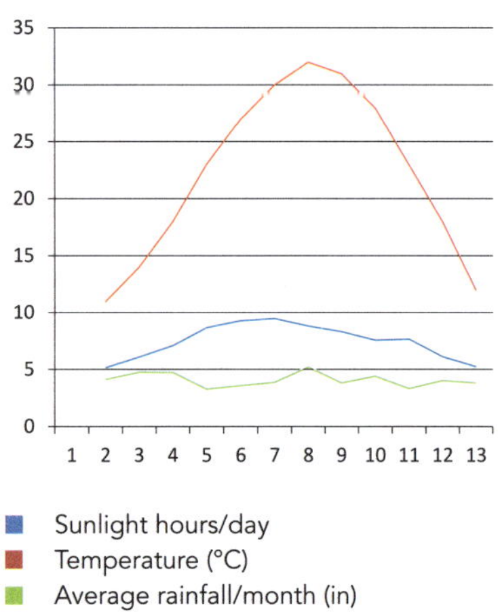

The site of the High Museum and Woodruff Arts Center is located at the intersection of 16th Street and Peachtree Street in downtown Atlanta. The High Museum features a collection of more than 17,000 works of art ranging from 19th- and 20th-century American and decorative art to contemporary photography and paintings, and was founded in 1905 as the Atlanta Art Association. In 1926 Mrs. Joseph M. High donated her family's residence on Peachtree Street to help the Association open their first permanent museum. In 1979, the Coca-Cola magnate Robert W. Woodruff made a large donation to build a new museum. The High Museum of Art's building was designed by the architect Richard Meier and opened in 1983.

In 2005, Renzo Piano designed the High Museum Expansion to increase the exhibition spaces and to create a vibrant art campus and public piazza, the "village for the arts" named The Woodruff Arts Center. The expansion included three new buildings, the Wieland Pavilion, the Anne Cox Chambers Wing and the Administrative Service Center, and doubled the museum's size to 29,000 square meters (312,000 square feet).

RPBW's museum extension is linked homogenously with Meier's museum. Both buildings are connected through sky bridges and the facades are clad with white aluminum panels. The top galleries of the extension are naturally lit through a grid of circular light scoops atop the roof, 800 on the Weiland Pavilion and 200 on the Anne Cox Chambers Wing. The north-facing skylights provide ambient illumination for the third-floor galleries with the necessary quantity of daylight for light-sensitive artwork.

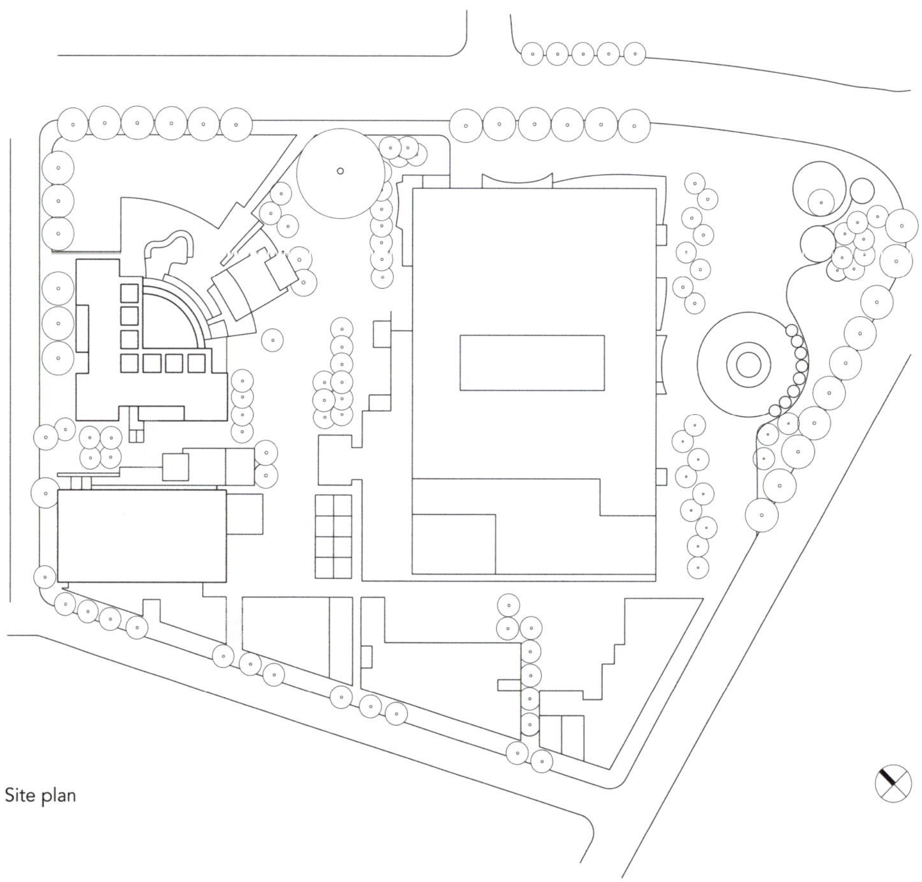

Site plan

Entry facade looking southwest

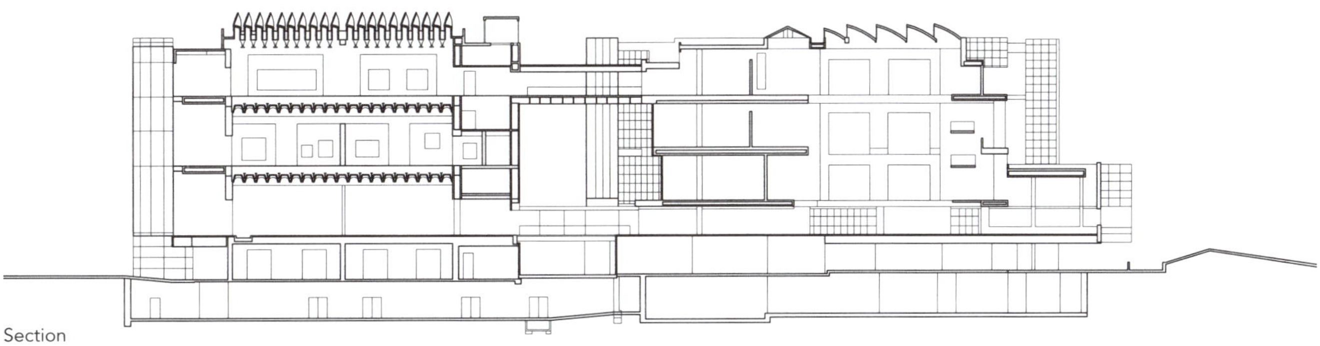

Section

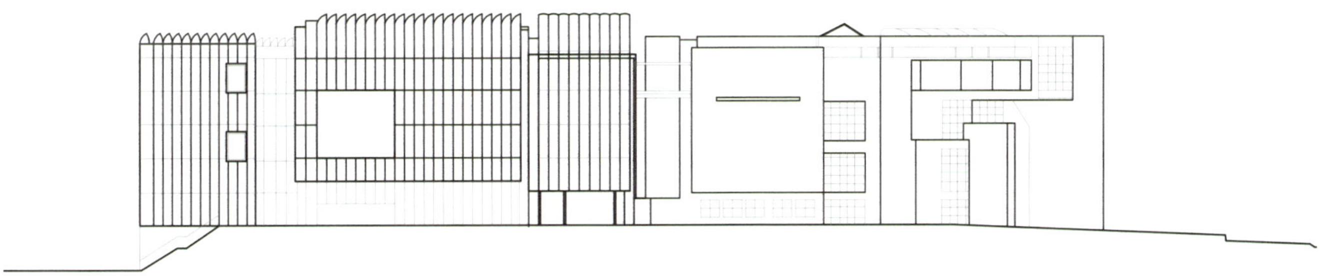

Elevation

The daylighting system with its skylights is entirely passive and has no mechanical systems. It comprises 1.82-meter (6-foot) high light scoops on the roof, circular glass skylights with a custom frit pattern and a tubular ceiling unit constructed of glass fiber-reinforced gypsum to diffuse and direct light from the skylight. The white aluminum light scoops oriented due north and 26 degrees off the building axis reflect indirect sunlight into the galleries off the white surface of the vela in front.

Aerial view

Wall section
Cut through a single light tube

1 Aluminum light scoop
2 Structural I-beams
3 Glass fiber-reinforced gypsum
4 Spot lighting
5 Aluminum rain screen facade
6 Gallery wall
7 Concrete flooring

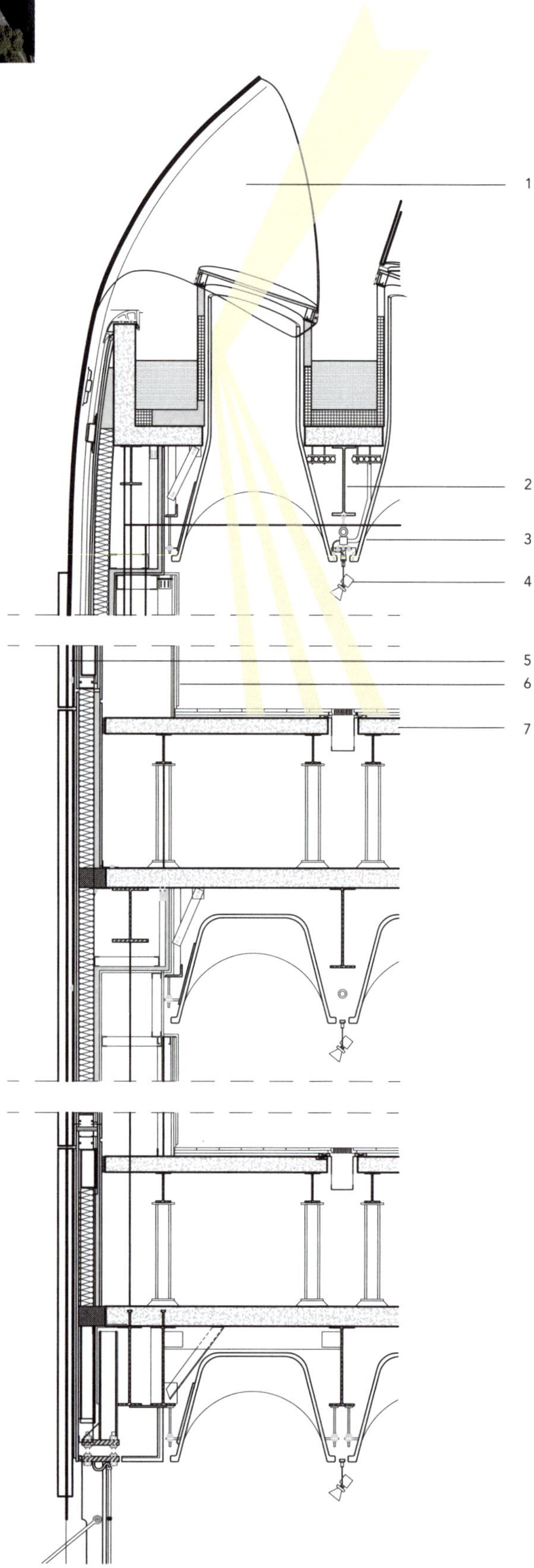

Third-floor gallery with skylight

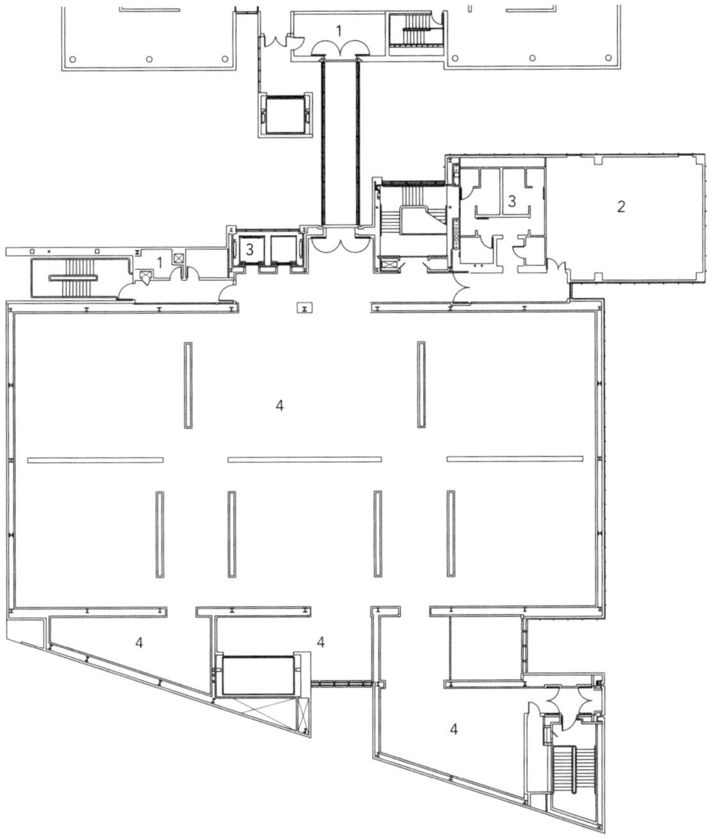

Second floor plan

1 Bridge foyer
2 Mechanical space
3 Elevators
4 Permanent gallery

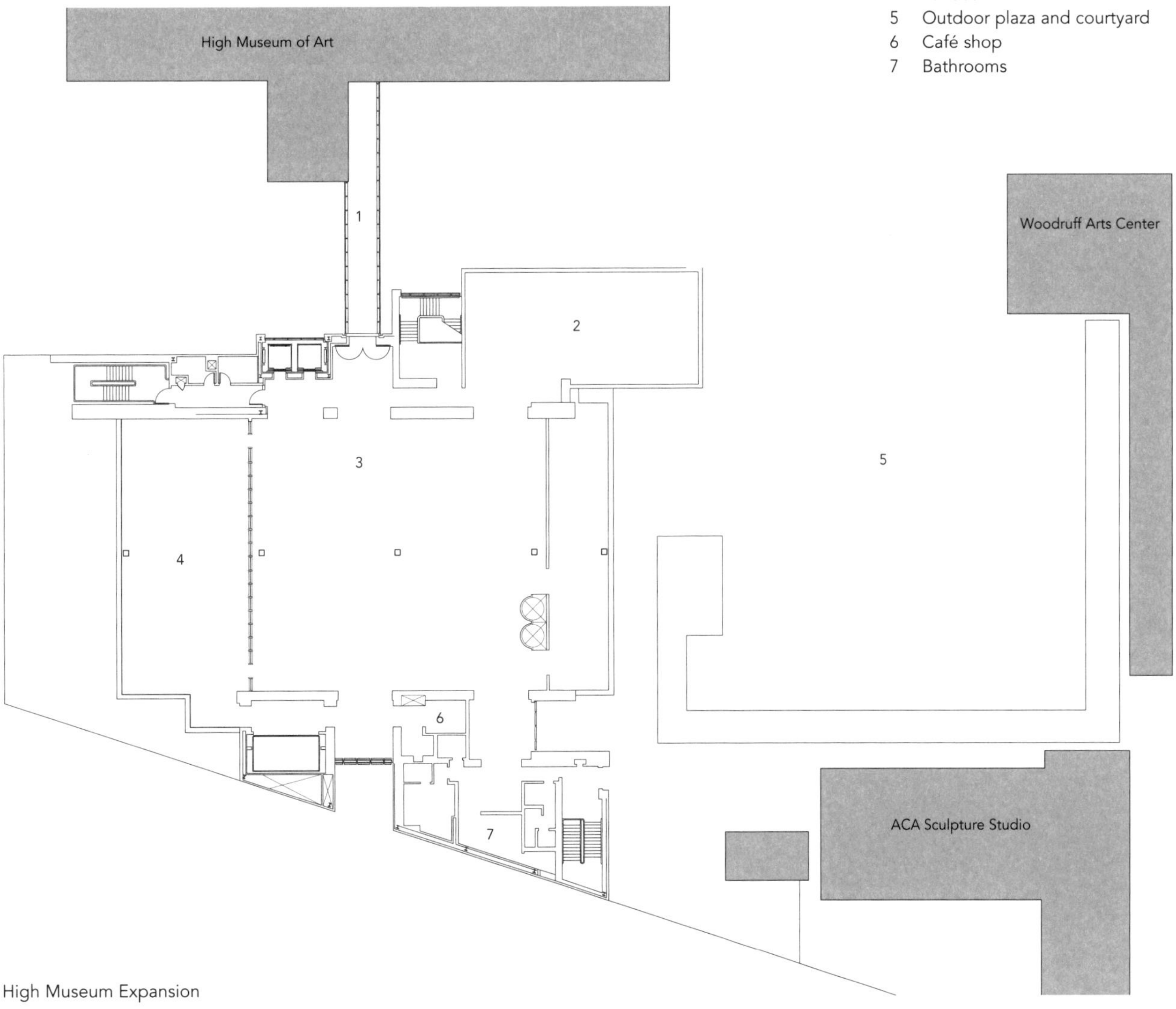

Ground floor plan

1 Bridge
2 Museum shop
3 Lobby
4 Terrace
5 Outdoor plaza and courtyard
6 Café shop
7 Bathrooms

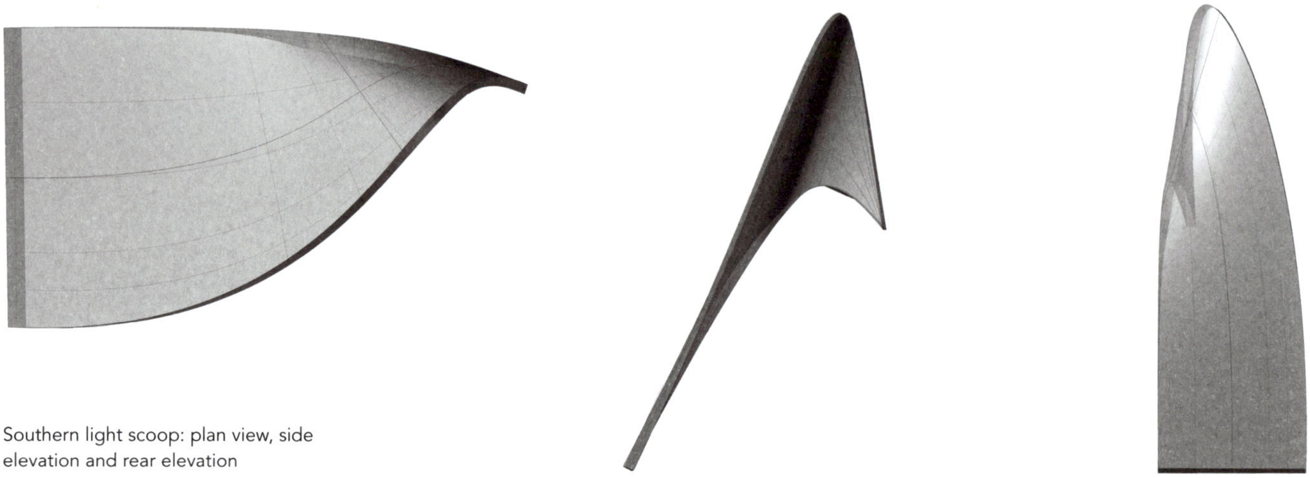

Southern light scoop: plan view, side elevation and rear elevation

View of third-floor gallery. Skylights evenly diffuse the natural light into the space.

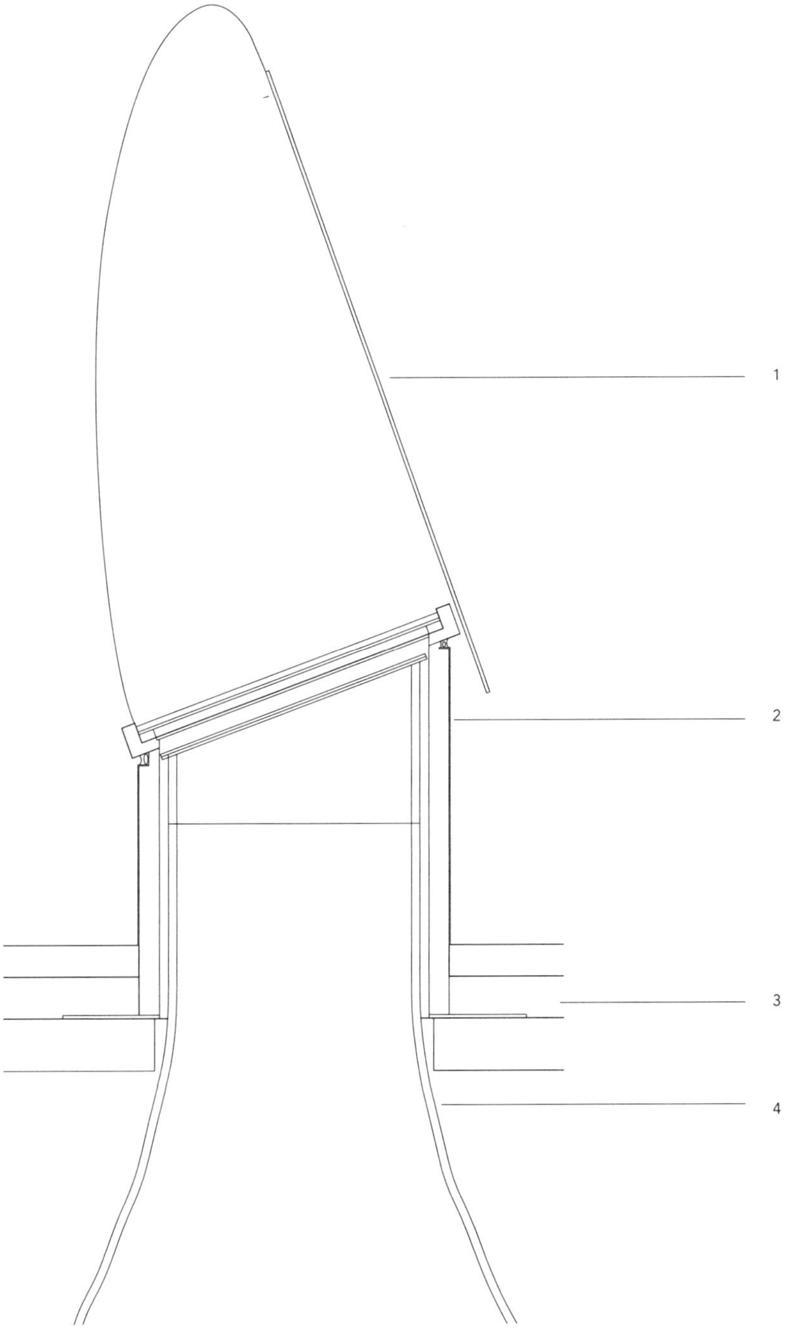

Section detail through light tube

1 Light scoop
2 Flashing and thermal insulation
3 Roof structure
4 Glass fiber-reinforced gypsum tube

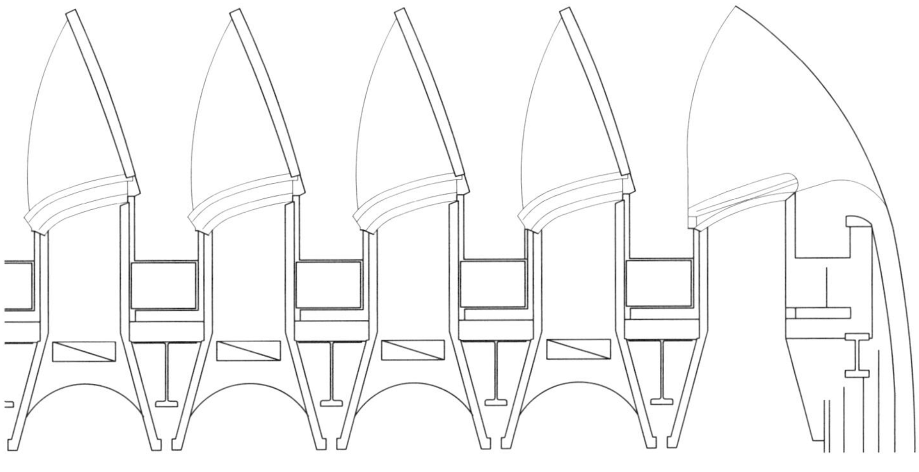

Elevation of light tubes showing joints and connections between tubes

Third-floor gallery space showing light tubes on roof

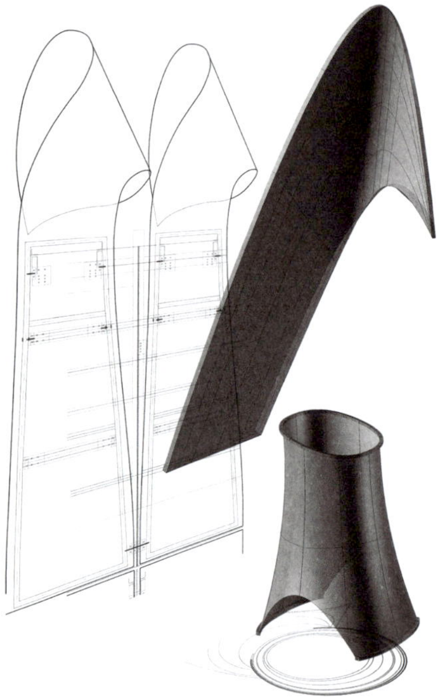

Exploded axonometry
Skylight system detail showing the connection between adjacent scoops and roof edge

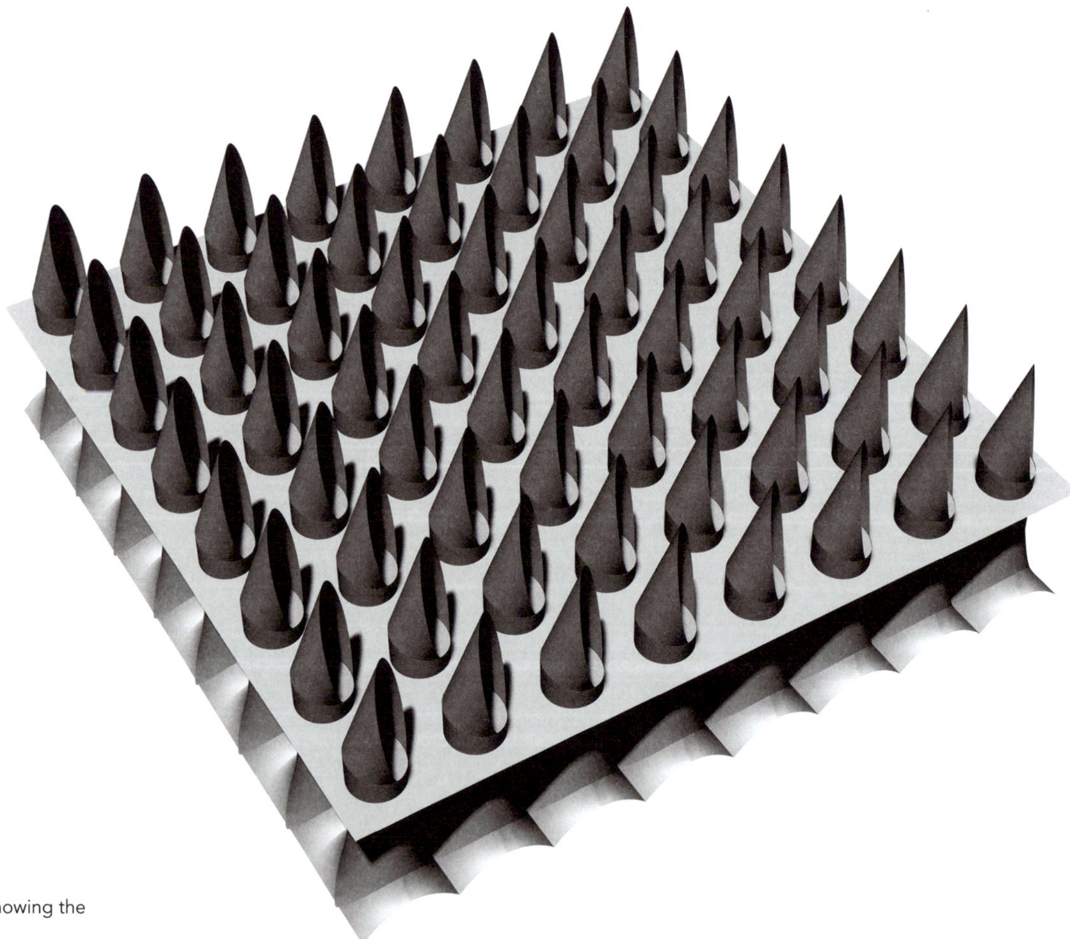

Abstracted section of the roof showing the light scoops and tubes

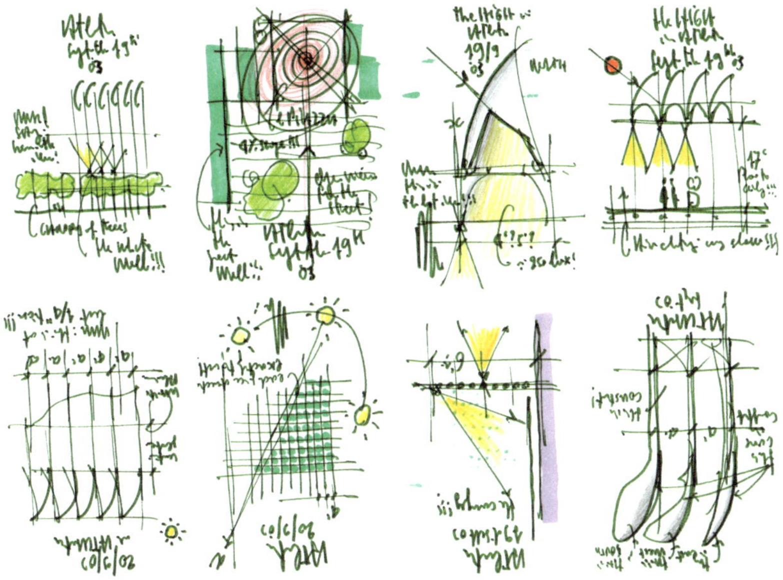

Renzo Piano sketches

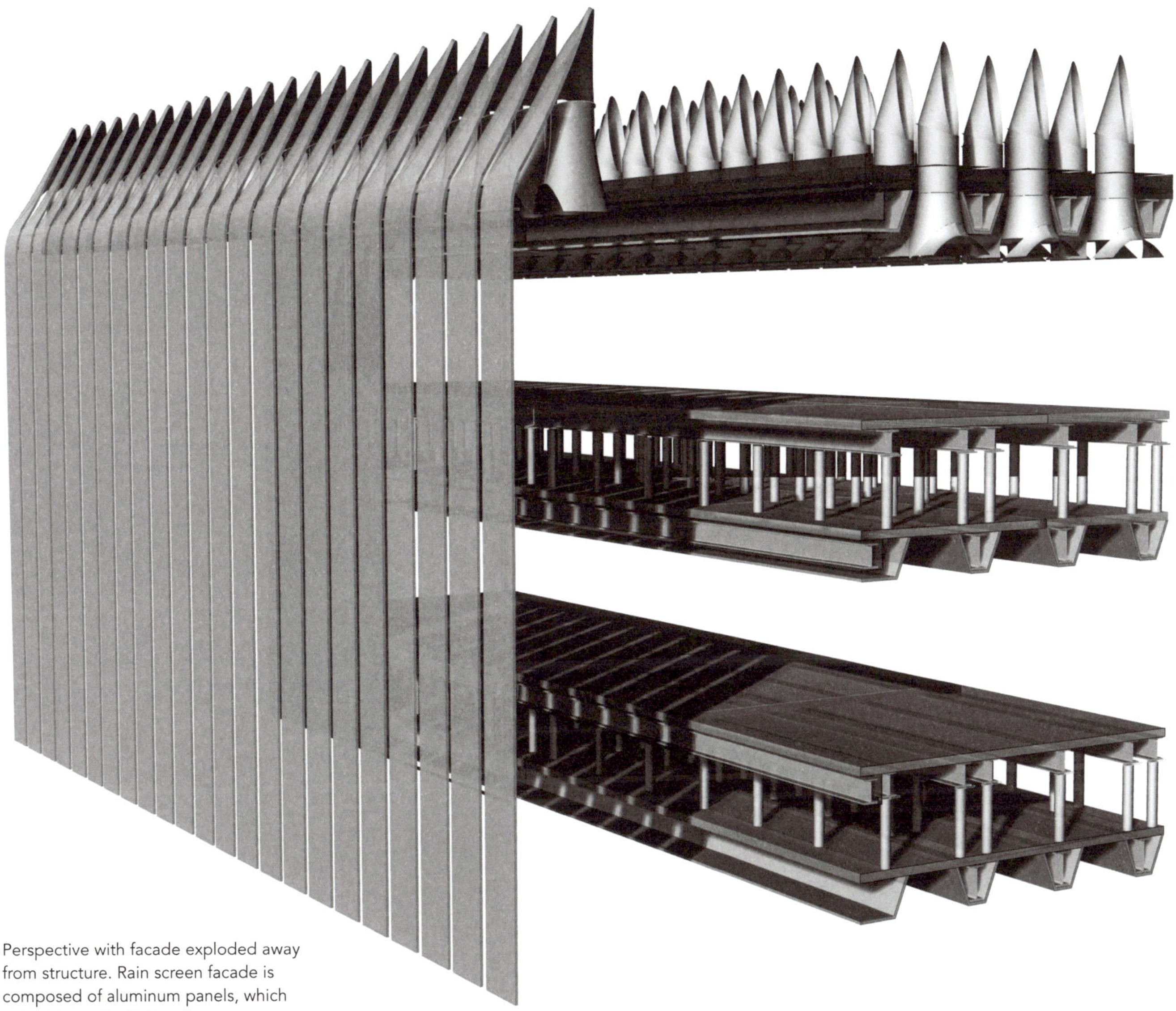

Perspective with facade exploded away from structure. Rain screen facade is composed of aluminum panels, which extend from the light scoops.

Zentrum Paul Klee
1999–2005

Bern, Switzerland

Geographical context within Switzerland

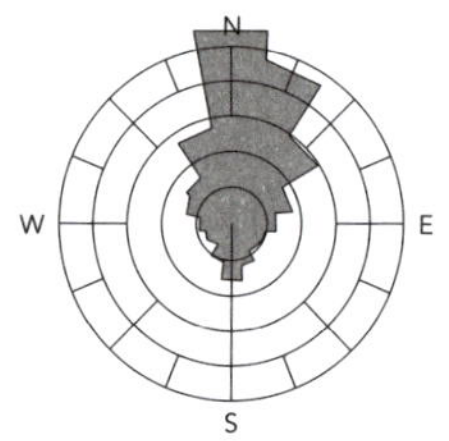

Wind rose: January

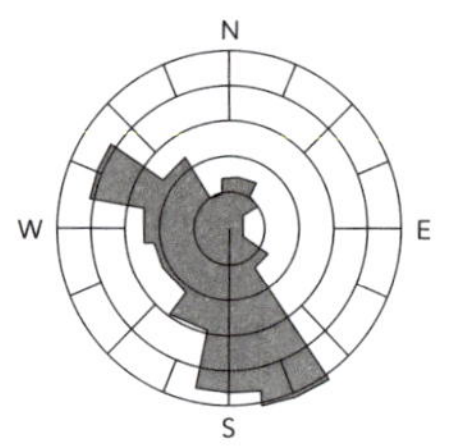

Wind rose: July

The Zentrum Paul Klee is located near Bern, the capital of Switzerland. With nearly 40% of Paul Klee's collection and more than 4,000 works of art, the museum is one of the world's largest monographic collections. The museum complex with its undulating roof blends into the rolling hills of the natural landscape and the distant profile of the Alps. The roof takes the form of three artificial hills and is barely visible from a distance. The curvilinear structure, up to 19 meters (63.3 feet) high, encloses the three main exhibition spaces, a concert hall, the conference center, an interactive children's workshop and the Paul Klee research center. The design intent was to create a peaceful place through the architectural form of the museum that mirrors Klee's passion for harmony of form, proportions and nature.

The museum houses the delicate artwork of Paul Klee and was specifically designed to protect the art from the negative effects of sunlight. The building faces west and allows sunlight to filter in through the 150-meter (492-foot) glassed facade. The entrance is between two of the "hills" and can be reached via a bridge that leads onto the major circulation path connecting each of the main galleries. The undulating roof consists of steel beams, each unique in its curvature and dimensions, and an aluminum roof system. The complex geometry of the series of waves situated on concentric circles required the development of a parametric computer model for the steel structure to aid the design process. The parametric data were ultimately also used to map the geometry of the curved I-beams into two-dimensional plans for the steel contractor.[1]

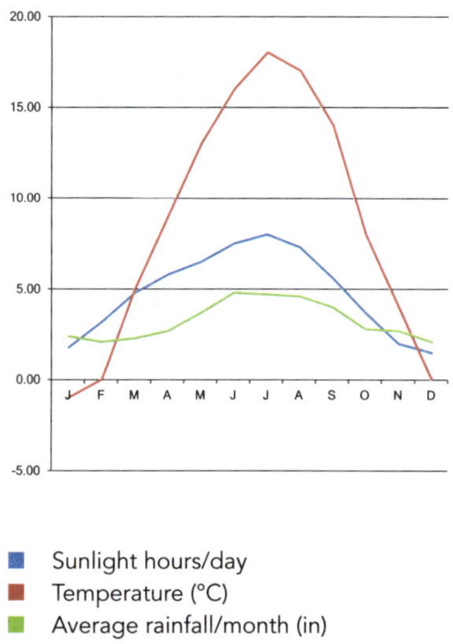

Site plan

1 Design-to-Production GmbH, Stuttgart/Zurich

Site view taken from the northeast corner of the property. The form created by the aluminum roof system blends with the landscape of the site, mimicking the terrain of the surrounding foothills.

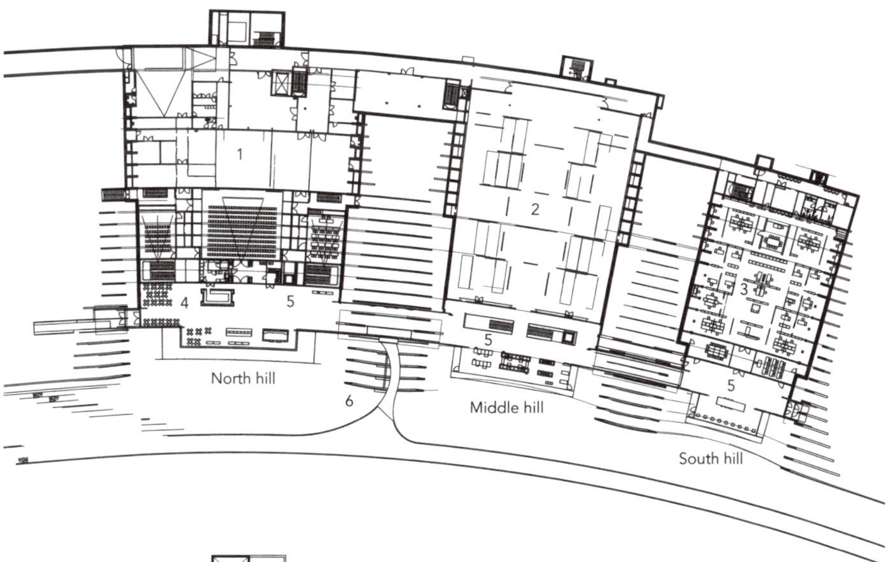

Ground floor plan

1 Restoration studio and workshops
2 Gallery spaces
3 Offices for administration and research
4 Café and ticket office
5 "Museum Street"
6 Main entrance

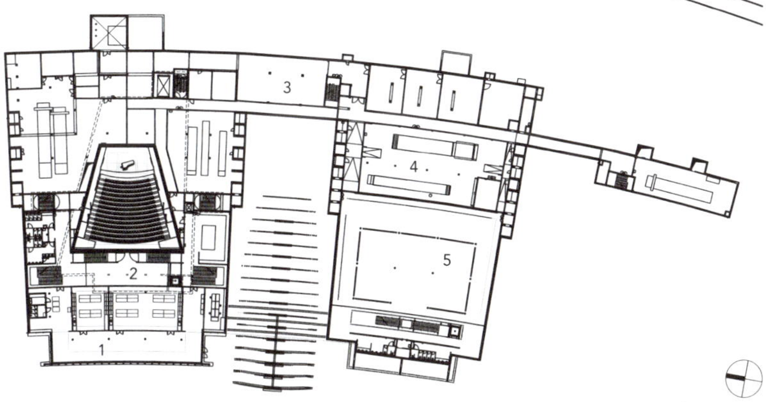

Lower level floor plan

1 Children's museum
2 Auditorium
3 Museum storeroom
4 Building services
5 Temporary exhibit area

View inside the gallery spaces. The delicacy of Paul Klee's works on paper required a controllable artificial lighting system for the gallery spaces. The light is diffused through a screen system that simulates the experience of natural light.

To modulate the landscape and embed the Zentrum Paul Klee's underground floors, 180,000 cubic meters (6,357,000 cubic feet) of earth had to be moved. The roof section, three hills wide, required 1,100 tons of steel girders and 1,000 tons of reinforcing steel and 10,000 cubic meters (353,000 cubic feet) of concrete to be put into place. The building's complex geometry resulted in an intricate design for the glass facade. Divided into an upper and a lower section along the entire length of the building, it defines the so-called "Museum Street", the spatial connection between all three hills and the different museum programs.

The long glass facade is daylit and controlled by motorized textile shading devices that filter natural light into the interior spaces. To protect Klee's delicate watercolors, paintings and drawings from the sun, the maximum illuminance values for the gallery spaces were set between 50 and 100 lumens. To achieve these requirements, only artificial light is used in the main hall under the middle hill and the exhibition hall on the lower floor of the building. The indirect base-lighting is installed in between the steel girders while individual artworks are accentuated by spotlights.

View of gallery and walkway washed with natural light, filtered by the building's facade to protect the artwork from harmful direct sunlight.

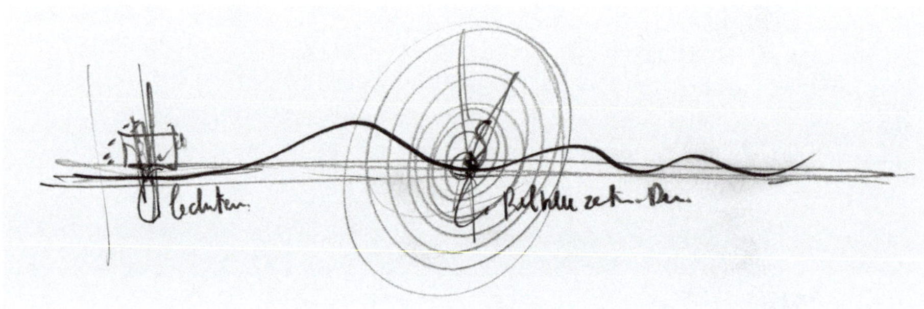

Renzo Piano sketch

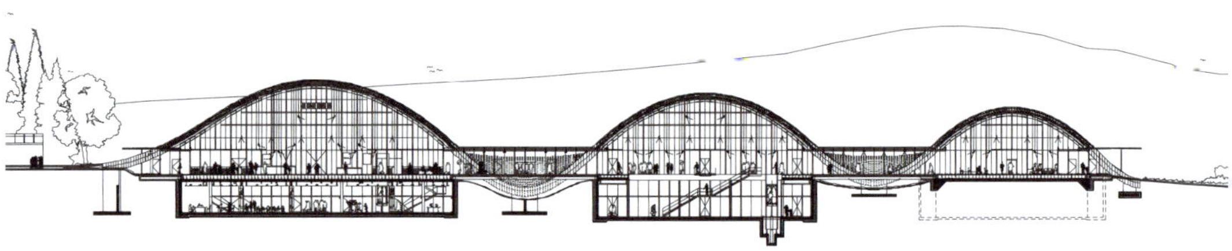

Section through museum

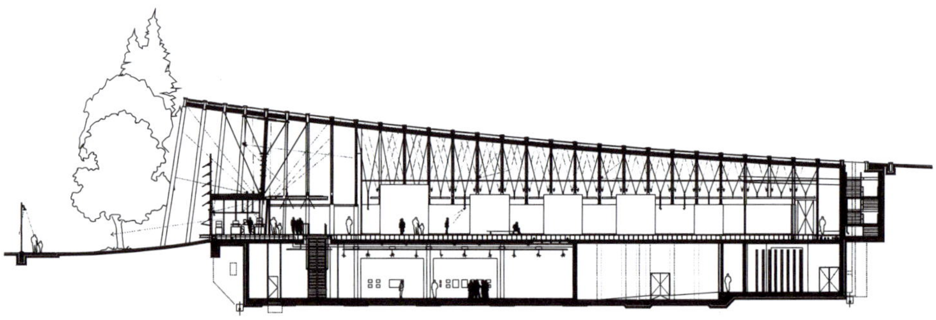

Section through auditorium

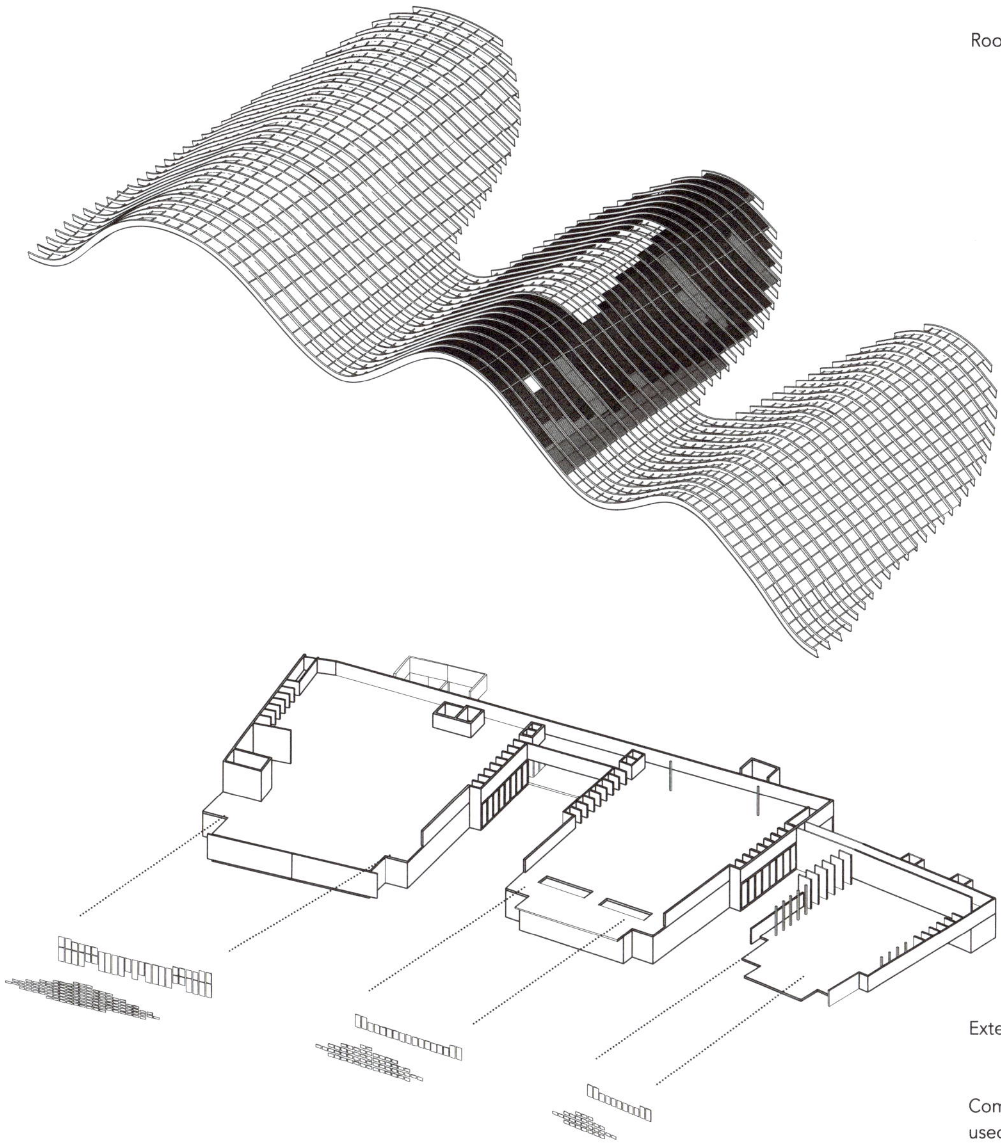

Roof system

Exterior walls

Computer-aided design technologies were used to define the complex geometry.

Roof structure showing steel beams

Exterior detail

1 Steel tension cable
2 Raised floor
3 Concrete slab
4 Steel beam
5 Curved I-beams
6 Stainless steel tension cable
7 Louvers
8 Timber decking
9 Curtain wall

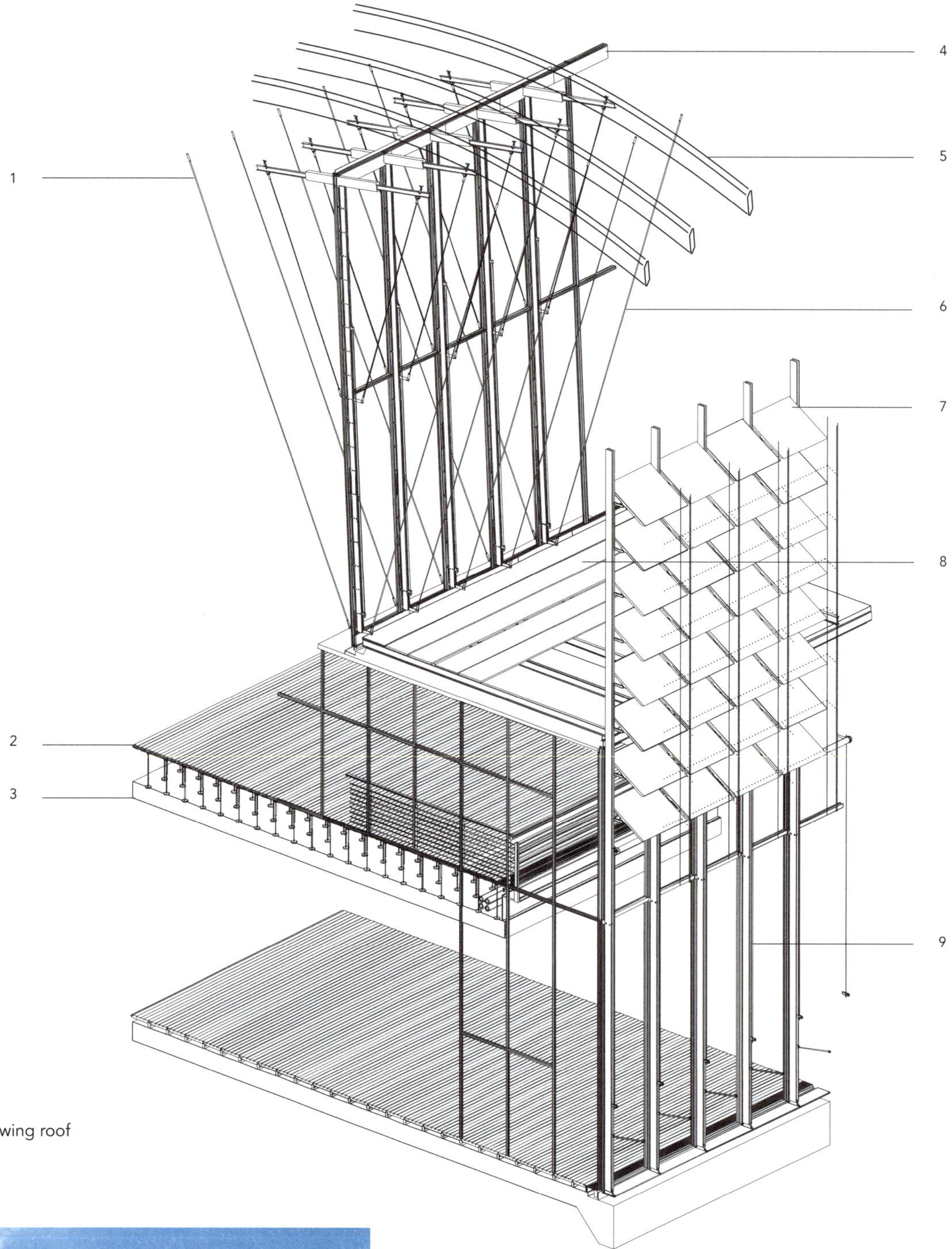

Exterior facade of building showing roof structure and shading device

The main pedestrian bridge integrated into the aluminum roof system

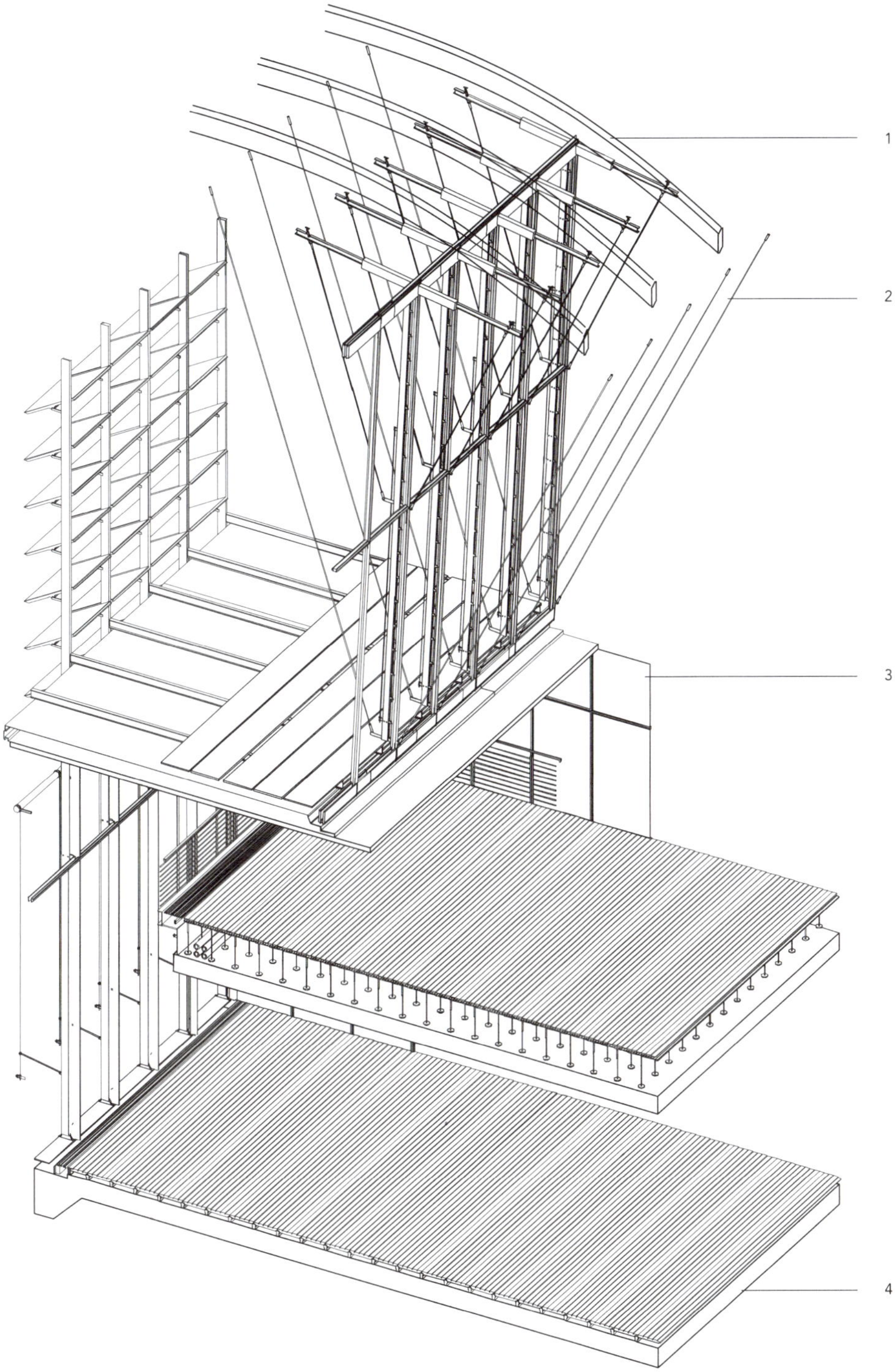

Interior detail

1 Curved I-beams
2 Stainless steel tension cable
3 Curtain wall
4 Site-cast concrete foundation wall

Children's workshop

Double-height "Museum Street" along the west facade

Building section showing roof and wall structure

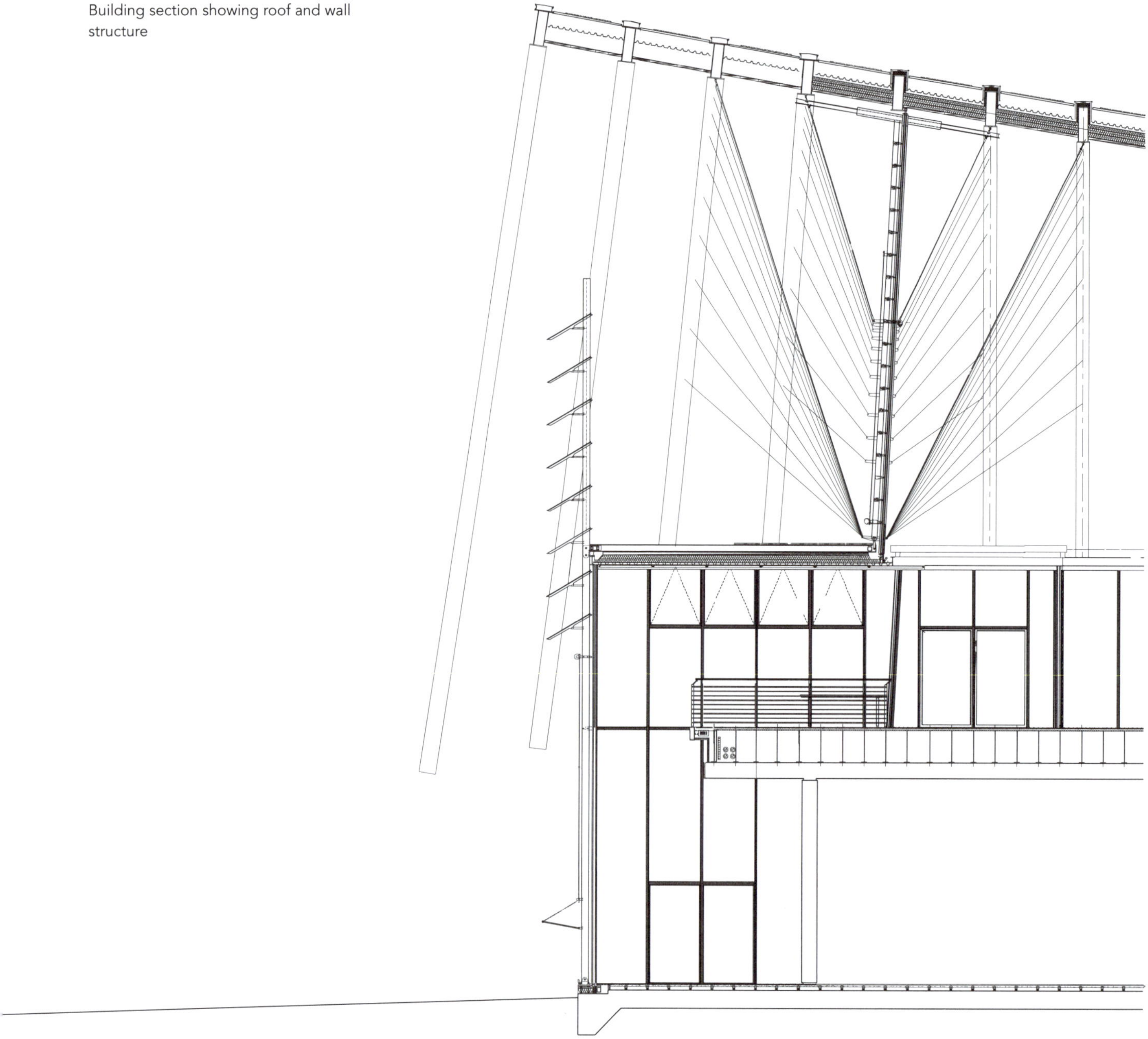

Integration of the roof structure and atrium facade

View of facade from interior atrium

Interior view from facade

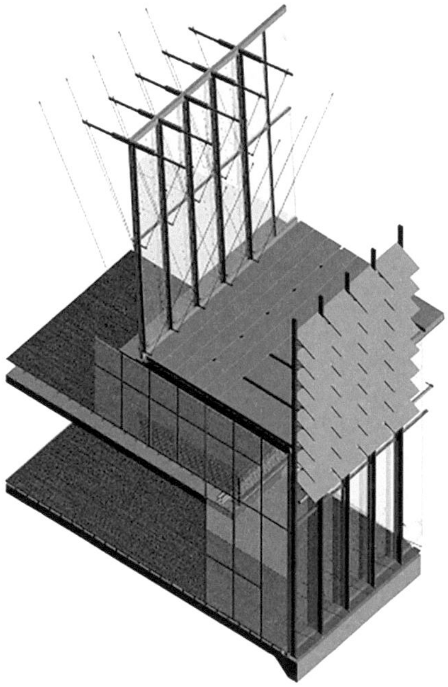

Building axon corner detail showing structure and facade shading panels

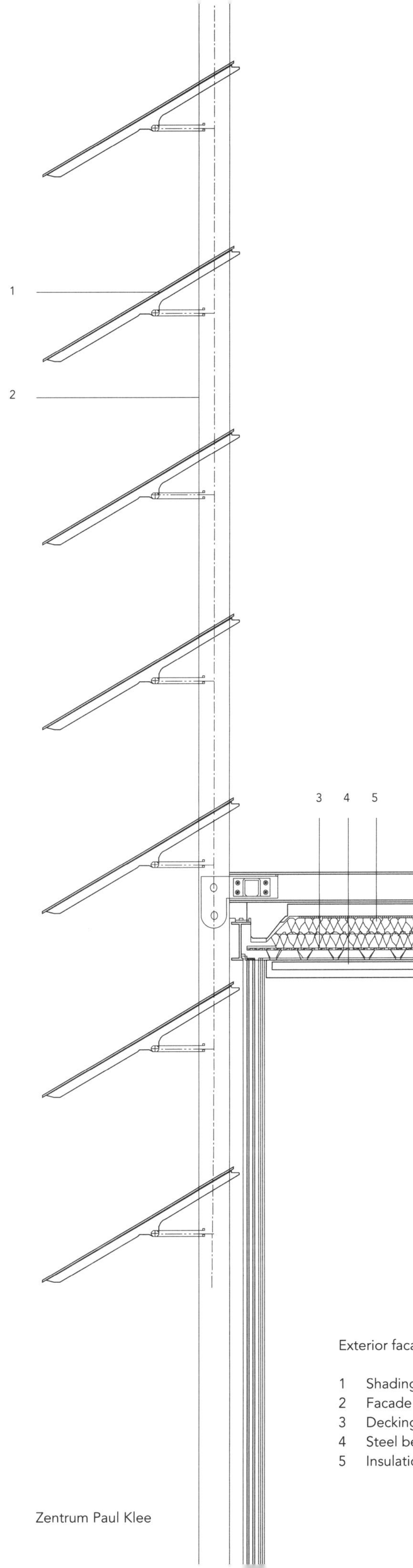

Exterior facade detail

1 Shading panel, glass
2 Facade structure
3 Decking
4 Steel beam
5 Insulation

Renovation and Expansion of the Morgan Library and Museum, 2000–2006

New York City, New York, USA

Geographical context within the USA

The Morgan Library and Museum is located on the corner of 37th Street and Madison Avenue in the heart of Manhattan, New York City. Originally an elegant group of buildings from 1906 and 1928, Renzo Piano's expansion, completed in 2006, connects and extends the existing complex. The Morgan Library and Museum houses various collections originally acquired by its founder, Pierpont Morgan. The collections range from Egyptian and Renaissance art to historical manuscripts and printed books. Piano's design incorporates four new galleries, the Engelhard Gallery, the Morgan Stanley Gallery East, the Morgan Stanley Gallery West and the Clare Eddy Thaw Gallery.

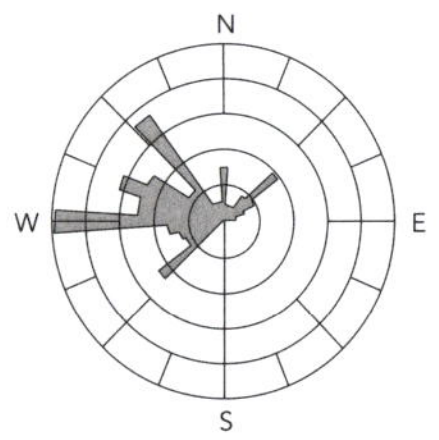

Wind rose: January

These additions create a new entrance and public spaces along Madison Avenue while adding 6,970 square meters (75,000 square feet) to the 14,030 square meters (151,000 square feet) of the Morgan complex. It allows the museum collection to expand as well as increase space for a library, reading room, an auditorium for chamber music and the museum's administration. More than half of the newly built space is located below ground and so it was necessary to excavate to a depth of 17 meters (56 feet). The central pavilion, flooded with natural light, has the beautiful atmosphere of an Italian piazza and connects the three historic buildings with the new pavilions.

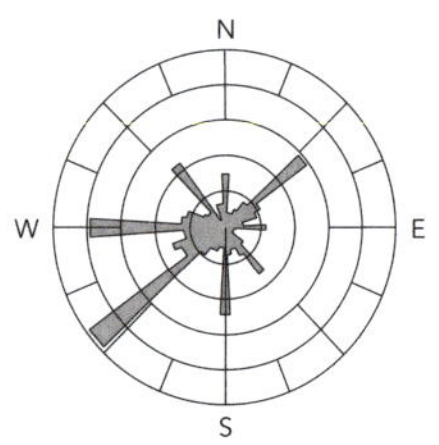

Wind rose: July

The building ensemble is covered with a high-transparency glass and louver system which filters daylight into the spaces. The faceted steel structure is coated in a rose-hued, off-white to sublimely match the Tennessee pink marble of the McKim building and annex. The pavilion facades, a combination of opaque steel panel, transparent low-iron glass and automated roller sunshades, seamlessly join the ensemble of old and new buildings.

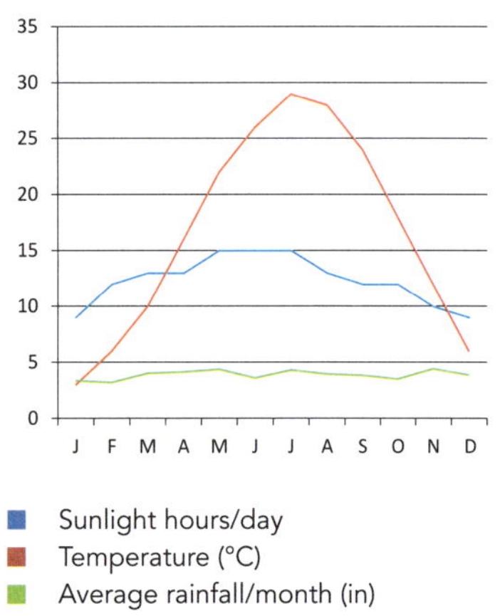

Site plan

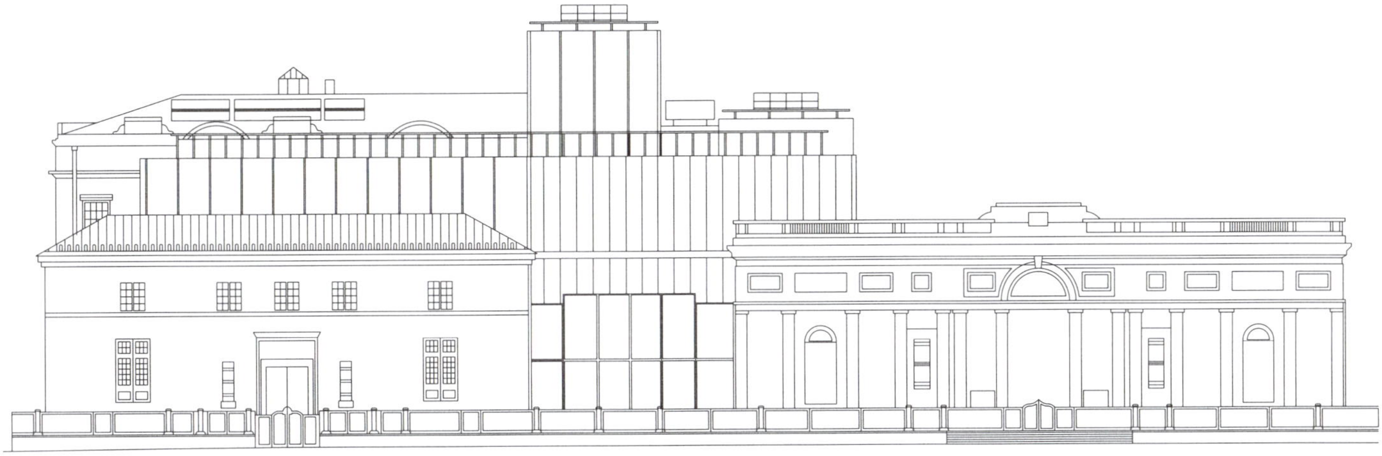

South elevation

Entrance facade along Madison Avenue, Manhattan

Section through the Morgan House, the Madison Avenue pavilion and the annex

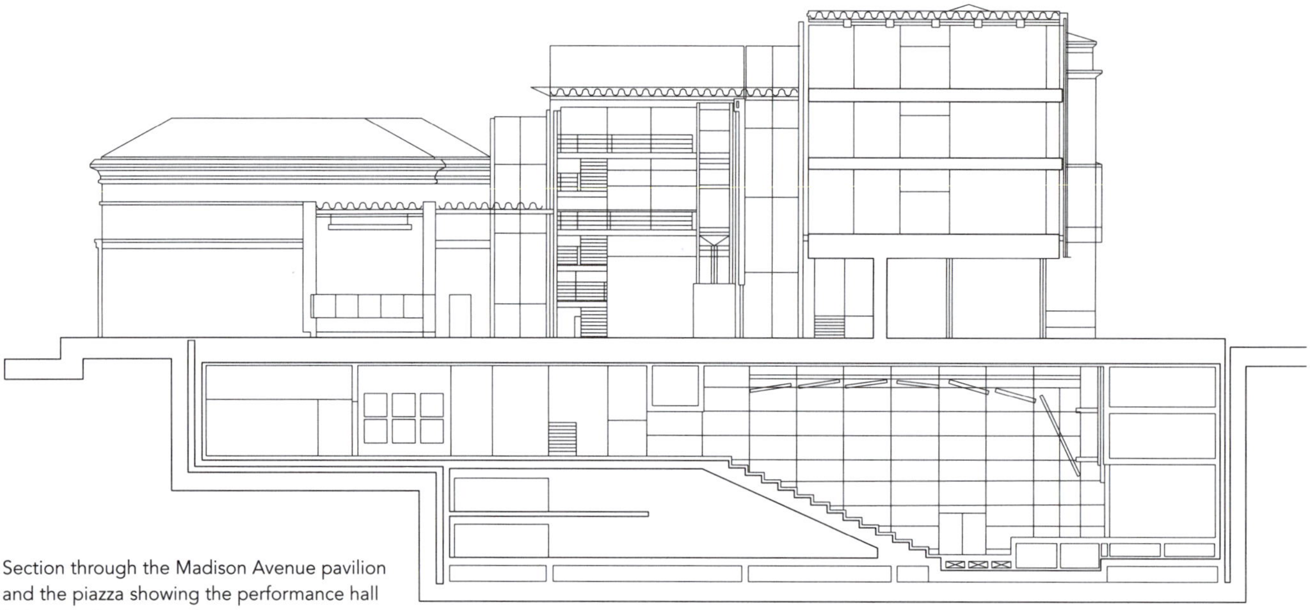

Section through the Madison Avenue pavilion and the piazza showing the performance hall below grade

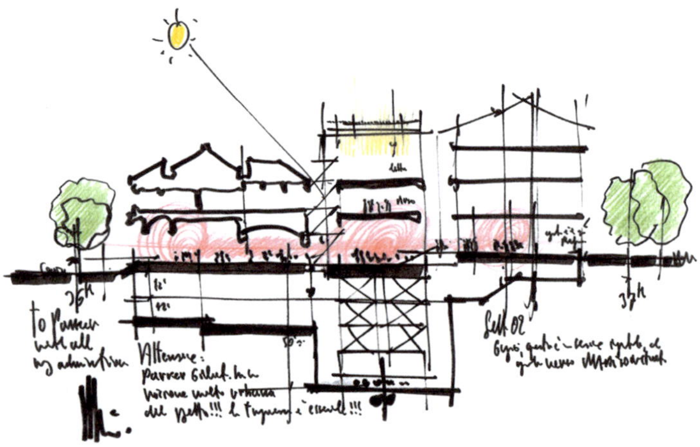

Renzo Piano sketch

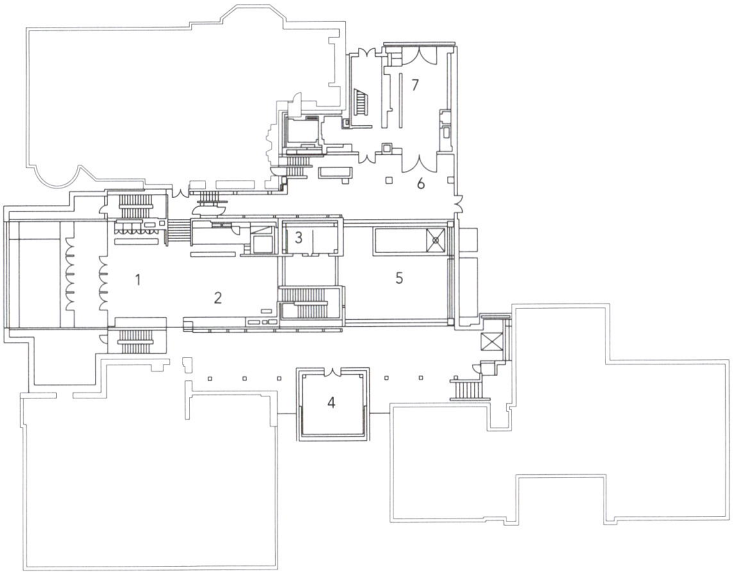

Second floor plan

1 Information desk
2 Lobby
3 Glass elevator
4 Cube gallery
5 Piazza
6 Café
7 Loading dock

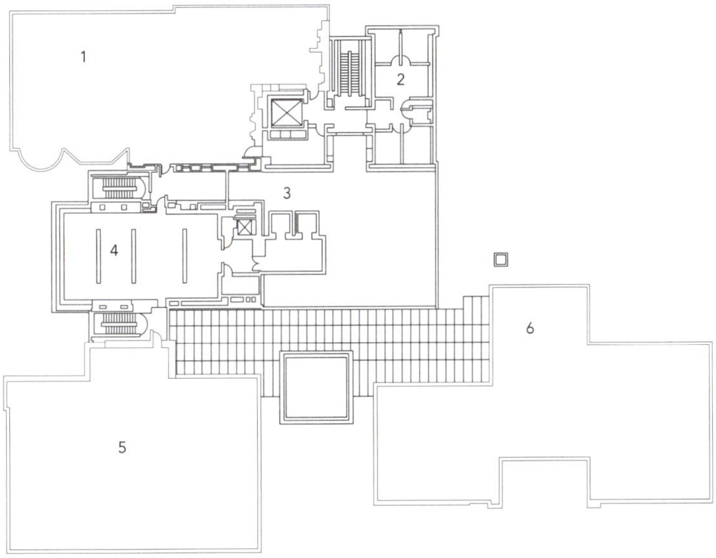

Ground floor plan

1 Morgan House – 1852
2 Office
3 Glass elevator
4 Reading room
5 Library annex – 1928
6 Original library – 1906

Interior view of piazza

Interior view from second floor overlooking piazza space

Exterior view of facade corner

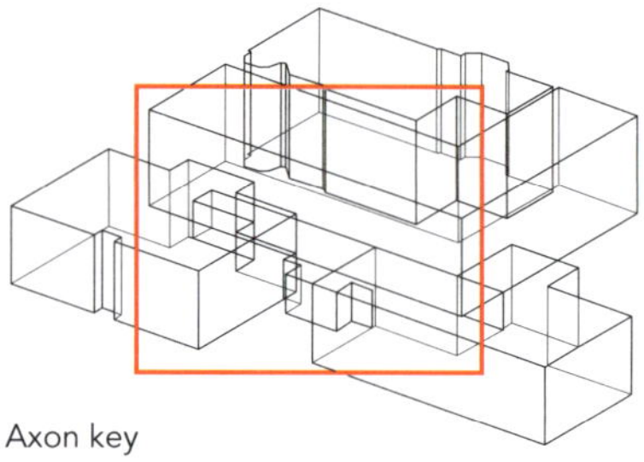

Axon key

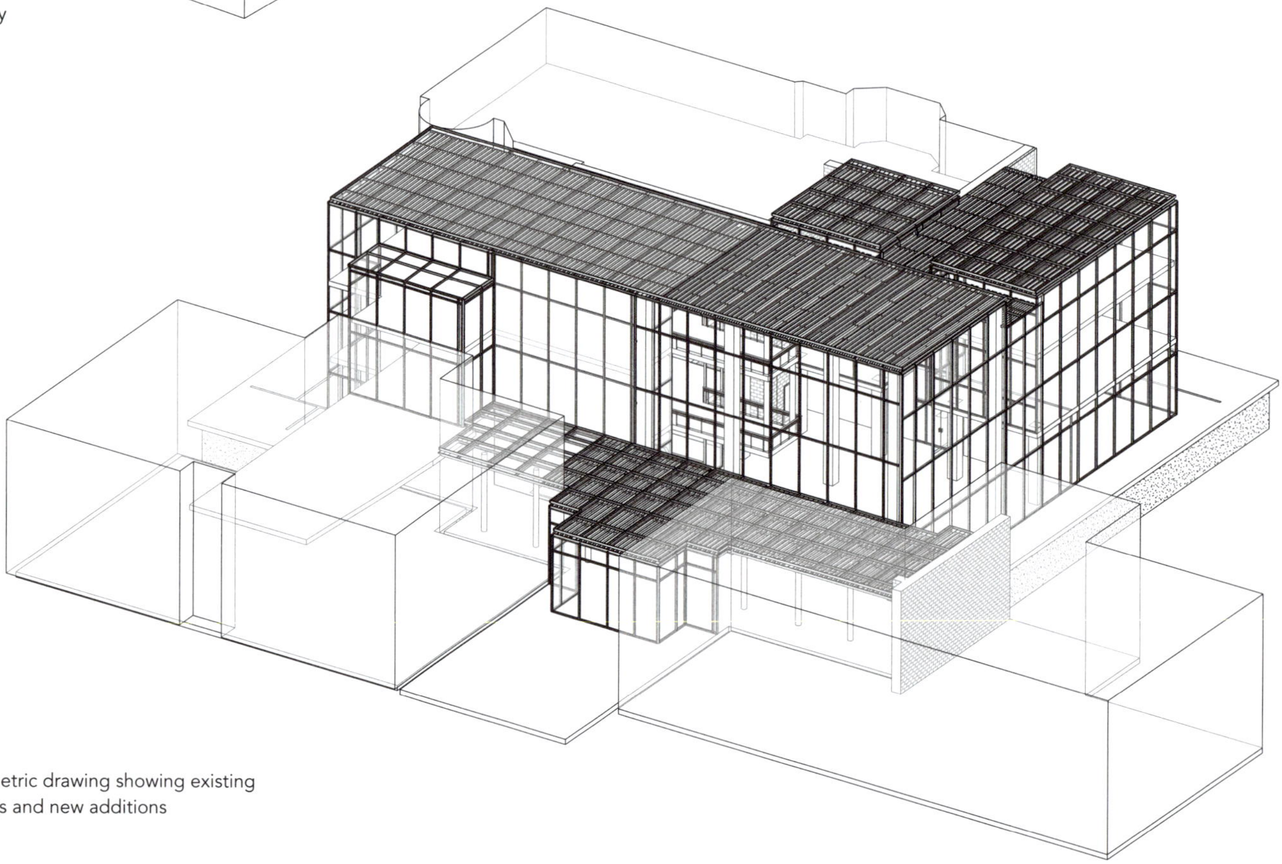

Axonometric drawing showing existing buildings and new additions

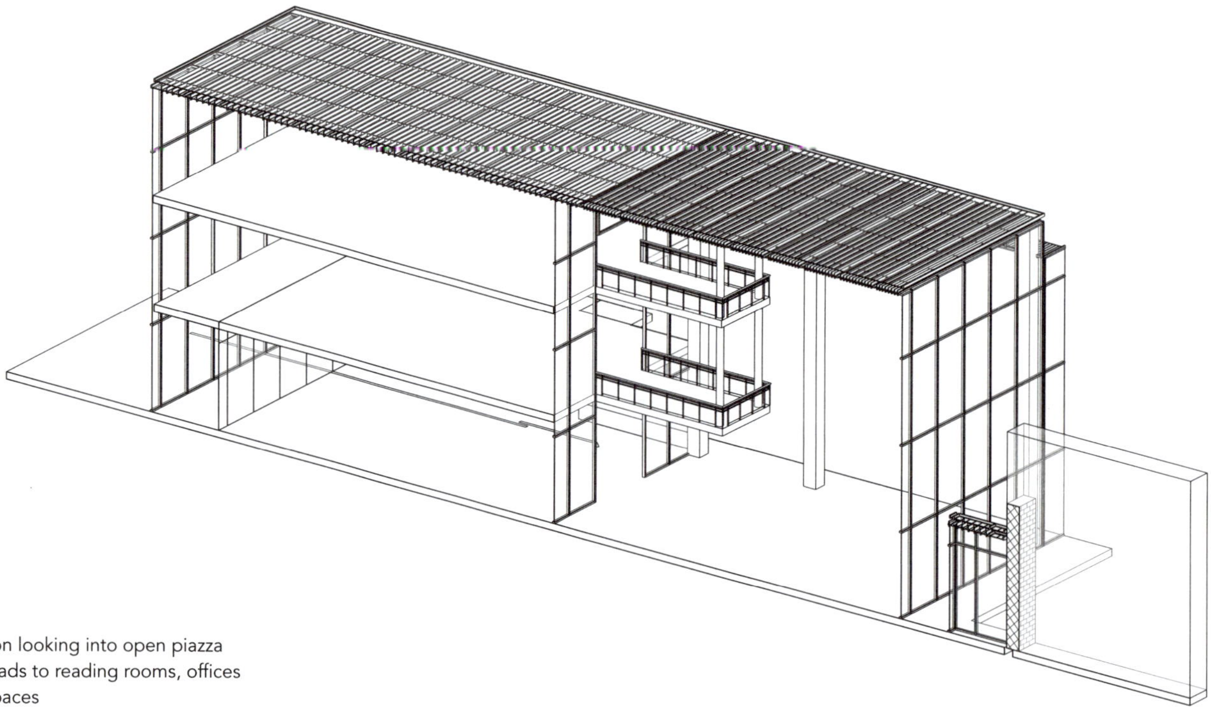

Corner section
Cutaway section looking into open piazza space which leads to reading rooms, offices and support spaces

View through the curtain wall to rear courtyard

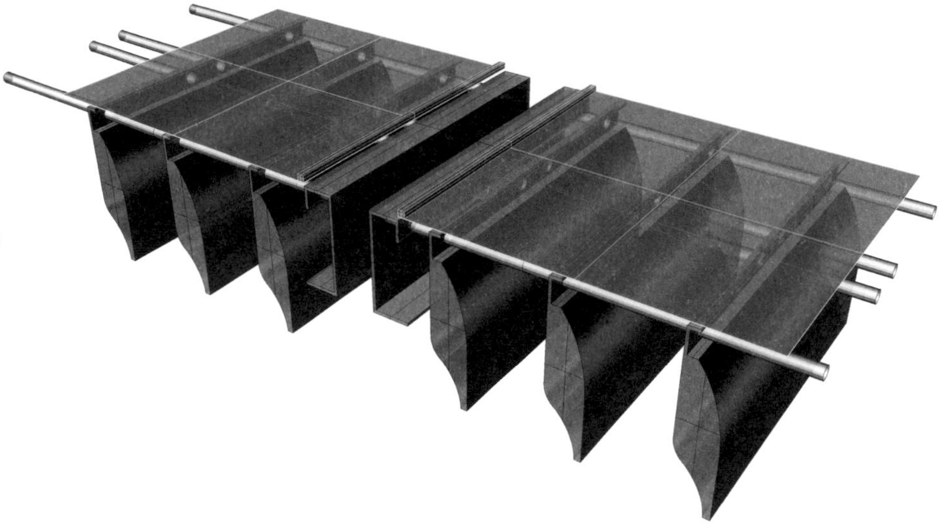

Detail of the interior solar shading fins. The shading system is extruded across the entire roof planes.

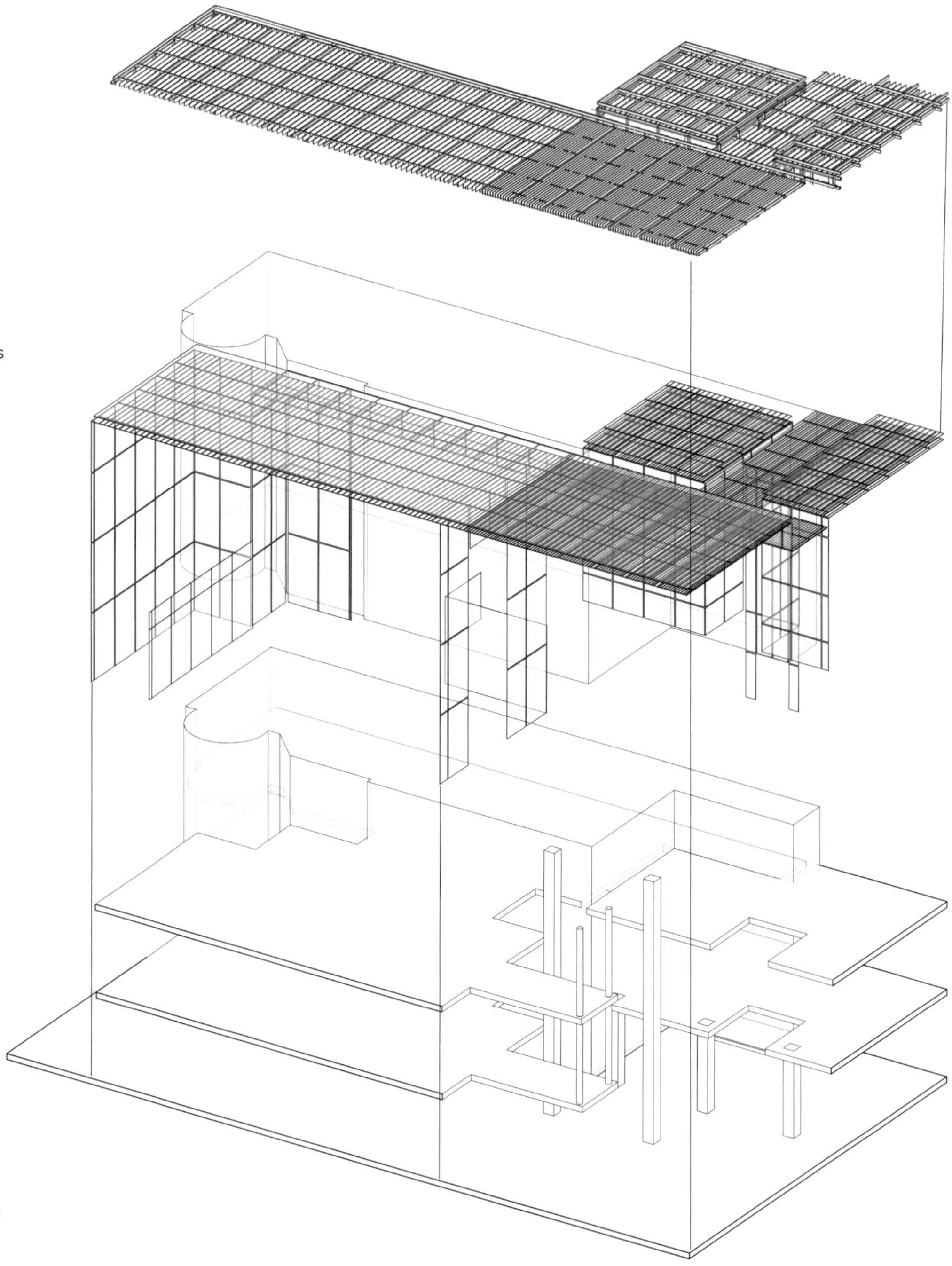

Horizontal steel grid

Roof glazing and internal shading fins

Vertical/horizontal mullion system and glass curtain wall

Floor slabs and column placement within piazza space

Exploded axon showing double layer of glazing, mullions and solar fins

Southeast facade of the Morgan Library complex

Interior view of the piazza

Cutaway section

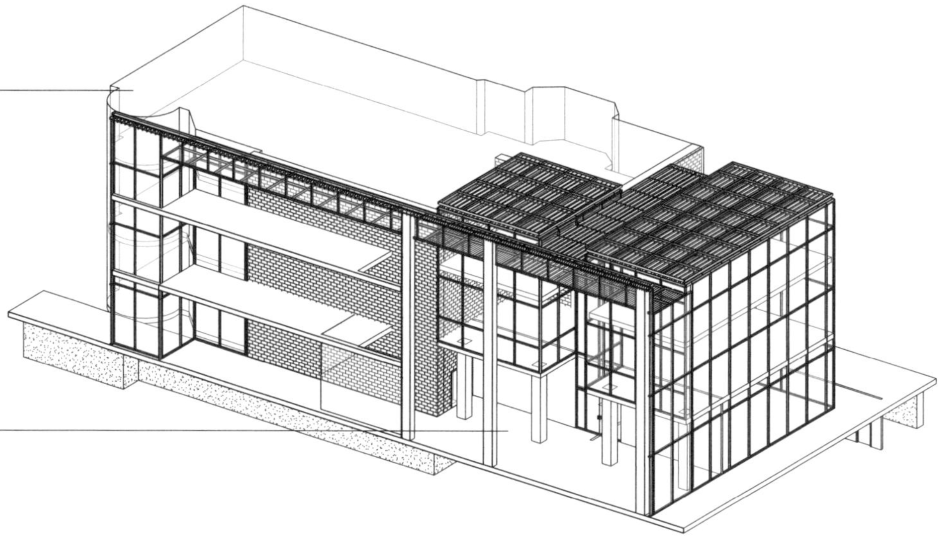

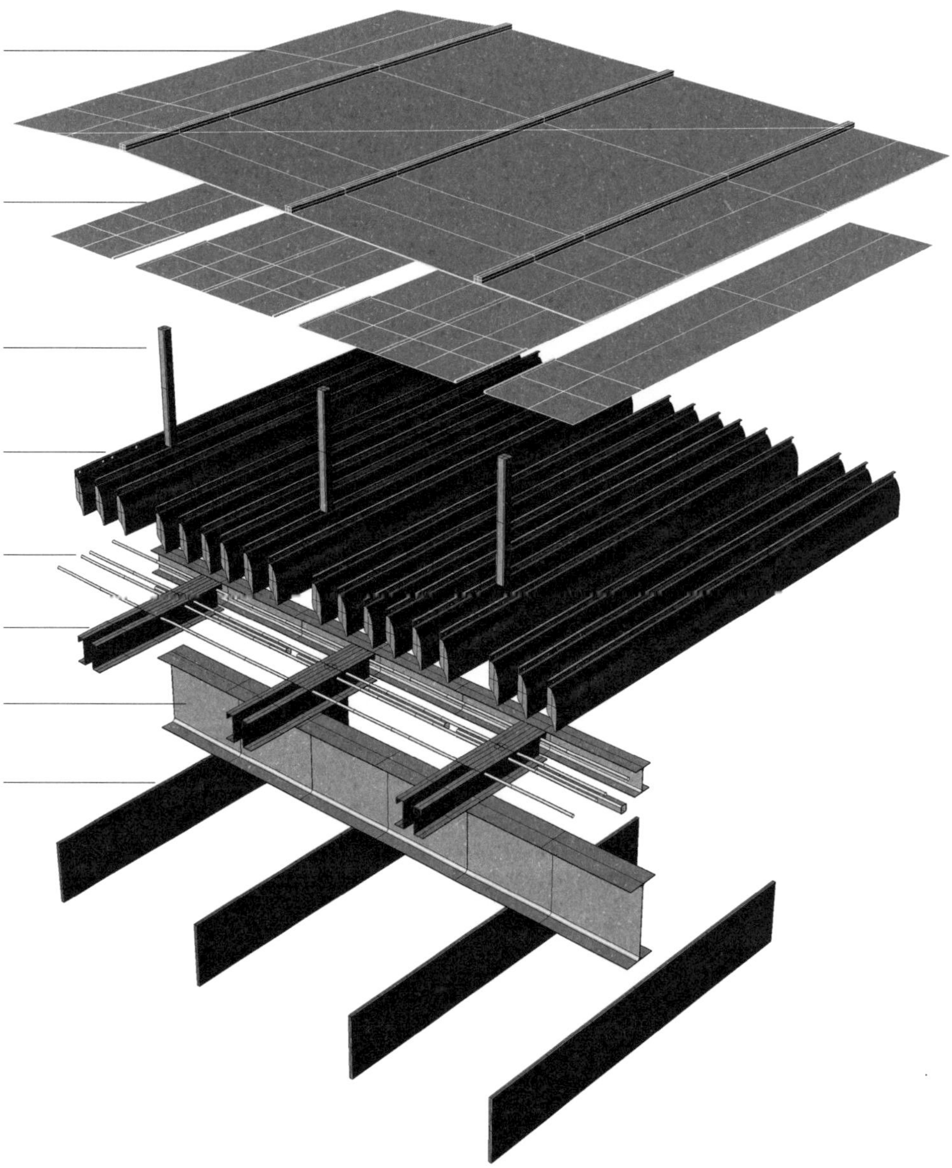

Exploded axonometry of solar shading roof detail

1 Steel shading grid
2 Glass roof
3 Structural columns
4 Solar fins
5 Solar fin structural supports
6 C-channel supports
7 Structural I-beam
8 Internal solar shading mullions

Internal view showing the transition between roof and facade

View from upper galleries

External view of facade

View of the piazza and garden facade

Roof detail
Roof system detail showing the layering of steel grill, glass roof, solar fins and steel structure

8 a.m.

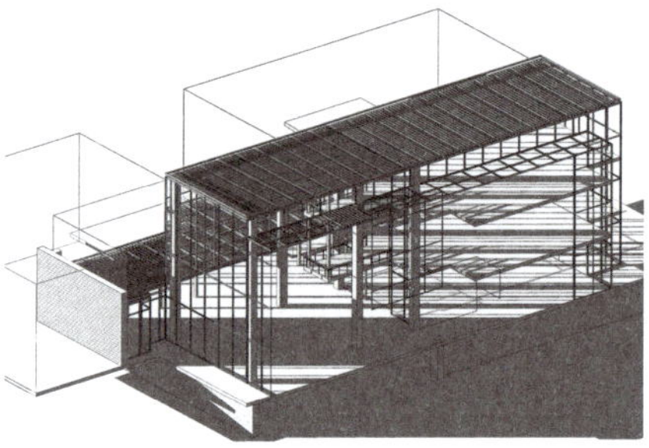

11 a.m

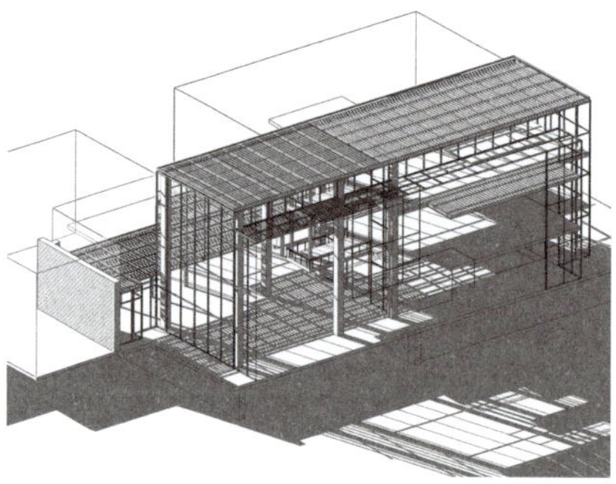

3 p.m.

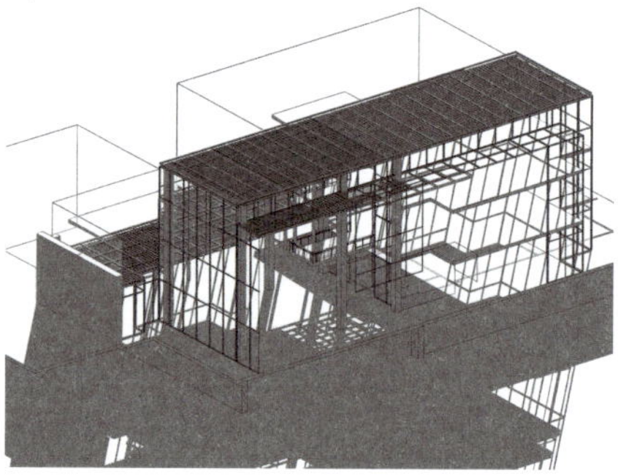

January solar/shadow studies

View of the roof structure showing the hinged steel grill

Interior view of facade

Roof detail
Detail of cross section of the glass roof system showing steel grill, glass panels, aluminum louvers and lighting track

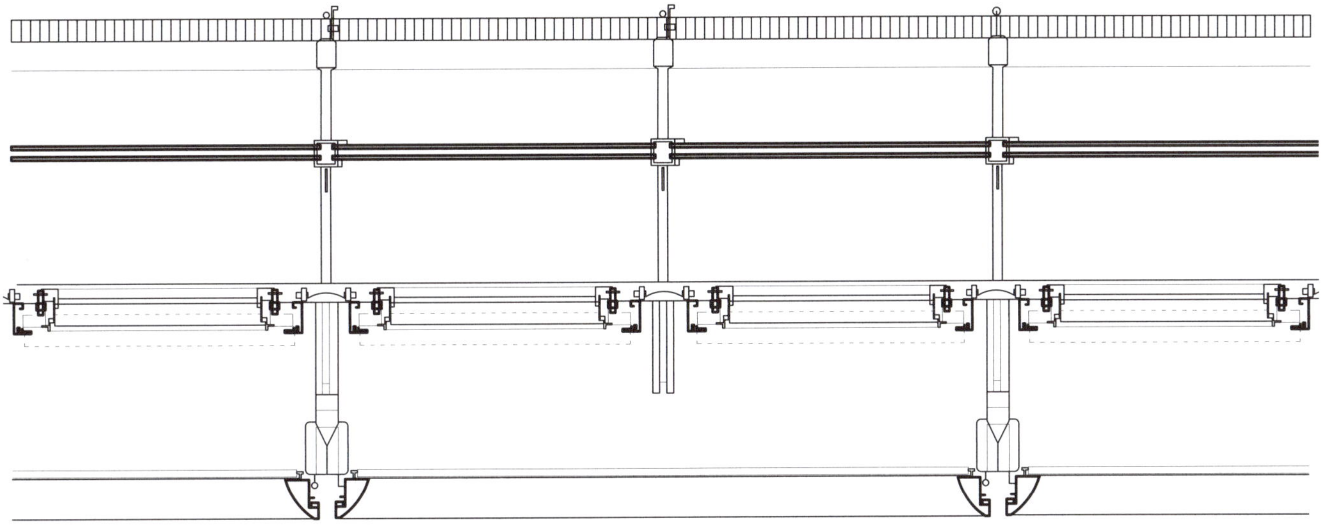

8 a.m.

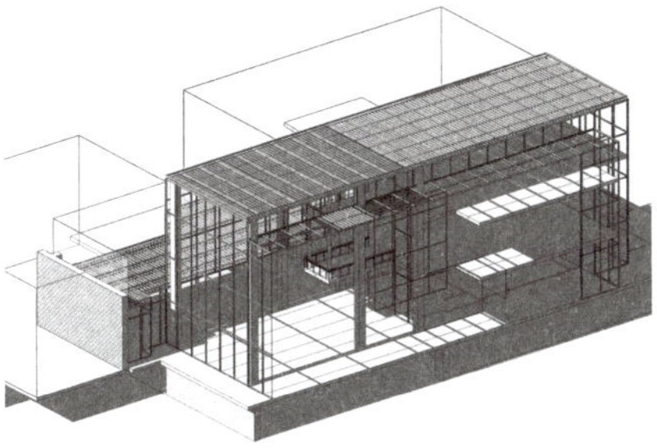

11 a.m.

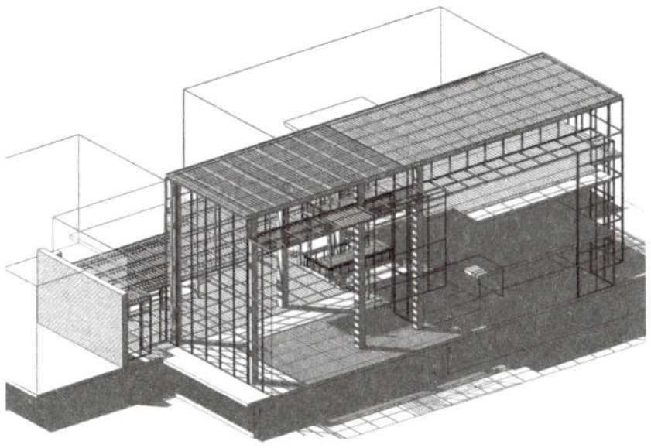

3 p.m.

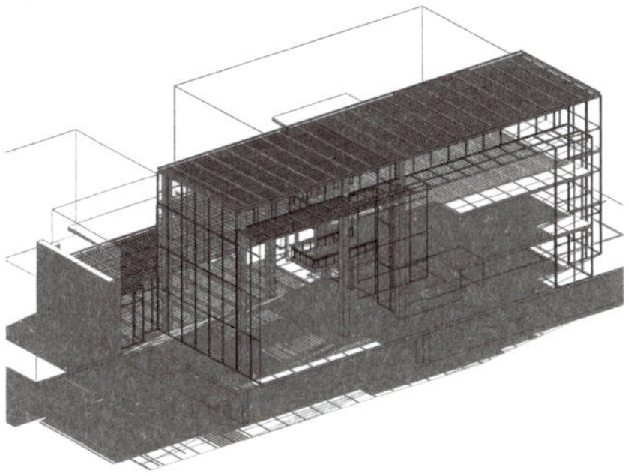

July solar/shadow studies

Glass roof and ceiling

External facade

Broad Contemporary Art Museum 2003–2008

Los Angeles, California, USA

Geographical context within the USA

In 2003, the Renzo Piano Building Workshop designed the expansion for the Los Angeles County Museum of Art (LACMA). This new gallery, known as The Broad Contemporary Art Museum and commonly referred to as The Broad, houses rotating exhibitions and art owned by the Los Angeles museum system. Located within central Los Angeles, The Broad links existing galleries and museums on the site into a cohesive campus with new public spaces and exhibitions, creating a visual identity for the LACMA. The Broad's sawtooth roof and plain travertine facade is somewhat reminiscent of industrial buildings.

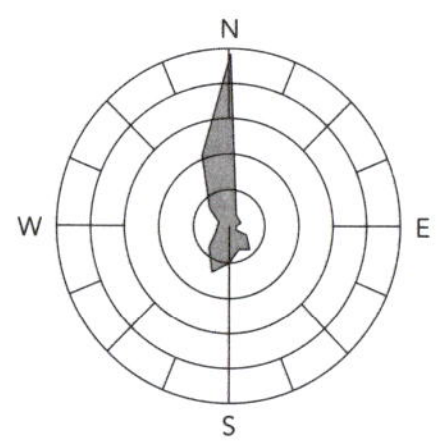

Wind rose: January

The Broad's museum collection is displayed in six large galleries over three floors. Each gallery is a free-span space 24 meters (80 feet) wide, with high ceilings and wooden floors. The red outdoor escalator and stairs takes visitors directly to the top-floor entrance. The third floor is flooded with natural light and contains a glass roof with large aluminum fins to diffuse light and block direct southern exposure. Located on a north-south axis, this orientation aids in limiting direct south light and prevents the galleries from overheating. The first- and second-level galleries, dedicated to special and temporary exhibitions, have no windows and rely solely on artificial lighting. The ground level opens out to the park and the neighboring Resnick Pavilion.

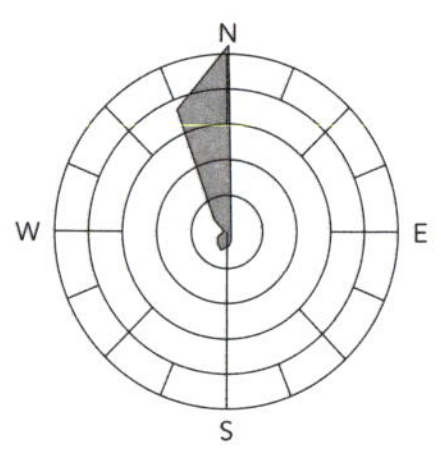

Wind rose: July

The roof system is composed of north-facing sawtooth skylights that channel north light into the third-floor galleries, vertical roller blinds and a horizontal glass roof. The low-iron glass has a fritted pattern to diffuse natural light and achieve very good color rendering (CRI). Diffused natural light illuminates the galleries and takes advantage of the varying intensity and color of natural light. External motorized shades reduce the overall amount of light transmission into the galleries to an appropriate level for displaying moderately light-sensitive art.

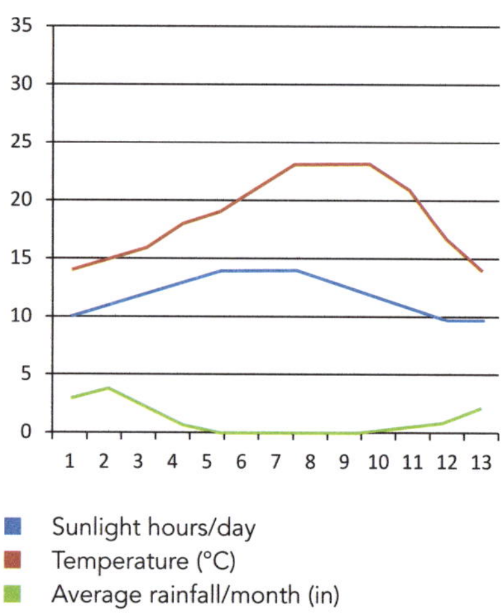

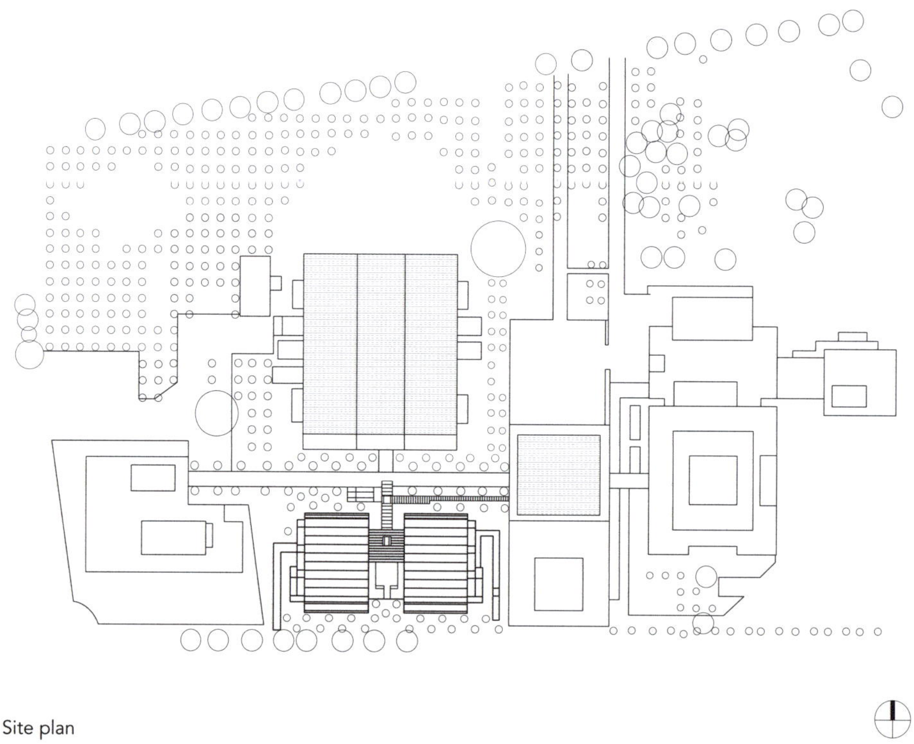

Site plan

1 West gallery
2 Stair circulation
3 Entrance lobby
4 Bathrooms
5 Central gallery
6 Escalator
7 East gallery

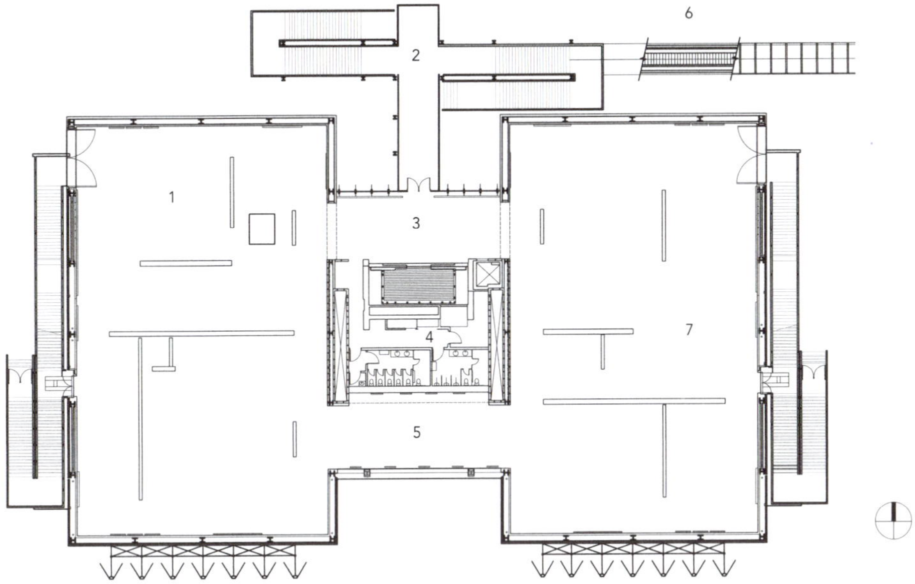

Third floor plan

View of museum plaza

The Broad's skylight system has a wide variation in light levels throughout the year. In this lighting scenario, it is more important to focus on the total illumination exposure received by the artwork in a year (annual lux-hours), rather than a targeted constant illuminance level (lux). This is not standard practice, according to the *Recommended Practice for Museum Lighting* (ANSI/IES RP-30-17). Based on the gained experience with the Broad, changes were made when designing a similar roofing system for the new Resnick Pavilion (LACMA Expansion – Phase II, 2006–2010).

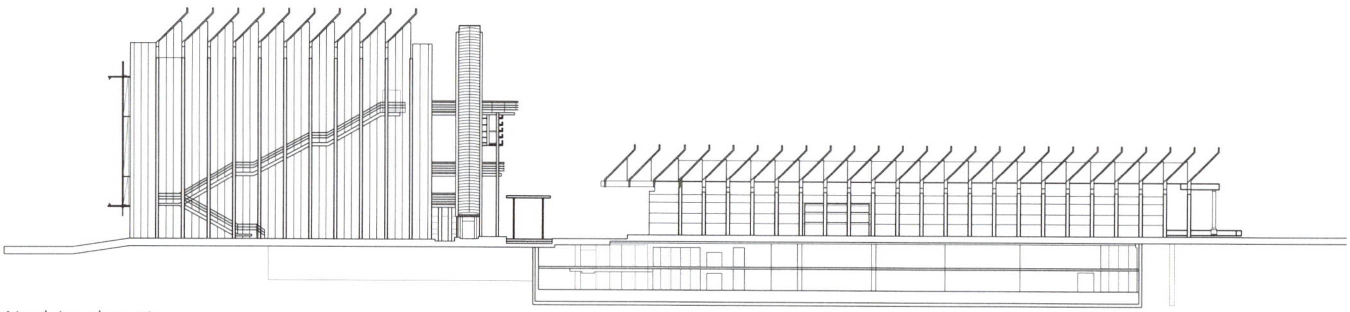

North/south section

View of northern facade

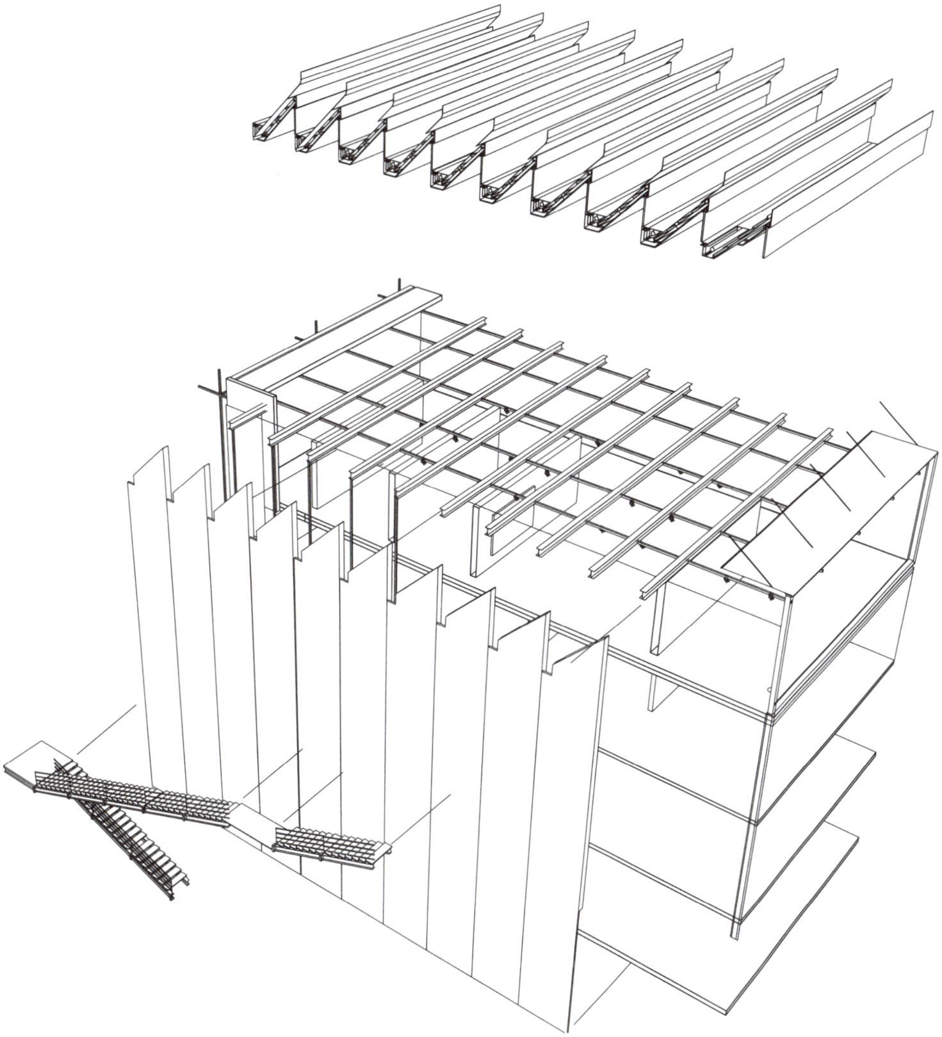

Exploded axonometry

Roof: Ten north-oriented aluminum louvers allow indirect light to enter the upper galleries. Additionally, a glass ceiling sits below the fins to create a transparent roof system.

Structure: A steel structure supports the roof system and facade cladding.

Facade: Italian travertine stone covers the exterior facade of the museum. The sawtooth shading creates the dominant form of the roof system.

Circulation: An exterior stair and escalator system creates direct access to upper-level galleries.

View showing south facade

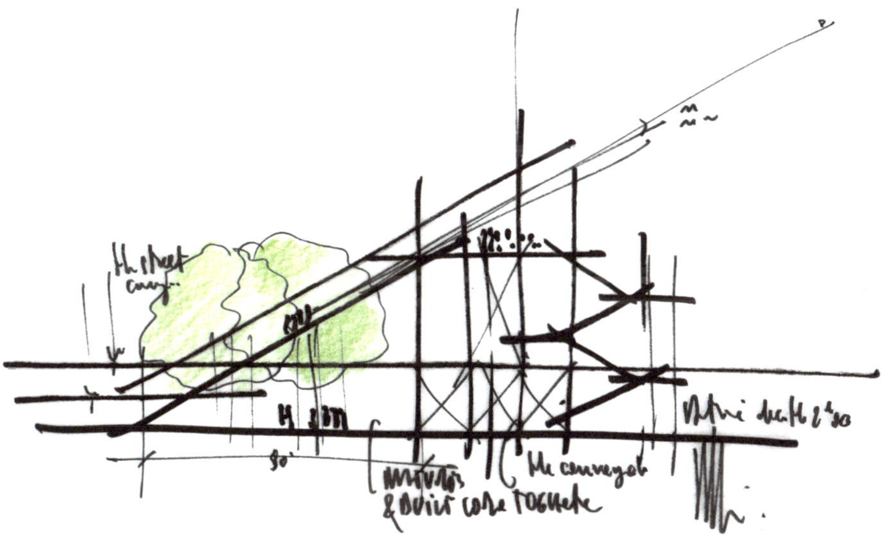

Renzo Piano sketch

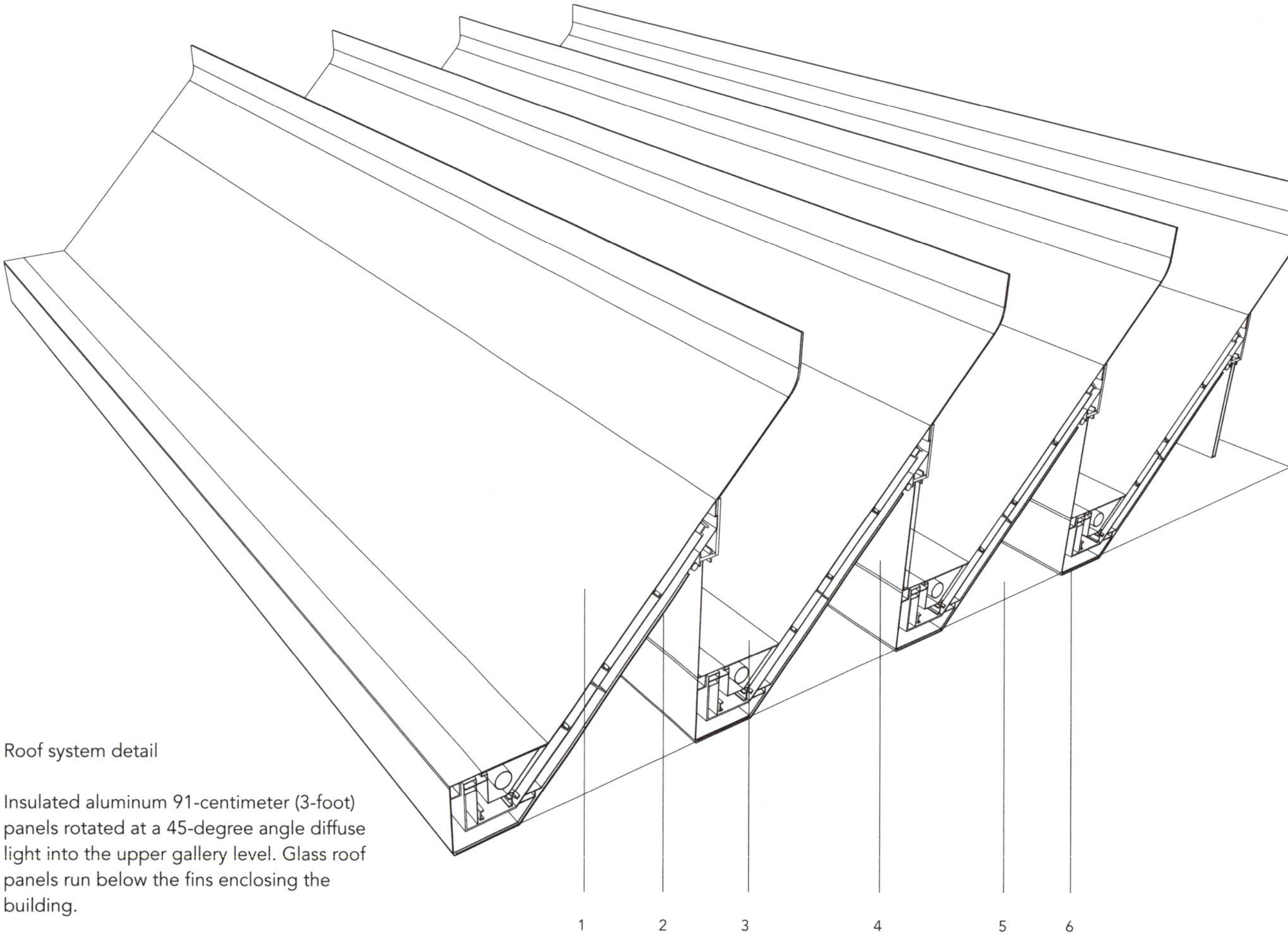

Roof system detail

Insulated aluminum 91-centimeter (3-foot) panels rotated at a 45-degree angle diffuse light into the upper gallery level. Glass roof panels run below the fins enclosing the building.

1 Aluminum panel
2 Insulation
3 Steel grid walkway
4 Roller shade
5 Glass ceiling
6 Aluminum structure

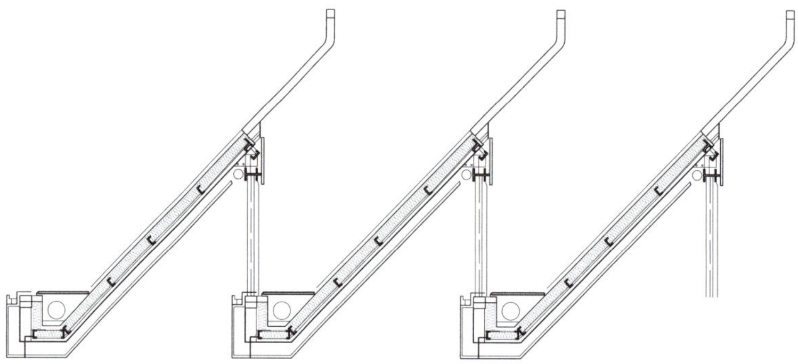

Roof detail

View showing exterior circulation leading to the upper-level galleries

Side elevation of roof

Computer rendering of roof structure

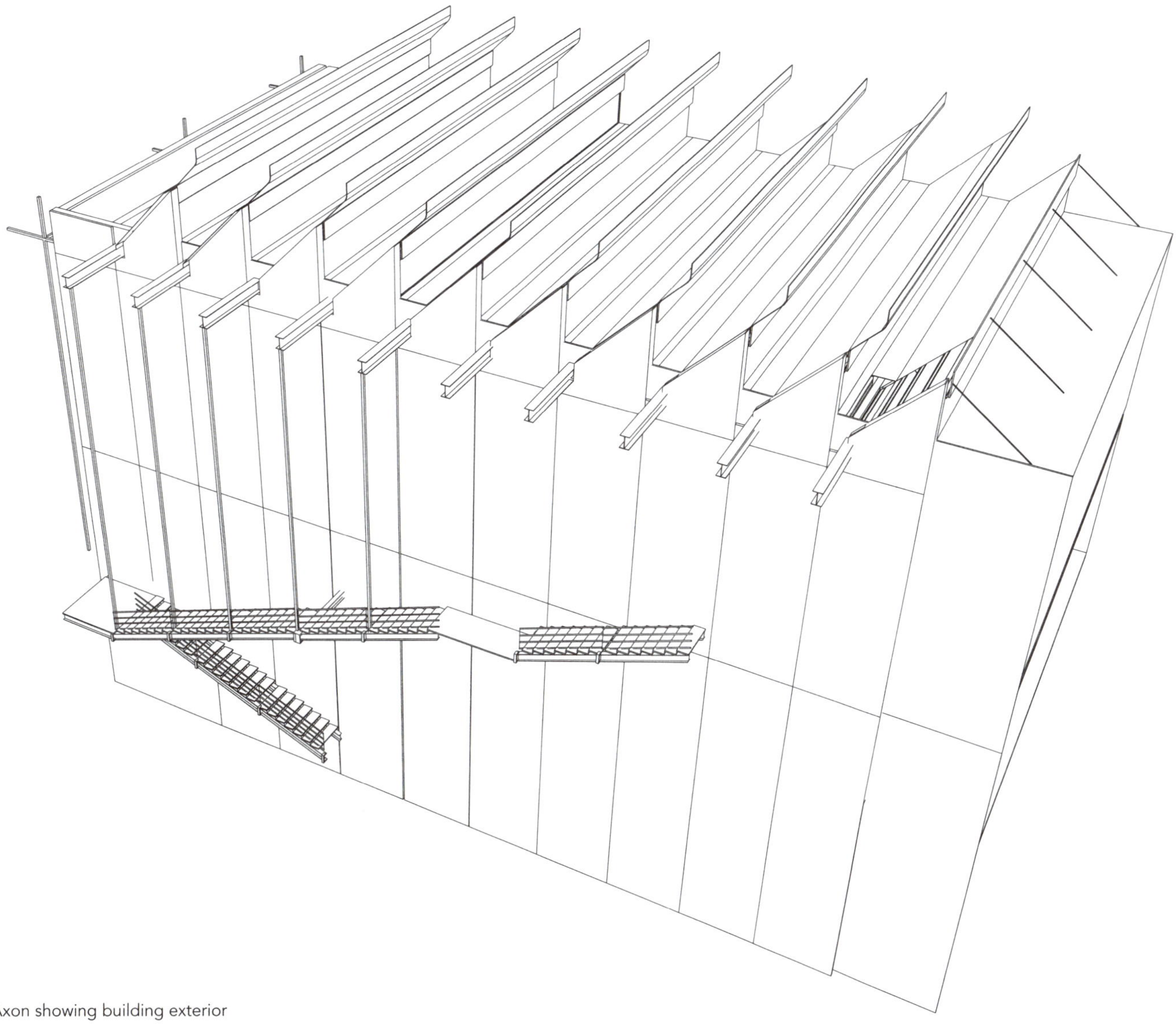

Axon showing building exterior

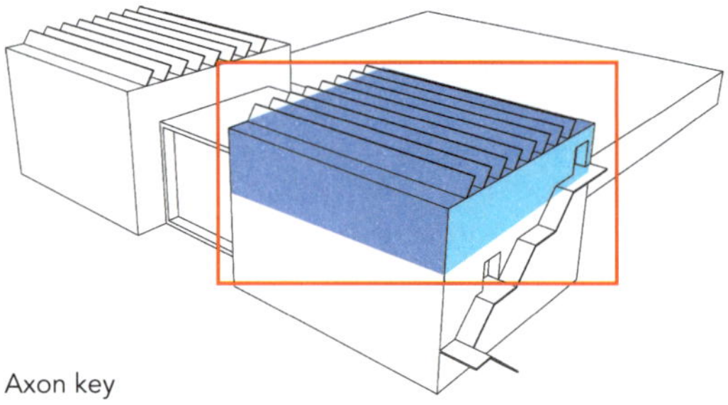

Axon key

Cutaway section showing the top two levels of the gallery space, exterior cladding and roof design

1 Aluminum louver
2 Roller blinds
3 Steel structure
4 Gallery lighting
5 Glass roof with screen
6 Travertine-clad facade
7 Freestanding gallery walls
8 Exterior circulation

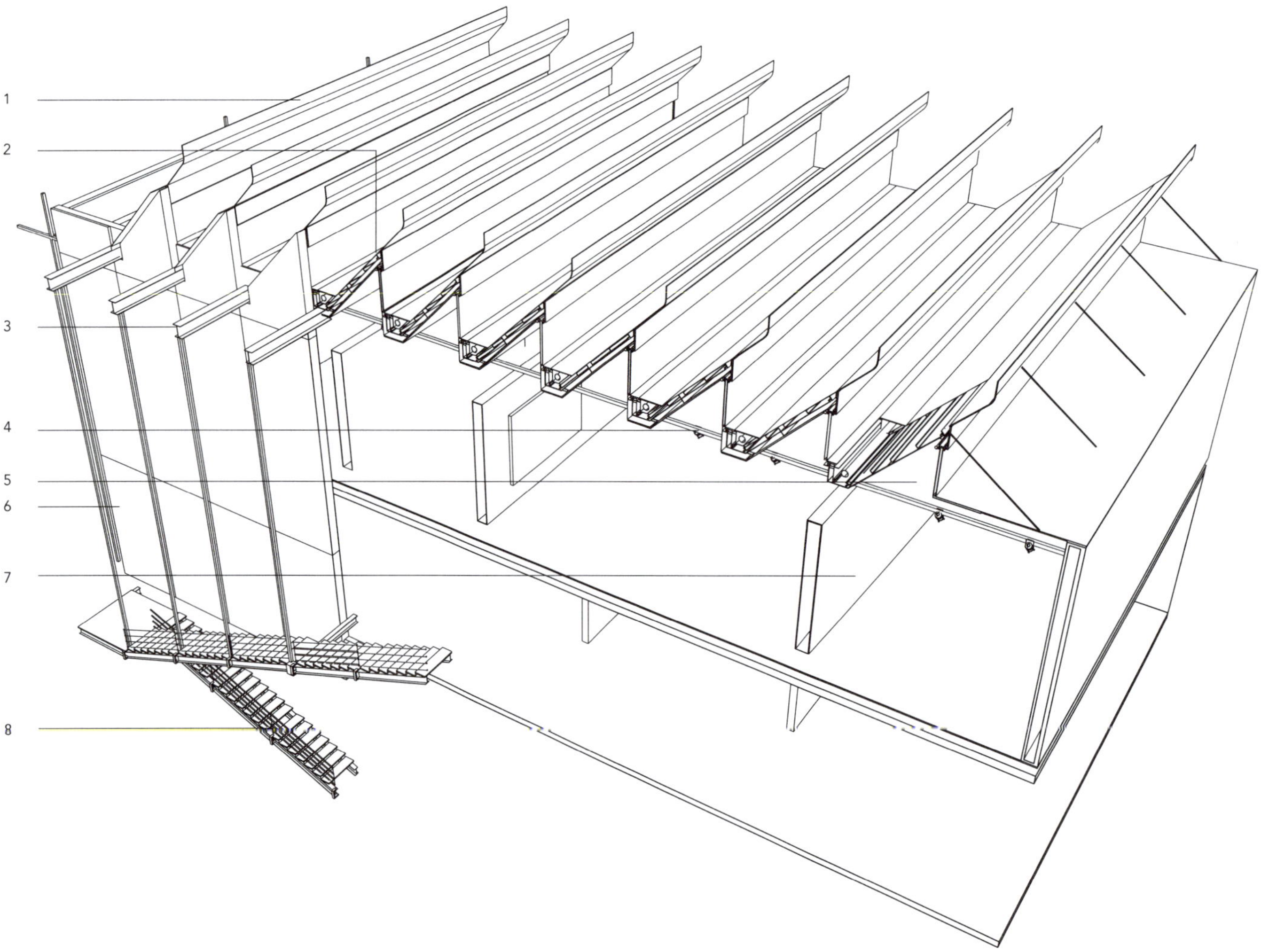

Zoom-in of glass roof and steel structure

Interior view of upper gallery space

Part II

Natural Light in Museums by Renzo Piano Building Workshop

General Considerations

No space, architecturally, is a space unless it has natural light.[1]

Louis I. Kahn

The use of daylight in museums has a long tradition. Starting with the first museum buildings[2] in Europe in the 18th century and until the 1950s, daylight was the preferred lighting option in showrooms due to the lack of suitable artificial lighting technology. However, direct sunlight on art objects has a damaging effect, so when technology made it possible, museums shifted to using artificial lighting instead.[3] A shift back to daylighting has happened since the 1980s due to the development of new daylight systems and light management.

Alte Pinakothek, Munich, Leo von Kenze. View into the gallery with skylight (1926)

The quality and the intensity of light (lighting conditions) in museums are the most important factors influencing the effect of the exhibition. In addition, good general lighting of the exhibition rooms is important for the spatial orientation of the visitors within the museum building and the spatial atmosphere. Particular attention must be paid to the materiality and type of the exhibitions in daylight and artificial lighting planning in exhibition rooms. Different art objects, such as paintings, sculptures or video installations, require different lighting conditions.

High Museum of Art, Atlanta. Interior of a top floor gallery

The ability to perceive an exhibition while simultaneously protecting the artwork from light represents a conflict of objectives in exhibition planning. Strong exposure to light can cause aging, discoloration and other damage to the exhibition objects. As a rule, limits are therefore set for the maximum illuminance[4] and maximum exposure time (duration of exhibition) for photosensitive exhibits.

New light simulation programs mean the planner is able to make accurate statements on light intensity, accumulated light quantity, light contrast and possible glare phenomena in an early design phase. In the past, a light simulation was only possible through models and mock-ups. Faulty lighting design repeatedly led to limitations in the exhibition concept or to subsequent redesigns and conversions to meet conservation and visitor requirements.

Light and Space

Space is oblivion without light. A building speaks through the silence of perception orchestrated by light.[5]

Steven Holl

Daylight and architecture need one another; only in their interaction can they be truly experienced by humans. Natural light, unified with architecture, opens the realm of time and space and evokes emotions through light flow, intensity, color and focus. The exhibition of art, paintings, manuscripts, facsimiles, photographs and sculptures requires knowledge of the architectural space, lighting technology and conservatorial needs. Successful lighting in museums encompasses the four dimensions of light:

- *Direction*: Art-centered highlights
- *Luminous intensity*: Precise conservatorial and curatorial illuminance values
- *Light color*: True color reception
- *Time*: Light color changes over the course of the day

The amount of light and the distribution of light in the room significantly determine our well-being. A full 80 percent of our sensory perception is linked to seeing. However, light not only brings spaces to life but also changes them depending on the chosen lighting concept. The type of daylight guidance (position of the light openings) and the daylight system decisively influence the effect and the quality of the

1 Louis I. Kahn, "Talk at the Conclusion of the Otterlo Congress (1959)," in: Robert Twombly (ed.), *Louis Kahn: Essential Texts*, W.W. Norton, London 2003, pp. 37–61.
2 The British Museum opened in 1759 as the second public museum in the world and the first public museum in Europe.
3 The New National Gallery by Mies van der Rohe is an example of a universal space with mostly artificial lighting, especially in the basement.
4 Illuminance (E) describes the quantity of luminous flux that falls on a surface. The luminous flux describes the quantity of light emitted by a light source. The quotient of the luminous flux (Φ) and the illuminated surface (A) determines the illuminance (E): $E = \Phi/A$. The unit for illuminance is lumen per square meter, lux (lx) (metric unit = lumen/m²) or foot-candles (Imperial unit = lumen/ft²). One foot-candle equals 10.8 lux. Illuminance can be calculated for any plane surface or measured using a lux meter. Common illuminance levels are: Full sunlight (100,000 lux), full daylight (10,000 lux), overcast day (1,000 lux), twilight (100 lux), full moon (1 lux), and starlight (0.01 lux).
5 Steven Holl, *Luminosity/Porosity*, Toto Shuppan, Tokyo 2006.

room. A successful lighting concept for daylight or artificial light makes spatial forms and paths visible, generates different spatial effects and spatial qualities and focuses the visitor's attention on the essentials of the space. Care must be taken to ensure that uniform lighting is monotonous, as exaggerated dynamic lighting causes disorientation.

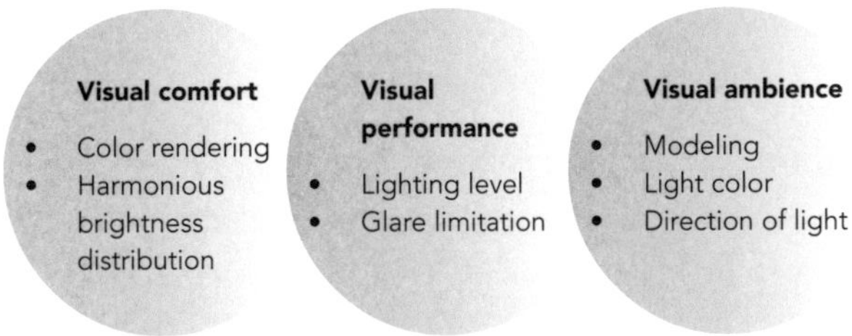

Good Lighting
Standard definition of quality characteristics that determine the quality of a lighting system[6]

Characteristics of Good Lighting

The quality of lighting or "good lighting" is based on the visual task that the human eye needs to perform.[7] Different lighting qualities are required depending on the visual task, such as reading or viewing light-sensitive artwork or sculptures in bright light. Good lighting is characterized by three basic quality features that are weighted differently based on the specific space and lighting requirements.

Visual comfort is defined by good color rendering, harmonious brightness and light distribution (contrast).
Visual performance is influenced by the illuminance levels and direct and reflected glare.
Visual ambiance is determined by light color, light direction and modeling (depth perception).

Good lighting is achievable by natural light, artificial light, or a combination of both and takes the visual, emotional and biological effects of light[8] into consideration. The characteristics of good lighting are:

- Adequate level of illuminance
- Harmonious brightness distribution
- Limitations of direct glare and reflections
- Light direction and modeling in order to perceive three-dimensional shapes
- Light color and color rendering
- Tunable light levels and color temperature

Modern lighting systems are also characterized by energy efficiency, seamless integration of daylight and artificial light as well as changeable lighting scenarios.

Daylight and Exhibition

When planning lighting in museums and exhibition buildings, a distinction is made between natural and artificial light sources. The design of daylight systems places high demands on daylight planning. On the one hand, a natural exposure of the exhibition space and good visibility of the exhibits is desirable. On the other, the protection against unobstructed UV irradiation of the art objects is of great importance. Meanwhile, the color rendering of an art object in daylight is unsurpassed compared to artificial light. Daylight comes closest to human viewing habits, allowing for an optimal indoor environment and a natural representation of the exhibits on display. In addition, daylight provides us with a wealth of perceptual information through constant changes in its intensity, spectral composition, color temperature and light distribution. By contrast, lighting using artificial light is usually uniform and static.[9]

6 See also: Fördergemeinschaft Gutes Licht, *licht.wissen 01: Lighting with Artificial Light*, Licht.de, Darmstadt 2016.
7 Ibid.
8 Ibid.
9 See also: Man Jin Choi, *Tageslichtoptimierung in Museen: Experimentelle Untersuchung des visuellen Museumsraumes unter Tageslicht aus der Sicht der ökologischen Optik*, Dissertation, TU Munich 2002.

Daylight and artificial lighting systems are usually combined with each other in order to illuminate a showroom and the displayed art objects evenly and without fluctuation. Sunlight is filtered and dosed by complex daylight systems or scattered and attenuated by passive or active shading systems (glare protection), and thus adapted to the museum's exposure requirements. Negative glare due to high luminance contrasts caused by strong differences in brightness between windows or luminous ceilings and objects can be avoided, as can direct irradiation of the exhibits with sunlight.

Architects and interior designers often use daylight as one of their design elements. In using daylight, they must carefully consider both *qualitative* and *quantitative* design aspects.

Qualitative design aspects
In 1929, the Swiss architect Le Corbusier said: "The history of architectural material... was the endless struggle for light... in other words, the history of the windows."[10] The use of natural light is one of the most critical design aspects in architecture. Not only are the aesthetics considered to be an aspect of qualitative daylight, but so is the influence of daylight on human health[11] and work performance. Daylight at a workplace has a positive impact on job satisfaction, productivity and well-being. Daylight has significantly higher visual acceptance values than electric lighting.[12] Daylight has a direct impact on human health as it affects circadian rhythms.

Quantitative design aspects
A daylight-flooded room requires both adequate levels of illumination and a balanced distribution of light. The Illumination Engineering Society (IES) and the Society of Light and Lighting (SLL) provide illuminance guidelines for each type of building and use of space. These guidelines set minimum and maximum illuminance values. The two most common metrics that IES has approved to evaluate daylight power are Spatial Daylight Autonomy (SDA) and Annual Sunlight Exposure (ASE). The latter is not applicable to museums, as direct sunlight is undesirable. SDA is a metric that describes the annual availability of indoor ambient light.

Museum Concept and Daylight: Uniform Exposure or Dynamic Light
Stimulation, color and visual comfort are crucial for a dynamic and stimulating perception in museums and galleries. The question, however, is: Where is the healthy balance between under- and overstimulation? On the one hand, lively light, strong color contrasts and overloaded visual impressions can easily overstimulate the viewer. On the other, a monotonously illuminated room is often boring and tiring for the visitor. How do you find the right balance in the lighting design of an exhibition space? Theories suggest that variety, novelty or atypicality contribute to visual complexity, which in turn translates into stimulation.

Art needs spaces in which viewers can concentrate, but they also need inspiration to arouse curiosity that invites them to linger. Likewise, the artwork needs the right amount of light and the right light color to be fully appreciated.

Light generates very different moods in exhibition spaces. For example, skylights in classic gallery rooms create diffused, soft light throughout the day for a neutral ambiance. This creates an ideal environment for obtaining a factual impression of the works of art, and numerous museums' daylight systems are based on diffuse skylights and ceiling lights. However, due to the low-contrast presentation form, a feeling of monotony can also arise in the rooms and in viewing the art.

Balanced light – creates moods
Soft (diffused) light is an essential part of lighting in museums, galleries and exhibitions. It produces low contrasts and little or no shadow. The larger the light-emitting surface, for example, a light ceiling, compared to the object being viewed, the softer the light is perceived to be, because there are no shadows.

10 Quote attributed to Swiss architect Le Corbusier (October 6, 1887 to August 27, 1965).
11 Myriam Aries, Mariëlle Aarts and Joost van Hoof, "Daylight and Health: A Review of the Evidence and Consequences for the Built Environment," *Lighting Research & Technology*, 47(1), 2015, pp. 6–27.
12 Apiparn Borisuit et al., "Effects of Realistic Office Daylighting and Electric Lighting Conditions on Visual Comfort, Alertness and Mood," *Lighting Research & Technology*, 47(2), 2015, pp. 192–209.

In order to create a contemplative mood in an exhibition space, the lighting has to capture this atmosphere and express a neutral and uniform attitude. As artists in their workshops often work with functional, diffused lighting, they therefore also strive for this same ambiance of light in their exhibitions. The uniform distribution of brightness on vertical surfaces creates a soft and harmonious room atmosphere in which the pictures form a unit with the wall. However, if an exhibition is not intended to be neutral, but rather to highlight works individually, then electric accent lighting represents a theatrical counterpart.[13]

Dynamic light – sets accents

In museums, particular attention should be paid to creating effective and yet gentle accent lighting free from damaging UV/IR radiation. Daylight systems and artificial lighting can generate accurate accentuation and three-dimensional modeling of artworks. The accentuated lighting allows even small details to come to the fore, thus creating depth and tension through their shadows. High-contrast light installations can even have an enhanced theatrical effect if the light on pictures is purposefully uneven and dynamic.[14]

Light and Visual Experience

Lighting can be divided into three aspects in terms of how it affects the visual experience. These are: the spatial distribution of the illuminance, the intensity of the light source, and the spectral distribution of the light.[15]

Spatial distribution of light – direction and modeling

Light enables us to see objects, but without directional light and shadows, we see objects merely as two-dimensional images. Light and shadow are necessary to see objects and surface structures accurately. Only directional light and the correct distribution of light and shade reveal the details of a sculpture or relief. A mix of diffused light distributed by the daylight system and directional light distributed by direct luminaires and downlights achieves optimal visual results and contributes to a pleasant visual ambiance.

Light intensity

Generally, museum visitors prefer higher illuminance levels to view artwork. This preference needs to be weighed against conservation concerns favoring lower light levels. The conservation specifications for maximum light exposure – 200 lux for moderately sensitive material such as oil paintings and 50 lux for highly sensitive materials such as paper – are based on a compromise between the long-term preservation needs and the ability to view art comfortably. The eye is able to adjust to different intensities of illuminance, but this adjustment requires time. This must be considered in a museum's design when planning transitions from brightly lit to more controlled gallery spaces. Within a gallery space, the eye uses the brightest surface as a reference point. Generally, the ceiling is much brighter than the exhibit walls, which lets a wall appear dark even when illuminance levels are high. A reduction in contrast between an exhibit wall and a painting reduces the time for pupils to dilate or to constrict.

Spectral distribution

Daylight and artificial light differ in the characteristics of their spectral energy distribution.[16] For example, daylight is rich in blue, but the actual color temperature varies dramatically with the time of the day. The spectral composition of sunlight changes primarily with respect to how directly sunlight is able to illuminate the earth's surface. Solar radiation varies from sunrise to sunset with the angle of the sun above the horizon.[17, 18] The most important argument in favor of natural lighting in museums is the viewer's ability to perceive artwork and color as faithfully as possible, and sunlight is the truest color-rendering source. The three major components of color are hue, saturation and brightness. Hue refers to the color appearance parameters of red, green and blue. Saturation describes the amount of gray in the color, while brightness refers to the degree of lightness or darkness of a color.

13 ERCO (ed.), *Culture – Light for Art: Planning Principles and Design*, https://www.erco.com/download/content/3-media/7-cluster-culture/erco-cluster-culture-en.pdf

14 Around 1940, Peggy Guggenheim used dynamic light in her first New York gallery, "The Art of This Century Gallery," to create a new approach to art and to visually convey pulsating life through pulsating light.

15 Steven Weintraub and Gordon Anson, "Technics: Natural Lighting in Museums: An Asset or a Threat?" *Progressive Architecture*, 5, 1990, pp. 49–54.

16 "Spectral power distribution is a pictorial representation of the radiant power emitted by a light source at each wavelength or band of wavelengths in the visible region of the electromagnetic spectrum.", in: Illuminating Engineering Society of North America, *Museum and Art Gallery Lighting: A Recommended Practice*, ANSI/IESNA RP-30-96, Illuminating Engineering Society of North America, New York 1996.

17 Günter Wyszecki and W. S. Stiles, *Color Science: Concepts and Methods, Quantitative Data and Formulae*, John Wiley & Sons, London 1967, p. 8.

18 Mark Karlen, James R. Benya and Christina Spangler, *Lighting Design Basics*, 3rd ed., John Wiley & Sons, Hoboken, NJ 2017, p. 103.

Ambient versus Task Lighting

Light in galleries has two functions: the illumination of the artwork (the "task lighting") and the general illumination of the physical space (the "ambient lighting"). Task lighting illuminates the artwork and may have no effect on the overall lighting of the space. Ambient lighting defines the general experience of light within a gallery, since natural light affects the psychological mood and changes the quality of natural light over time. These two functions, while related, are quite different and need to be reviewed separately.

Daylight and the Exhibition Concept: Permanent Exhibition – Rotating Exhibitions

The conservation guidelines and requirements for daylight and artificial light in museums can vary considerably. Often, museums have specific guidelines for their exhibition depending on the exhibition concept or the photosensitivity of the objects to be exhibited.[19] Depending on the museum's exhibition concept, permanent or rotating exhibits, and type of exhibited objects, the maximum permitted illuminance tags are set. A distinction, therefore, is made between the maximum illuminance (PITI), which is the maximum light level value at a specific point in time measured on the exhibit wall or object, and the average annual illuminance (AAI), which is the total exposure of artifacts over time.

In permanent exhibitions, works of art remain in the space and are displayed throughout the year. From a conservational point of view, it is necessary to comply with the upper limit of average annual illuminance.

With rotating exhibits or exchange exhibitions, the maximum value for AAI can be exceeded because the art object is exposed to light only occasionally. For exhibits in temporary exhibitions, attention must be paid to the maximum illuminance.

The Triple Effect of Light in Museums

Good lighting in museums has a positive effect on the viewing performance of humans and creates a comfortable environment.

Visual functions

- Illuminate task area in conformity with conservational standards
- Illuminate sufficiently for viewing
- Create no glare or reflections
- Provide good contrast on art objects
- Use correct light color and render color correctly
- Provide sense of direction and orientation in space

Emotional perceptions

- Enhance the architecture and experience
- Use light as a design element
- Create dynamic scenarios
- Distribute brightness harmoniously

Biological effects

- Stimulate or relax the viewer
- Provide a sense of time and circadian rhythm

Light and Materials

> *I think light is as material as anything else.*[20]
>
> James Turrell

Light and materials depend on each other. Materials directly influence the light quantity and quality. Two important properties of materials are color and surface texture. Reflective materials and glossy surfaces reflect the light like a mirror, allowing reflected images of the light source to be seen on the surface. Matte surfaces such as natural

19 The Museum and Art Gallery Lighting Committee of the Illuminating Engineering Society of North America, *Recommended Practice for Museum Lighting*, ANSI/IES RP-30-17, Illuminating Engineering Society, New York 2017, p. 8.

20 Laura J. Millin (ed.), *James Turrell: Four Light Installations*, The Real Comet Press, Seattle 1982, p. 18.

stone, wood and plaster detract the light evenly in all directions. Light is defined by hue, reflectance value and light intensity. The value determines how much light is absorbed and how much is reflected. A white wall reflects about 80 percent of the incident light and a dark wall about 10 percent. Colored surfaces add some color to the reflected light.

Kimbell Art Museum, Louis I. Kahn, Fort Worth (1966–72). Light modulates material contrasts: the surfaces of the walls in the museum are made of travertine, the arch of exposed concrete. According to the direction (direct or indirect) and nature of the light (daylight or artificial light), either the contrasts between the materials are emphasized or the materials appear to blend into each other.

Location of the Daylight Source

In general, the two daylighting concepts in museums are lighting through side windows and lighting through roof openings and skylights. Skylights are combined with light-guiding systems which, in combination with light-scattering, UV-filtering glass ceilings, allow only diffused daylight to pass through and specifically block sunlight. Light-guiding systems are light-directing devices in the roof area as well as light-reflecting ceiling cavities, which divert the daylight via multiple reflections into the exhibition space and distribute it evenly throughout the room through light-diffusing glass ceilings. A distinction is made between rigid and non-adaptable light-guiding elements and mobile systems that dynamically modulate daylighting and are also used as thermal sunscreens. In general, in a light-guiding and shading system, a distinction is made between sun protection (for example, shading by external louvers), glare protection (contrast and direct light beam), light filtering (adjustment of the illuminance) and light scattering (luminance distribution).

Lateral windows in exhibition rooms are only practical if objects on display are not shaded by people or other objects and if only indirect light filters through the facade. This can be ensured by the arrangement of high lateral skylights or by the north orientation of the facade, which allows the daylight to pass without any fluctuation in the exhibition space.[21]

Daylighting System Typologies

Modern museum design requires daylit art galleries with diffuse daylight for comfortable viewing and acceptably low rates of damage. In principle, daylighting systems[22] can be categorized by the geometry of the light ceiling. In surface systems, the entire ceiling of the gallery is glass; in linear systems, the linear skylight is either horizontal (roof glazing strip) or vertical (sawtooth); and in point systems, the daylight system consists of individual skylights. In vertical systems, the light enters the gallery through vertical openings (single window or glass facades).

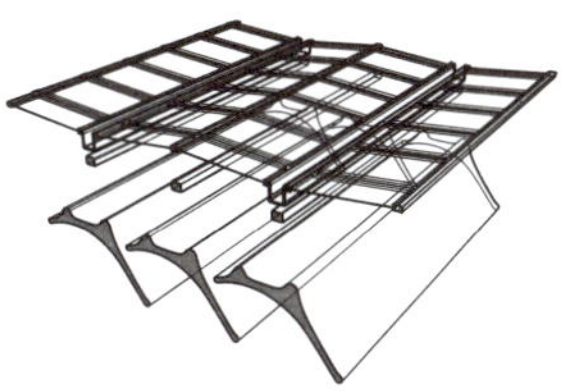

Surface system
- Daylight ceiling
- Daylight ceiling with velarium

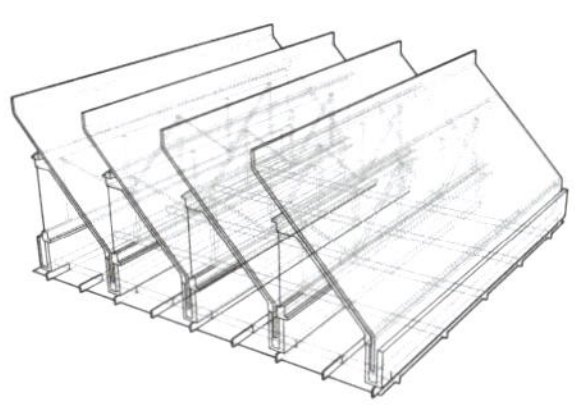

Linear system
- Glazing strip
- Sawtooth skylight

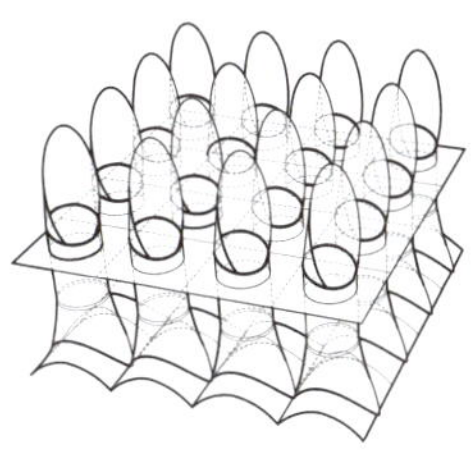

Point system
- Single skylights
- Skylight cluster

Daylight-diffusing skylights such as glass roofs, linear horizontal skylights, and point skylights receive the sum of direct sunlight, blue-sky light and cloud-reflected light. They modulate the light through translucent materials and louvers. Polar-oriented skylights (sawtooth skylights) use the northern orientation and external shading to prevent direct sunlight entering the gallery space. The advantage is that the source of the light is less variable throughout the day in comparison to direct sunlight. Because the sheds diffuse the sunlight, clear glazing can be used to allow the occupant to observe the sky condition.

21 Doris Haas-Arndt and Fred Ranft, *Tageslichttechnik in Gebäuden*, C.F. Müller Technik, Heidelberg 2006.
22 Christopher Cuttle, *Light for Art's Sake: Lighting for Artworks and Museum Displays*, Butterworth-Heinemann, Boston 2007.

Side-lit galleries (vertical systems) are good for displaying three-dimensional artwork like sculptures and reliefs; the lateral light flow reveals superbly the form and texture. Side-lit galleries can be problematic for picture galleries; a picture facing a window causes the image of the window to reflect in the picture. Pictures need to be tilted forward to avoid the veiling reflection.

Light Management Systems

A light management system combines the daylight control system (active shading and blinds) and electric lighting (direct and indirect luminaires) and makes sure that exhibits which are sensitive to light are exposed only to the luminance level required for good perception. Presence-based control systems restrict illumination to the time when visitors are present. Daylight sensors and blind management control the amount of daylight accordingly to the required conservational level and balance between architectural experience, human well-being, gentle illumination of exhibits and energy costs. Daylight also has a significant benefit for the museum staff, resulting in improved well-being and productivity.[23]

Daylight – Electric Light

Daylight is carbon-free and cost-free, and when used properly can and does play an important role in energy conservation. The use of daylight in museums can offset a considerable amount of electric lighting, which can account for up to 20% of total energy consumption. The uncontrolled use of daylight in museums and galleries, however, has disadvantages. Sunlight has the potential to overheat a room or to flood it, causing the artworks to be over-illuminated. Museum projects must effectively develop and implement active and passive lighting solutions to control the extremes of light, heat and UV radiation. RPBW museum projects effectively control daylight and show the value of experience in developing and implementing active and passive lighting solutions.

Electrical lighting technology has undergone an unprecedented change in recent years. LED lighting and new lighting and control systems offer benefits to museums and galleries, in particular saving energy and maintenance costs.[24]

Daylight	**Electric light**
Benefits	Benefits
• Improved visitor experience • Carbon-free and cost-free • Link to the outside world and sky conditions • Improved staff well-being • Variation in lighting condition and ambiance of galleries • Changing color temperature during the course of the day • Correct light color and color rendering	• Enhanced flexibility in lighting scenarios • Ability to tune lighting according to visitor and curator preference • Tailored lighting specific to application • Tunable color temperature and illuminance level • Presence-based control systems reduce illumination exposure to artwork • Lighting only during operating hours • Retrievable pre-programmed lighting scenes
Drawbacks	Drawbacks
• Potential to overheat the gallery space • Potential to over-light gallery • Dynamic lighting scenario does not fit exhibit	• Potentially high maintenance/life cycle costs • Potentially high energy costs if not using high-efficiency luminaire systems • Potentially monotone and tiring lighting scenarios

Lighting Concepts for Museums

The lighting design in museums depends on several planning parameters: the architecture language and intention, the gallery space and proportions, the interior design and color scheme, the available daylight and the type of exhibition. The way the ambiance is shaped is vital for the spatial impression and the enjoyment of art. Lighting design in museums is a combination of daylighting and electric lighting and

23 L. Edwards, P. Torcellini, *A Literature Review of the Effects of Natural Light on Building Occupants*, NREL/TP-550-30769, National Renewable Energy Laboratory, Colorado 2002.

24 ARUP lighting design, *Rethinking Lighting in Museums and Galleries*, https://www.arup.com/-/media/arup/files/publications/r/rethinking_lighting_in_museums_and_galleries.pdf

can be defined by six lighting concepts.[25] This depends on the exhibited artwork, the museum's program and the desired visitor experience; a specific lighting concept is required. The lighting design for a specific ambiance in a gallery space combines different lighting aspects into an overall design concept. All six lighting concepts are important and form the visual characteristics of a space.

- Ambient illuminance
- Visual perception
- Illumination hierarchy
- Flow of light
- Sharpness of light
- Luminous elements

Ambient illuminance describes the overall subjective impression of lighting within a space. Diffuse lighting illuminates the room evenly and non-directionally, without producing shadows.

Visual perception means the ability of the viewer to see small objects and fine details. For good visual performance, a minimum of illuminance and contrast are necessary.

Illumination hierarchy structures the lighting design concept and defines the different light levels within the gallery space. Light draws attention towards the important objects on display and away from insignificant things.

Flow of light describes the directionality of lighting to enhance the visual impact of three-dimensional surfaces or objects by generating highlights and shading patterns.

Sharpness of light describes the sharply defined borders of light and shadows on surfaces.

Luminous elements are luminaires or other sources of light perceived by the viewer.

Conservation and Light

Conservation and Daylighting – a Contradiction?
Collections are most susceptible to light damage while on display. The length of time displayed as well the intensity of light are the two main factors to consider for protection. The Illuminating Engineering Society of North America (IESNA) suggests that: "The artifact should be visible when on display. There is no point causing a little damage (with insufficient light) for no purpose (the artifact cannot be seen). The institution must decide how much light damage in how much time is acceptable, i.e., what lifetime is desirable. The institution must acknowledge the sensitivity of each artifact, or group of artifacts, as accurately as possible."[26]

Effects of Light Exposure
Light is essential for the perception and enjoyment of art in museums and galleries. Simultaneously, light exposure can result in cumulative and permanent damage to light-sensitive artifacts and artwork. Even sustaining low light levels over a long period of time can cause as much degradation as intensive light levels over a short period.[27] Light is radiant energy and causes irreversible changes through radiant heating or photochemical action. Artifacts with organic materials are particularly susceptible to damage by light.[28]

Radiation heat increases the surface temperature of an object and can cause discoloration, cracking and deterioration. Photochemical action changes the object at a molecular level and can cause embrittlement. "Since all damage is cumulative and

25 Christopher Cuttle, *Light for Art's Sake: Lighting for Artworks and Museum Displays*, Butterworth-Heinemann, Boston 2007, pp. 51–112.
26 Illuminating Engineering Society of North America, *Museum and Art Gallery Lighting: A Recommended Practice*, ANSI/IESNA RP-30-96, Illuminating Engineering Society of North America, New York 1996, p. 1.
27 National Gallery of Art, *Effects of Light Exposure*, https://www.nga.gov/conservation/preventive/effects-of-light-exposure.html
28 https://llfa.eu/

irreversible, the duration and intensity of light exposure must be monitored and limited."[29]

Daylight contains visible light (400–760 nm), ultraviolet radiation (wavelengths shorter than 400 nm) and infrared radiation (wavelengths longer than 760 nm). Light will always have a damaging effect on light-sensitive materials, regardless of how low the light exposure is, but the risk of light damage can be reduced. Strategies to reduce light damage include:[30]

- Reducing the amount of visible light an object receives – lowering the illuminance or light intensity
- Reducing the time an object is exposed to visible light – lowering the cumulative effect
- Eliminating all invisible radiation – blocking ultraviolet and infrared radiation

Reducing the Amount of Visible Light

The human eye requires the minimum amount of 50 lux to adequately perceive the shape and color of an object. Therefore, art conservation experts have recommended that the maximum value for very delicate materials should be 50 lux. For items that are moderately sensitive, the maximum recommended level is 200 lux. Materials insensitive to light are not affected by the amount of light, but levels should not exceed 300 lux, since it becomes more difficult for the human eye to adapt to great differences between light levels from one gallery space to another.

Reducing the Time of Exposure

While daylight intensity is not constant, the damage that results from light exposure is a combination of the light intensity and the length of time an object is exposed to light. "For example, objects exposed to a light intensity of 100 lux for six months will suffer the same amount of damage as an object exposed to twice that intensity for half the time (i.e., 200 lux for three months)."[31]

Therefore, it is crucial to control the time museum objects are exposed to light by keeping the total annual light exposure levels to a minimum. Annual exposure hours are based on the annual opening hours per year for a standard museum. The annual exposure hours multiplied by the recommended maximum for spot light readings give a total sum for the recommended maximum number of lux/hours of exposure over the whole year. Examples of annual maximum number of lux/hours of exposure are:[32]

50,000 lux/hours for highly sensitive materials (50 lux)
480,000 lux/hours for moderately sensitive materials (200 lux)

Annual light exposure levels can be a practical matrix when the light level in the exhibit space cannot be reduced sufficiently. By limiting the display period, the total light exposure can be restricted and remains within the annual exposure maximum. After an object has reached its recommended annual exposure hours, it should be removed from display and placed into dark storage.[33]

Eliminating Invisible Radiation

Ultraviolet (UV) radiation is extremely harmful for objects sensitive to optical radiation. UV is measured in microwatts per lumen, "the amount of the UV component within one lumen of light. To eliminate UV radiation, a filter is needed that reduces the UV component in the natural and electric light. Because UV radiation does not contribute to the visual appearance of artwork",[34] it should be reduced to as close to zero microwatts per lumen as possible.

Infrared (IR) radiation is the form of energy we feel as heat. Heat impacts the air's relative humidity and the moisture content of materials and objects. Heat produced by infrared radiation will cause objects to dry even when the room temperature and

29 The National Gallery of Art, *Effects of Light Exposure*, https://www.nga.gov/conservation/preventive/effects-of-light-exposure.html
30 Scottish Museums Council, *Fact Sheet Conservation and Lighting*, Museums Australia Victoria, 2003, https://amagavic.org.au/assets/Info_Sheet_3_Conservation_and_Lighting.pdf
31 Ibid.
32 Ibid.
33 Ibid.
34 Ibid.

humidity of the room or display case are kept constant.[35] All light sources produce heat to some extent. Direct unfiltered sunlight has a high IR content and should therefore be avoided even for short periods. The heat emitted by luminaires can create hot spots on objects or increase temperature within display cases. To limit the negative effects of IR exposure, natural light needs to be IR-filtered by applying low-emissivity coatings to windows and skylights, and luminaires should be mounted at a safe distance from the art object and vitrines.

Categories of Light Sensitivity of Material

To preserve light-sensitive materials, it is important to identify the light sensitivity of the object displayed. The table below gives recommendations for maximum illuminance levels for specific materials.

Material/exhibit	Sensitivity	Recommended lux level
Most ceramics, glass, stone and metals	Low	200 lux or more
Oil and tempera paintings, undyed leather, lacquer, wood, horn, bone, ivory, minerals and modern black and white photographs	Medium	150–200 lux
Watercolor paintings, dyes, stamps, manuscripts, prints and drawings, vulnerable textiles, photographs, fur and feathers, miniatures, transparencies and unprimed thinly colored paintings on canvas	High	50 lux or less

Table 1: Typical Categories of Light Sensitivity[36]

The Categorizing of the Sensitivity of Colored Material to Light and UV Energy

The exposure to light (radiant energy) can result in cumulative and permanent damage to light-sensitive objects. "This energy causes irreversible change, either through radiant heating or photochemical action."[37]

Illuminance	Damage	Low sensitivity	Medium sensitivity	High sensitivity
50 lux	Just noticeable fade Almost total fade	300 yr – 7,000 yr 10,000 yr – 200,000 yr	20 yr – 700 yr 700 yr – 20,000 yr	1.5 yr – 20 yr 50 yr – 600 yr
150 lux	Just noticeable fade Almost total fade	100 yr – 2,000 yr 3,000 yr – 70,000 yr	7 yr – 200 yr 200 yr – 7,000 yr	6 mo – 7 yr 15 yr – 200 yr
500 lux	Just noticeable fade Almost total fade	30 yr – 700 yr 1,000 yr – 20,000 yr	2 yr – 70 yr 70 yr – 2,000 yr	6 mo – 2 yr 5 yr – 60 yr
5,000 lux window or study lamp	Just noticeable fade Almost total fade	3 yr – 70 yr 100 yr – 2,000 yr	2 mo – 7 yr 7 yr – 200 yr	5 d – 2 mo 6 mo – 6 yr
30,000 lux average daylight	Just noticeable fade Almost total fade	2 mo – 10 yr 20 yr – 300 yr	2 wk – 1 yr 1 yr – 30 yr	1 d – 2 wk 1 mo – 1 yr

Table 2: Time until Fading in Materials Sensitive to Light[38]

(Abbreviations: year-yr, month-mo, week-wk, day-d)
Note: Exposure is assumed to be approximately 8 hours per day, 3,000 hours per year.

Total Exposure Limits

Annual cumulative daylight illuminance should be above 50,000 lux-hours but not exceed 480,000 lux-hours for medium sensitive materials. Medium to highly sensitive objects are illuminated using minimum quantities of light (50 lux), and because they are damaged faster, the duration of their exposure to light should be shorter. Because daylight exposure is cumulative, it is important to limit the total annual lux-hours and not only the maximum illuminance target. Glazing should eliminate all ultraviolet radiation (wavelengths of 400 nm and below).

35 Ibid.
36 The Museum and Art Gallery Lighting Committee of the Illuminating Engineering Society of North America, *Recommended Practice for Museum and Art Gallery Lighting*, ANSI/IES RP-30-17, Illuminating Engineering Society, New York 2017, p. 31.
37 The National Gallery of Art, *Effects of Light Exposure*, https://www.nga.gov/conservation/preventive/effects-of-light-exposure.html
38 The Museum and Art Gallery Lighting Committee of the Illuminating Engineering Society of North America, *Recommended Practice for Museum and Art Gallery Lighting*, ANSI/IES RP-30-17, Illuminating Engineering Society, New York 2017, p. 106.

Type of materials	Maximum illuminance	Lux-hours/year
(Neither value should exceed) Highly sensitive displayed materials: textiles, cotton, natural fibers, furs, silk, writing inks, paper documents, lace, fugitive dyes, watercolors, wool, some minerals.	50 lux	50,000
	Note: Approximately (50 lux) × (8 hours per day) × (125 days per year). Different levels (higher or lower) and/or different periods of display (4 hours for 250 days) may be appropriate, depending upon material.	
Moderately susceptible displayed materials; textiles with stable dyes, oil paintings, wood finishes, leather, some plastics.	200 lux	480,000
	Note: Approximately (200 lux) × (8 hours per day) × (300 days per year). Lower levels may be appropriate, depending upon material.	
Least susceptive displayed materials: metal, stone, glass, ceramic, most minerals.	Depends upon exhibit situation	

Table 3: Recommended Total Exposure Limits in Terms of Illuminance Hours per Year to avoid Light Damage to Susceptive Museum and Art Gallery Artifacts[39]

Art and Architecture

Today it is common sense that the quality of light in museum galleries has a substantial impact on the visitor's perception and experience of the artifacts exhibited, as it influences how their visible attributes are revealed. The experience of art under natural light can be more comfortable and satisfactory than under artificial lighting. Because of the ever-changing nature of daylight, the visitor's experience will be unique every time. Additionally, daylighting enables the visitor to view paintings and drawings close to the lighting conditions under which they were created.

"We knew," wrote Louis Kahn, "that the museum will always be full of surprises. The blues would be one thing one day; the blues would be another thing another day, depending on the character of the light. Nothing static, nothing static as an electric bulb, which can only give you one iota of the character of light. So, the museum has as many moods as there are moments in time, and never as long as the museum remains as a building will there be a single day like the other."[40]

The role of museum architecture goes beyond functionality; it is to develop a story through form and aesthetics, not to overlay art but to serve as a framework. Daylight openings and their control systems give identity to museum galleries because they generate an integrated experience of the space. When they allow views of the urban environment, they connect the visual experience to the location.

39 Illuminating Engineering Society of North America, *Museum and Art Gallery Lighting: A Recommended Practice*, ANSI/IESNA RP-30-96, Illuminating Engineering Society of North America, New York 1996, p. 14.

40 Nell E. Johnson and Louis I. Kahn, *Light is the Theme: Louis I. Kahn and the Kimbell Art Museum*, Kimbell Art Foundation, Fort Worth 1975, p. 16.

Kimbell Art Museum Expansion, 2007–2013, Renzo Piano Pavilion

Design Principles of the Daylight Systems

Shading Concepts – Daylight Control Systems

Shading Concept

Scoop System
1. Light well used to bounce diffused light
2. Light scoop mounted outside the structure to catch sunlight
3. Glass integrated into light well

Fin System
1. Fixed diffusing louvers, constructed of ferro-cement, metal or translucent glass
2. Glass building envelope
3. Translucent ceiling constructed of cloth, glass, or metal designed to diffuse light evenly

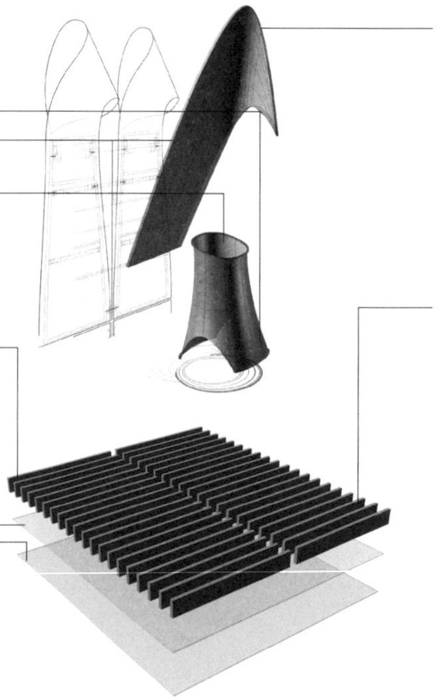

Projects with Scoop Systems

Nasher Sculpture Center
High Museum Expansion

Projects with Fin Systems

The Menil Collection
Cy Twombly Pavilion
Beyeler Foundation
Morgan Library and Museum

Two primary roof design systems by RPBW

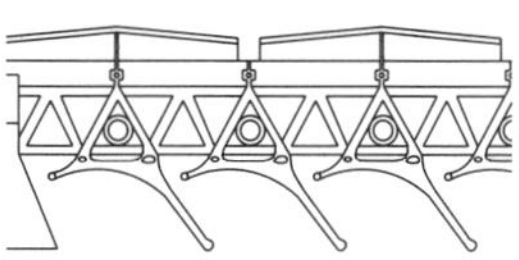

The Menil Collection
300 25 mm (1") ferro-cement fins bounce light into gallery and lobby spaces.

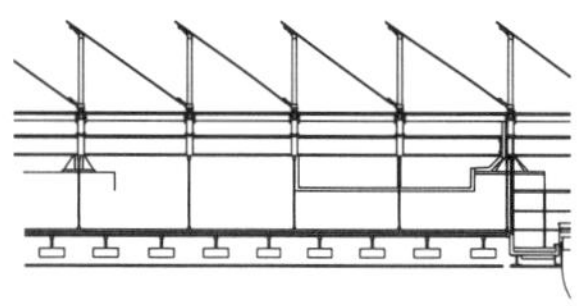

Beyeler Foundation
12 mm (0.47") fritted glass fins diffuse light into gallery spaces.

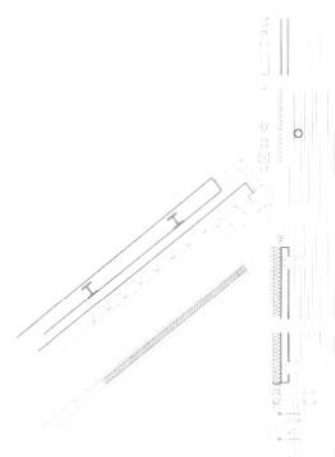

Jean-Marie Tjibaou Cultural Center
244 Iroko wood rib louvers provide shade in library and activity spaces.

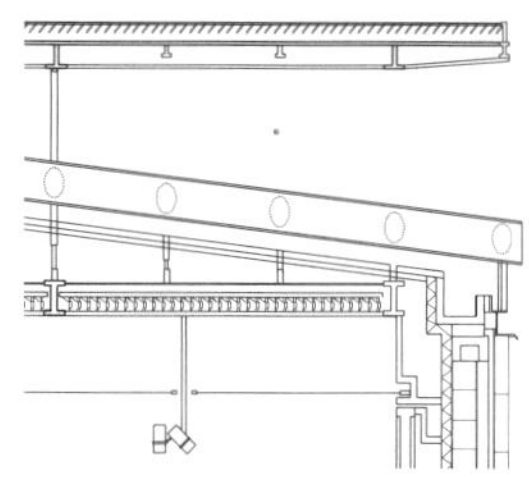

Cy Twombly Pavilion
Fritted glass and steel louvers provide shade in gallery spaces.

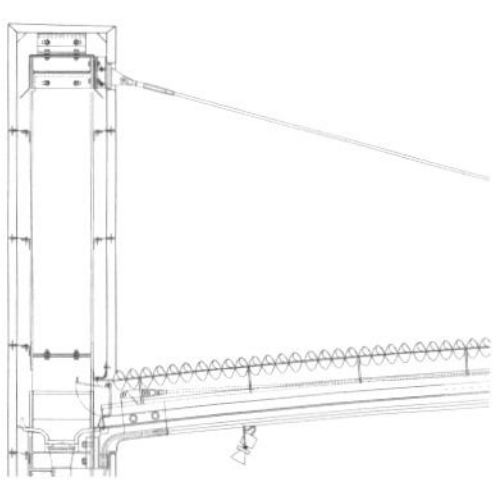

Nasher Sculpture Center
912 cast aluminum sun filters capture and bring light into gallery and lobby spaces.

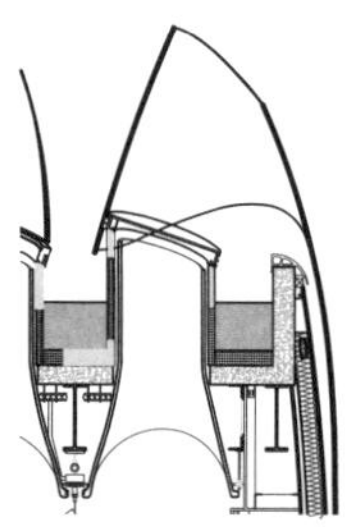

High Museum Expansion
1,000 aluminum light wells bounce light into gallery spaces.

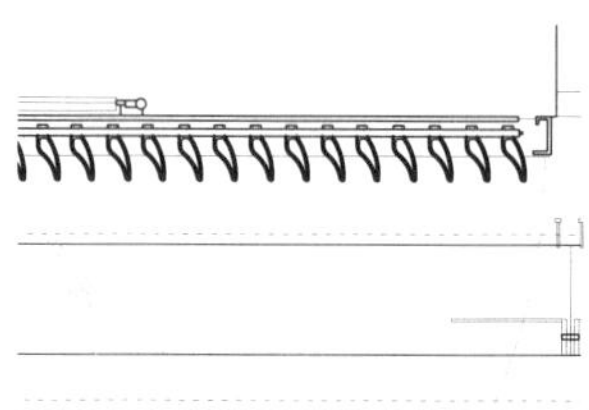

Renovation and Expansion of the Morgan Library and Museum
Glass and aluminum louvers filter light into lobby and reading spaces.

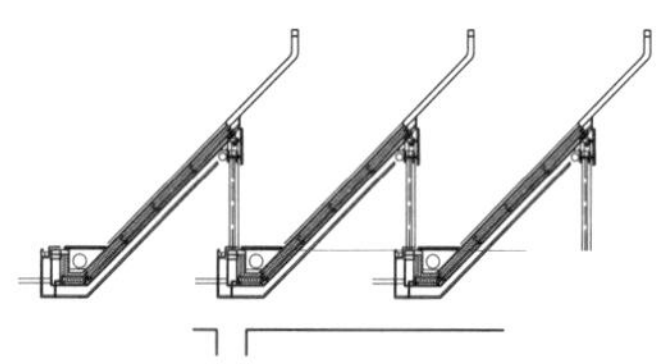

Broad Contemporary Art Museum
Aluminum fins bounce light into gallery spaces.

Daylight System Typologies

Horizontal daylight systems can be categorized into three systems: A) Surface ceiling systems, in which the glass ceiling and the shading system/light control system are flat; B) Linear ceiling systems, in which the glass ceiling or the shading system/light control system is linear and; C) Point (punctiform) ceiling systems, in which the light is guided by point-like skylights. Vertical systems allow daylight penetration through windows and facade openings.

Daylight system	Illustration of principle	Illustration of system	Functional principle
Surface system Daylight diffusing ceiling Skylight ceiling with internal shading The Menil Collection	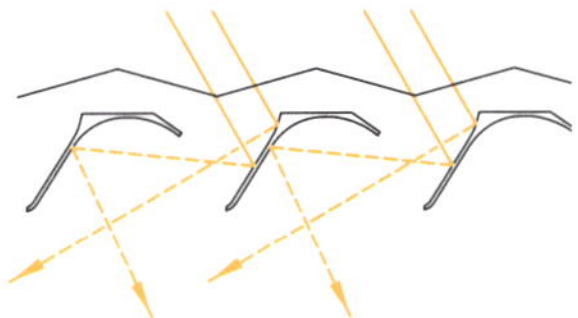	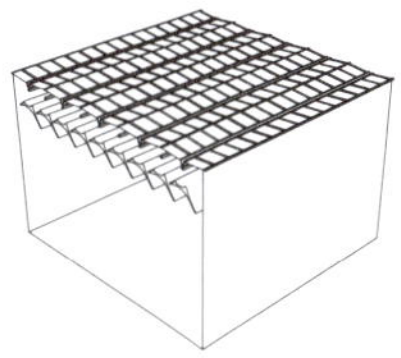	Multilayer surface roof composition consists of slightly sloped exterior skylights and large interior fiber cement fins: • Passive illuminance control • High illuminance levels • Veiling reflections on the upper walls possible
Surface system Restricted daylight diffusing ceiling with velarium Skylight ceiling with external and internal shading Beyeler Foundation	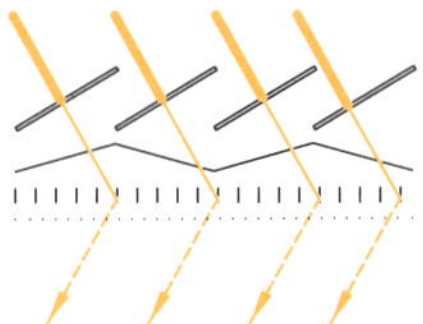	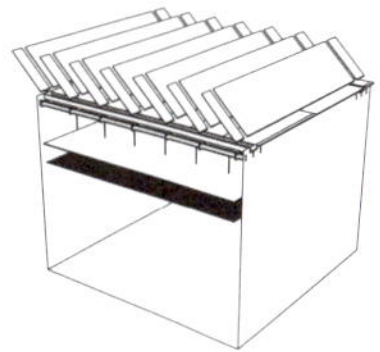	Multilayer roof composition consists of external translucent glass louvers facing north, a horizontal glass roof, interior aluminum louvers, a translucent laminated glass ceiling and a ceiling screen: • Plenum between the skylight and glass ceiling holds the motorized and photocell-controlled louvers. • Plenum climate controls the gallery space. • Diffusing ceiling screen avoids veiling reflections.
Linear system Polar-oriented skylights Sawtooth Broad Contemporary Art Museum	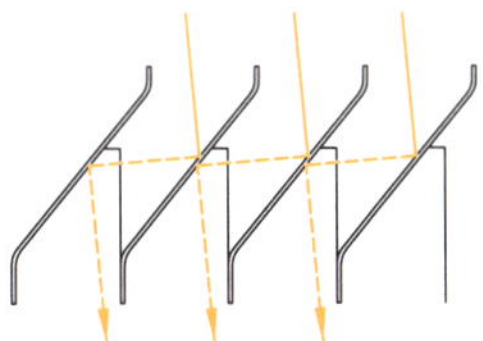	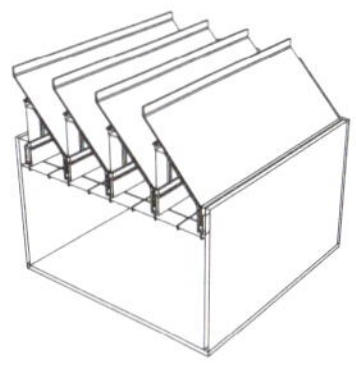	Sawtooth roof comprised of a series of ridges inclined towards the south, channeling north light into the galleries and excluding direct sunlight. Vertical motorized blinds control illuminance level: • Manual override and high wind speeds can retract the external blinds resulting in high illuminance levels.
Point system Multiple skylights Light cones High Museum Expansion	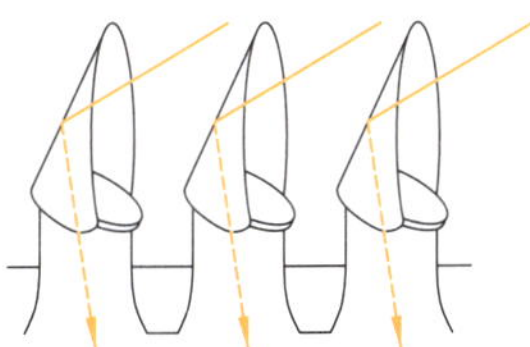	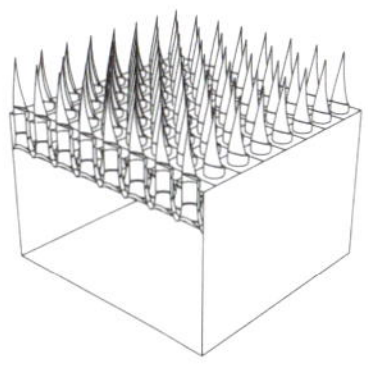	The point system consists of exterior sunshades, glass skylights and a light tube integrated into the ceiling. The north-oriented sunshades and light tubes reflect the sunlight several times before it enters the gallery: • Illuminance levels are not controllable.
Vertical system Side-lit room Window Jean-Marie Tjibaou Cultural Center	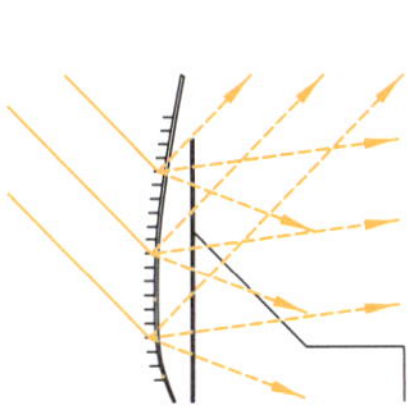	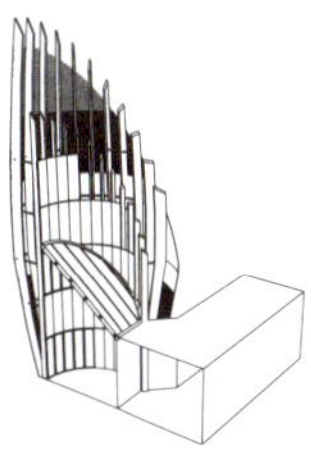	Daylight falls through vertical facade openings to side-light the gallery spaces. The exterior shell-like structure and the wooden shading panels filter light into the interior spaces: • Windows located next to artwork can cause disabling glare. • Directional lighting generates strong shadows.

Definitions

The terms defined here appear in the order of the following daylight analyses of the museums by RPBW.

Exhibition Concept
Light sensitivity of exhibit material; permanent or rotating exhibitions. Target light levels are based on the light susceptibility of the displayed art work and the exhibit concept. Highly susceptible displayed materials: maximum 50 lux, 50,000 lux-hours/year. Moderately susceptible displayed materials: 50–200 lux, 480,000 lux-hours/year. Low susceptible displayed materials: 50–300 lux.

Section Diagram
The section diagram shows the architectural geometry of the gallery and how natural light enters the buildings through the roof daylight systems. It shows how light fins and baffles bounce and reflect daylight into the gallery space.

Daylighting System
Single layer or multilayer system; linear shading or light-well shading (louver, cone or waffle); horizontal surface skylight/glazed roof, linear skylight or point skylight.
Aperture to Floor Area Ratio (AFR): % of gallery floor.

Daylighting Control System:
Daylight shading, modulation, scattering and light filtering concept.

Electric Illumination
Electric illumination concept, location of luminaire.

Material Properties
Light reflectance values (LRV) for walls, floors, exposed structure
Visible Light Transmittance (VLT) for glass and shading screens
Color Rendering Index (CRI) of skylight glass.
CRI defines the ability of transmitted daylight through the glazing to portray a variety of colors compared to those seen under daylight without the glazing. Scale is 1–100. A low CRI causes colors to appear washed out, while a high CRI causes colors to appear vibrant and natural.

Overhead Skylight Glass
LRV, VLT and other properties of skylight glass; specular or diffuse reflection.

Light-Guiding and Shading System
Baffles and shading: external/internal; kinetic or static system
Baffles and shading: location under or above skylight; construction material
Control logic for baffles and shading: manual or automated

Quantitative Daylight Analysis
Point-in-Time Illuminance and Annual Illuminance

False Color Luminance Map
The false color luminance map shows surface reflectance ranges. The colors represent different luminance values (lux) in absolute terms, showing surface brightness and glare potential.

Luminance Scale
The visual scale of the false color luminance map shows the luminance value associated with each color.

Point-in-Time Illuminance (PITI)
Matrix Definition: Point-in-time illuminance calculates the light level values at a specific date and time, under a specific external environmental lighting (sky) condition. The date and time is set to June 21 at noon, summer solstice ("worst-case scenario," highest overlit probability). The false color luminance map shows overlit areas above the target threshold of 200 lux and underlit areas below the target threshold of 50 lux, gradient shows illuminance between 0 and 1000 lux.
Recommended Illuminance Target: Values are based on ANSI.[1] The illuminance target threshold is between 50 and 200 lux for moderately susceptible displayed materials and between 50 and 300 lux for low susceptible displayed materials. In general, levels above 300 lux are not recommended in exhibit spaces because of the difficulty of the human eye to adapt to changing light levels between exhibits and high contrast values on exhibited objects.[2] The recommended light levels are a compromise between the need to see exhibits and the need to preserve the objects. All light exposure will cause damage to sensitive objects. There is no minimum level at which damage will not occur.

Average Annual Illuminance (AAI)
Matrix Definition: Light acts cumulatively, and so the total exposure over time is the critical factor for artifact damage. The sensitivity of colored material to light and UV energy is based on ANSI and is categorized as low sensitivity, medium sensitivity and high sensitivity.[3] AAI is the average daylight illuminance during occupied hours, averaged over the course of the year. A threshold and/or maximum illuminance metric is established to preserve the artifact from any lighting damage.
The annual illuminance target threshold for medium sensitive displayed materials is between 50 and 200 lux (averaged). Gradient shows illuminance between 0 and 1000 lux.
Recommended Total Exposure Limits: The recommended illuminance targets are based on IESNA[4] and categorized as highly susceptible, moderately susceptible and least susceptible displayed materials.
The maximum (cumulative) total lux-hours annually for highly susceptible displayed materials is 50,000 lux-hours/yr and 50 lux maximum illuminance; the maximum total lux-hours annually (cumulative) for medium sensitive materials is 480,000 lux-hours/year and 200 lux maximum illuminance.
Average annually illuminance calculation: lux × hours/day (operating hours) × operating days/year.

Useful Daylight Illuminance (UDI)
Matrix Definition: UDI is a modification of Daylight Autonomy and is "founded on an annual time-series of absolute values for illuminance predicted under realistic skies generated from standard meteorological datasets."[5] This metric bins hourly time values based upon three illumination ranges: 0–25 lux (daylight level is insufficient to perform visual task), 50–200 lux (daylight level is sufficient to perform visual task) and over 200 lux (daylight level is above target threshold for sensitive art). The false color luminance map shows overlit areas above 200 lux and underlit areas below 50 lux. The spatial UDI map shows the percentage of operating hours when daylight illuminance levels are between 50 and 200 lux, considered "useful" for galleries with sensitive artwork.
Recommended Targets: The recommended target is a high percentage of floor and wall area that meets the UDI criteria at least 50% of the time annually.
The illuminance target threshold for UDI should be between 50 and 200 lux, unless the exhibits have a low susceptible level. UDI falling short of the lower limit (< 50 lux) indicates the need for artificial lighting. UDI exceeding the upper limit (> 200 lux) indicates the potential for occupant discomfort and the probability of daylight glare. Generally, a UDI percentage of 50% or better is considered well daylit and indicates a potentially lower annual energy consumption for lighting.

Daylight Dimming Potential (DDP)
Matrix Definition: The matrix shows the percentage of time when the illuminance exceeds 200 lux (in white) within the operating hours of 8 a.m. to 6 p.m., 6 days/week. The calculation takes the gradual increase of e-lighting under consideration. Calculated were 100% e-lighting below 50 lux daylight and 50% e-lighting below 200 lux daylight.
Recommended Targets: A high DDP percentage shows the potential for energy savings for electric lighting.

Annual Illuminance Frequency (AIF)
Matrix Definition: The percentage values represent the annual daytime hours with illuminance within range (50–200 lux). The x-axis shows the range in illuminance levels while the y-axis shows the annual frequency. The AIF matrix is based on the annual UDI simulation. Note that the maximum hourly illuminance value may not be on June 21 at noon, but may be on a different day and time depending on the specific geographical location and climate.
Recommended Targets: A high percentage of illuminance within the target range reflects good daylight conditions during operating hours.

Qualitative Daylight Analysis
Glare and Visual Comfort

Physiological Glare: Annual Daylight Glare Probability (DGP)
Matrix Definition: The DGP metric is used to evaluate comfort and the probability of persons being disturbed by glare. The DGP index was based on experiments with real human subjects and classifies a whole space in terms of daylight glare comfort classes (imperceptible glare, perceptible glare, disturbing glare and intolerable glare). It shows the percentage of persons disturbed at different vertical eye illuminance (lux). Glare is a subjective human sensation described as "light within the field of vision that is brighter than the brightness to which the eyes are adapted"[6] and caused by a significant ratio of luminance between the task (that which is being looked at) and the glare source. Factors such as the angle between the task and the glare source and eye adaptation have significant impacts on the experience of glare.
Based on the DGP, the Illuminance Value Contrast (IVC) evaluation uses the point-in-time glare simulation with a camera viewpoint to investigate the overall brightness of the view, position of "glare" sources and visual contrast at a specific point in time.
DGP Graph: The x-axis corresponds to different days of the year; the y-axis to time of day. Red and orange fields correspond to hours with intolerable or disturbing glare, respectively.
Recommended Targets: Direct or indirect glare has a negative impact on the visual comfort and should be avoided. The DGP percentage value should be between .4 and .35 (perceptible glare to imperceptible glare).

Psychological Glare: Illuminance Value Contrast (IVC)
Matrix Definition: The point-in-time glare simulation (IVC) shows the visual comfort of a person under the simulated conditions at the camera viewpoint. A satisfactory brightness perception is primarily a function of controlling the relative luminance between the displayed objects and their surroundings and has little to do with the actual illuminance exposure that the material receives. A luminance ratio of 3:1 between the displayed object and its surroundings creates a pleasing sense of emphasis and favorable brightness perception.
The IVC shows contrast values between walls, floor and ceiling. The ideal contrast value (contrast ratio) threshold lies between 1:2 and 1:4. A contrast value below the threshold is too low and a contrast above the threshold can be visually disturbing.[7]
Recommended Targets: The recommended contrast value (contrast ratio) should be between 1:2 and 1:4 for uniformity targets and for vertical flat viewing surfaces such as paintings. For three-dimensional objects, the variation of illuminance from several directions is important to provide the light contrast (highlights and shadows) to reveal the object's plasticity.[8] The foreground-to-background luminance ratio should not exceed 1:10 and should preferably be 1:5.[9]

1 The Museum and Art Gallery Lighting Committee of the Illuminating Engineering Society of North America, *Recommended Practice for Museum Lighting*, ANSI/IES RP-30-17, Illuminating Engineering Society, New York 2017, p. 31.
2 National Park Service, *Museum Handbook*, Chapter 4 "Museum Collections Environment," NPS, Washington, DC 2019.
3 The Museum and Art Gallery Lighting Committee of the Illuminating Engineering Society of North America, *Recommended Practice for Museum Lighting*, ANSI/IES RP-30-17, Illuminating Engineering Society, New York 2017, p. 106.
4 The Museum and Art Gallery Lighting Committee of the Illuminating Engineering Society of North America, *Recommended Practice for Museum Lighting*, ANSI/IES RP-30-17, Illuminating Engineering Society, New York 2017, p. 31.
5 Azza Nabil and John Mardaljevic, "Useful Daylight Illuminance: A New Paradigm for Assessing Daylight in Buildings," *Lighting Research & Technology*, 37(1), 2005, pp. 41–57.
6 HarperCollins, *Collins Thesaurus of the English Language – Complete and Unabridged*, 2nd ed., HarperCollins, New York 2002.
7 The Museum and Art Gallery Lighting Committee of the Illuminating Engineering Society of North America, *Recommended Practice for Museum Lighting*, ANSI/IES RP-30-17, Illuminating Engineering Society, New York 2017, p. 91, errata 1, 11/2017.
8 Ibid., p. 28.
9 Ibid., p. 28.

The Menil Collection 1982–1986

Houston, Texas, USA
29.737081°N, -95.398338°W

Exhibition Concept

Low to medium light sensitivity of exhibit; sculpture and paintings; permanent and rotating exhibitions. Illuminance threshold: 50 to 200 (300) lux; maximum lux-hours/year: 480,000.

Section Diagram

The section diagram shows natural light entering the building through the roof daylight systems. Light fins (fiber cement) bounce and reflect diffused daylight into the gallery space.

Daylighting System

Multilayer linear roof composition consisting of exterior tilted skylights and interior large fiber cement fins. Aperture to Floor Area Ratio (AFR) is 100%.

Daylighting Control System

Interior curved fins control the daylight from the glass skylights. The curve of the louver blocks and scatters the light, reflecting it off the neighboring louver.

Electric Illumination

The electric illumination consists of spotlights attached to a linear track at the underside of the fins.

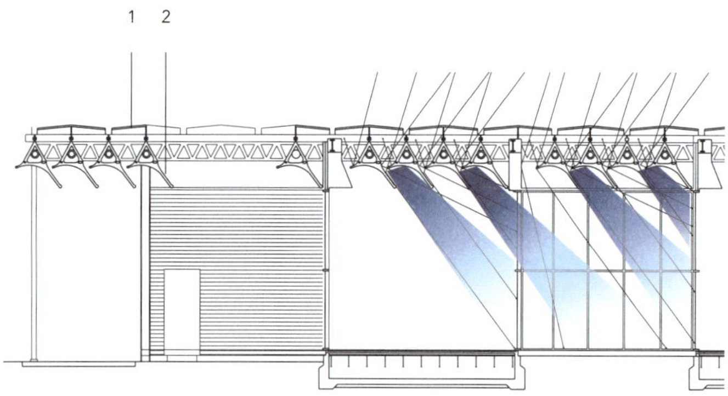

Section through Gallery Space

1 Double pane low-e glass with UV coating
2 Light fins (fiber cement)

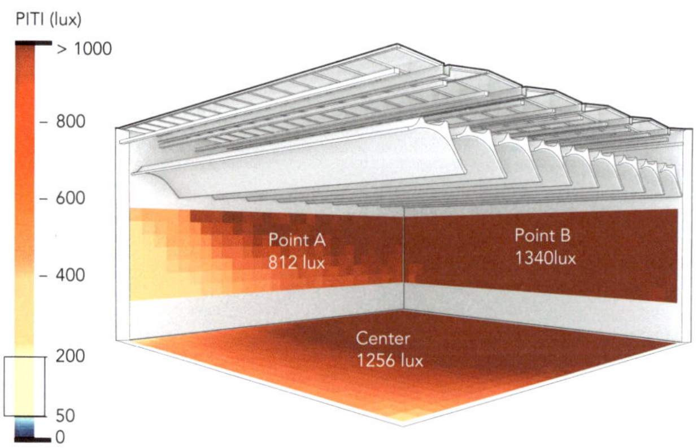

Point-in-Time Illuminance (PITI)

June 21, noon light levels projected onto floor and wall surfaces

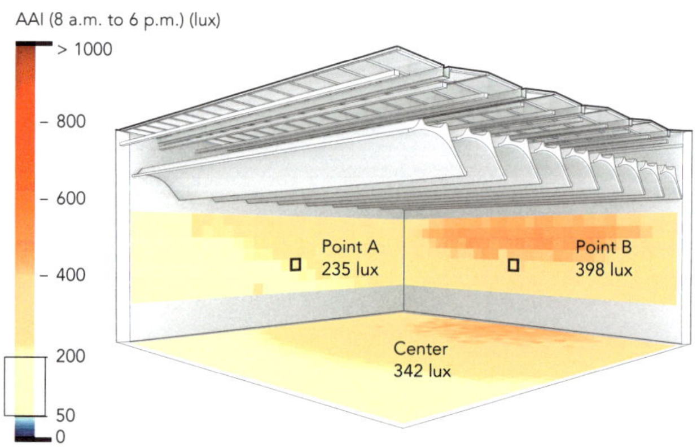

Average Annual Illuminance (AAI)

Light levels projected onto floor and wall surfaces

Location
Climate: Hot and humid
Building orientation: North-south
Louver orientation: East-west
Material Properties
Walls and surface finishes: Wall: SW 7757 High Reflective White, LRV 92.6% Floor: DuraSeal 199 True Black, LRV 4.0%
Exposed structure: White paint, LRV 80%, white ferro-cement fins, LRV 80%
Overhead Skylight Glass
Skylight glass: VLT 50%, double pane low-e glass (1 5/16) with UV coating
Reflection: Specular
Glass around the perimeter wall: Opaque Glass above roof overhang: Laminated, clear
Light-Guiding System – Control Logic
External shading: Kinetic system (manual) Skylights covered as needed by perforated steel covers; 0%, 50%, 75%, 100% blockout. Simulation with 50% perforation.
Internal shading: Static system
Location of louvers: Under the skylight

Quantitative Daylight Analysis
Point-in-Time and Annual Illuminance

Point-in-Time Illuminance (PITI)	
PITI June 21, noon (West-facing wall)	812 lux
PITI June 21, noon (Center of gallery)	1,256 lux
Average Annual Illuminance (AAI)	
Average daylight level (West-facing wall)	235 lux
Accumulated lux-hrs annually	358,900
Recommended total exposure target (480,000 lux-hrs annually)	Below
Useful Daylight Illuminance (UDI)	
Percentage daytime hours with daylight levels of 50–200 lux (West-facing wall)	45%
Daylight Dimming Potential (DDP)	
Percentage of daytime hours with daylight levels above 200 lux (Center of gallery, 8 a.m. to 6 p.m.)	64%

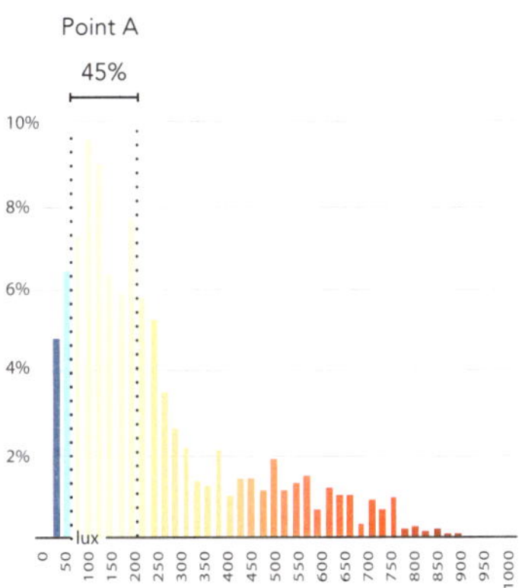

Illuminance at Point A (west-facing wall) falls within the target range 45% of the year with a peak hourly value of 936 lux and a cumulative annual exposure of 358,900 lux-hrs.

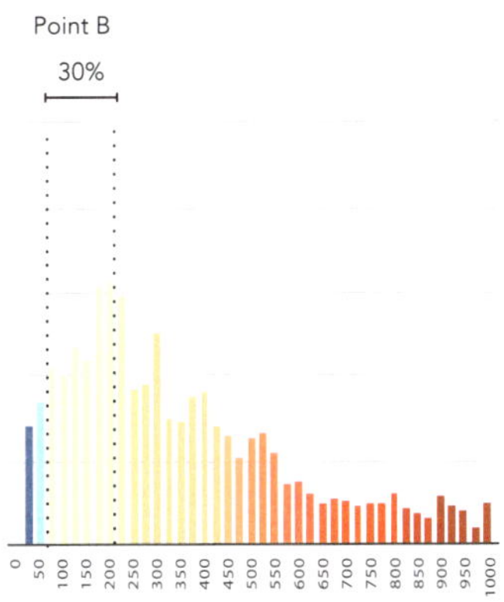

Illuminance at Point B (north-facing wall) falls within the target range 30% of the year with a peak hourly value of 1,564 lux and a cumulative annual exposure of 1,452,000 lux-hrs.

Annual Illuminance Frequency (AIF)
The percentage values represent the annual daytime hours with illuminance within the target range.

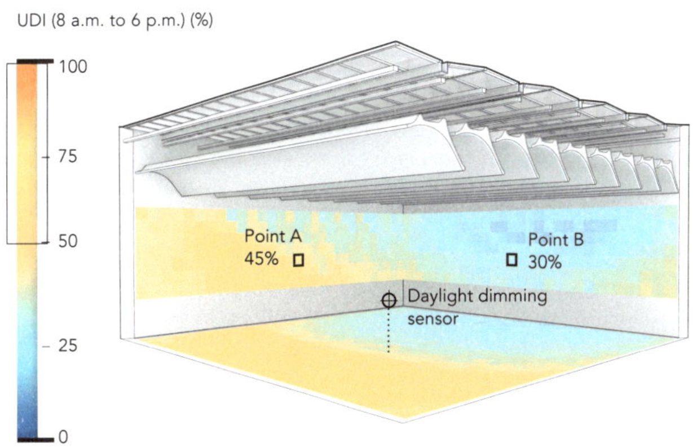

Useful Daylight Illuminance (UDI)
The spatial UDI map shows 30–45% of the operating hours receiving daylight illuminance levels of 50–200 lux.

Qualitative Daylight Analysis
Glare and Visual Comfort

Physiological Glare
Annual Daylight Glare Probability (DGP)
Annual DGP simulation shows no direct or indirect glare on walls or floor.
Probability of disturbing glare: 30%.

Psychological Glare
Illuminance Value Contrast (IVC)
Point-in-time glare analysis shows luminance ratios for a gallery space. The contrast values are between 1:2 and 1:4 and show good contrast of luminance on the object.

Summary
The daylight system consists of a glass roof and fixed diffusing ferro-cement fins under the skylight. The fixed fins allow for a greater daily and annual luminance fluctuation. Positioning the fins inside the building under the glass roof exposes the glass to full sun exposure and heat gain.
The quantitative daylight analysis shows a dynamic lighting situation on the simulated walls and floor. Peak illuminance of 936 lux (PITI) on the west-facing wall is above the illuminance target recommendation, while the accumulated exposure of 358,900 lux-hrs (AAI) is below the recommended levels, indicating high variability in annual daylight levels. The north-facing and west-facing walls show significant difference in accumulated lux-hours annually.
The UDI and the AIF show that the center of the west-facing wall receives target daylight levels of 50–200 lux for 45% of the time annually. A lower UDI for the north-facing wall can be attributed to more hours when daylight illuminance exceeds 200 lux.
The qualitative daylight analysis shows no perceptible glare (DGP) during the occupancy hours year-round. Note that a south-facing view was also analyzed, demonstrating consistent results. The lighting simulation (IVC) shows a dynamic contrast on the exhibit walls with contrast values of between 1:2 and 1:4 on most of the target zone. The annual daylight dimming potential is high, at 64% of the gallery opening hours.

Recommendations
The initial concept for the galleries was to house rotating exhibitions. The daylight system is excellent for sculptures and low sensitive artwork. The daylighting values exceed the recommended total exposure limits for moderately susceptible displayed artwork (textiles, oil paintings, leather etc.). The fixed louvers are not able to modulate or adjust the daylighting conditions.
Sun exposure of artwork needs to be addressed by close monitoring of the annual lux-hours exposure. The manual interchangeable perforated metal screens covering the outside skylights were meant to control the Visible Light Transmittance but proved to be impractical.

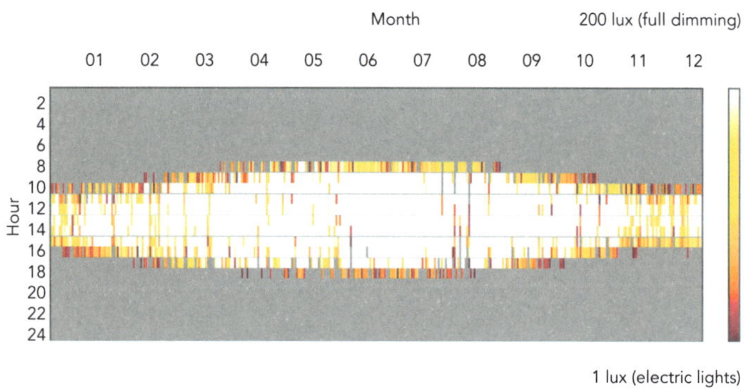

Daylight Dimming Potential (DDP)
Daytime hours when illuminance exceeds 200 lux (in white) indicate the potential to dim electric lighting 64% of the time annually.

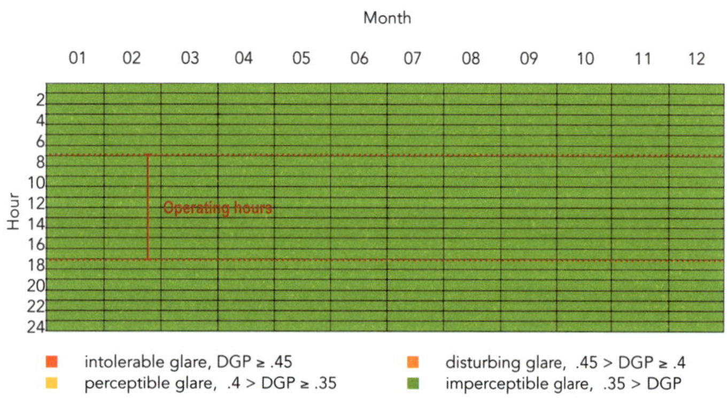

Annual Daylight Glare Probability (DGP)
Annual hourly DGP from the camera viewpoint indicates no perceptible glare.

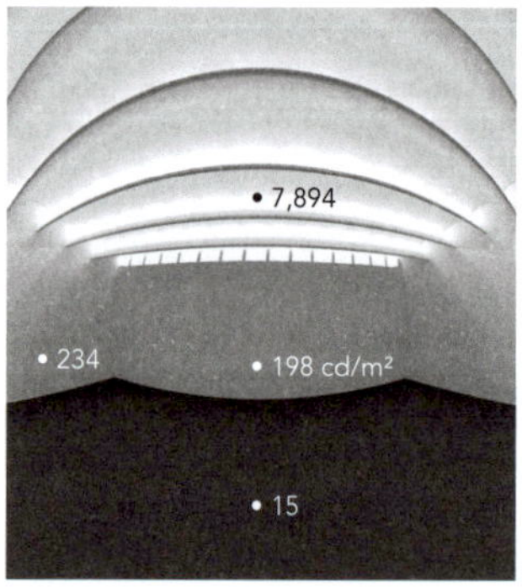

Illuminance Value Contrast (IVC)
The rendering shows highest contrast ratios when looking north on June 21 at noon.

Gallery View
The photo shows significant contrast on visible exhibit wall.

Beyeler Foundation 1991–1997

Riehen, Basel, Switzerland
47.587960°N, 7.651042°E

Exhibition Concept

Medium to high light sensitivity of exhibit; sculpture, paintings and drawings; permanent exhibitions. Illuminance threshold: 50 to 200 lux; maximum lux-hours/year: 480,000.

Section Diagram

The section diagram shows natural light entering the gallery space through a multilayered roof system. Each inclined exterior glass sun-shading panel reflects light to lower the overall brightness. The reflected light is diffused across the gallery.

Daylighting System

Multilayer linear roof composition consisting of external translucent sawtooth glass louvers facing north, a horizontal double-glazed roof, interior horizontal aluminum louvers, a translucent laminated glass ceiling and a perforated metal and paper ceiling screen. Aperture to Floor Area Ratio (AFR) is 100%.

Daylighting Control System

The inclined and fritted glass sunshades (1) prevent direct sun penetration and maintain optimum admittance of diffused light during operating hours. The glass roof (2) consists of double pane low-e glass with UV coating. Computer-motorized aluminum louvers (3) control light levels in each gallery and keep light levels within predetermined limits. The louver system is situated between the glass roof (2) and glass ceiling (5) in a thermal buffer zone (4) above the art galleries. The visible ceiling is the lowest layer in the system and consists of a grid of perforated metal panels (6), which incorporate a paper that diffuses light once more and adds a layer of opacity to the lofted thermal buffer zone. The combined daylighting system prevents 98% of the solar radiation from reaching the gallery spaces.

Electric Illumination

Electric illumination complements the daylighting strategy, as daylight decreases, the tri-phosphor linear fluorescent luminaires in the loft thermal buffer zone increase to maintain ideal lighting levels. The lighting system is augmented by small low-voltage spotlights positioned on stems at the junctions of all ceiling panels to highlight and add directional light for enhanced contrast and effects to the sculpture.

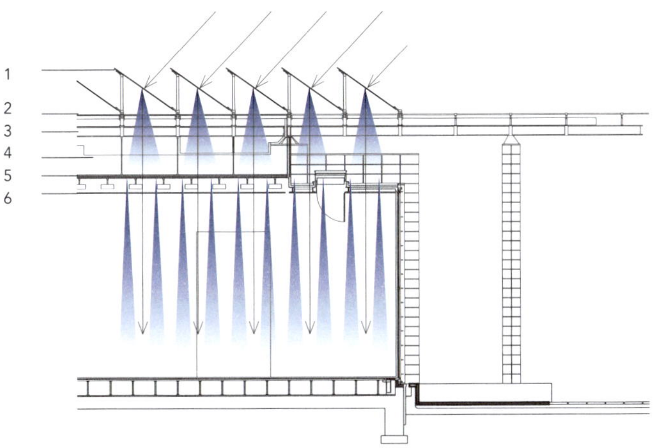

Section through Gallery Space

1 Sunshading: 12 mm (0.47") screen-printed opaque glass, inclined
2 Weatherproof layer: Double pane low-e glass with UV coating
3 Aluminum louvers: Computer-motorized to control light levels in each gallery
4 Thermal buffer zone: 1.4 m (6 ft) high loft space between the glass ceiling and the roof
5 Laminated glass ceiling: Allows access to the louver motors and electric lights
6 "Velum" suspended ceiling grid: Perforated metal panels incorporating a light softening paper

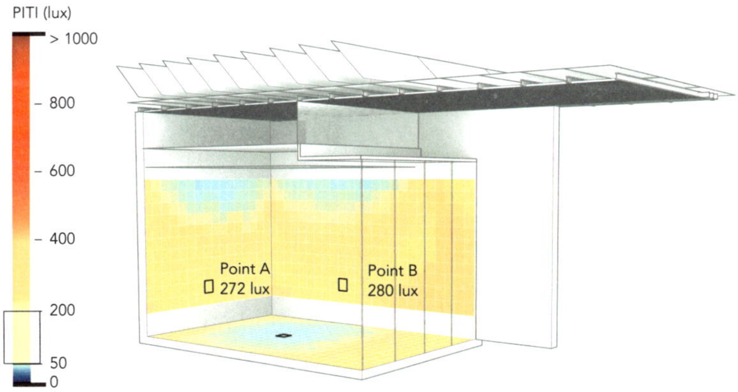

Point-in-Time Illuminance (PITI)
June 21, noon light levels projected onto floor and wall surfaces

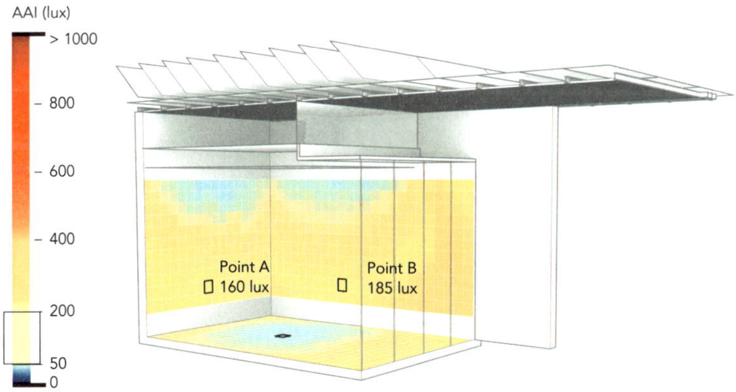

Average Annual Illuminance (AAI)
Light levels projected onto floor and wall surfaces

Location
Climate: Temperate
Building orientation: North/northeast
Louver orientation: South/southwest
Material Properties
Walls and surface finishes Wall: SW 7757 High Reflective White, LRV 92.6% Floor: Natural oak, LRV 37.9%
Exposed structure: White paint, LRV 80%
Overhead Skylight Glass
Skylight glass: VLT 50%, double pane low-e glass with UV coating
Reflection: Specular
Light-Guiding System – Control Logic
External shading: Static system, fixed 12 mm (0.47") tempered glass panels, white ceramic frit screen-printed 50% coverage,[1] diffusing, VLT 40%
Internal shading: Kinetic system; computer-motorized aluminum louver blades
Location of louvers: Under skylight, white paint, LRV 80%
Glass ceiling: Laminated glass, clear, VLT 90% "Velum" suspended ceiling grid: Perforated metal panels incorporating a light softening paper, diffusing, VLT 50%

Quantitative Daylight Analysis
Point-in-Time and Annual Illuminance

Point-in-Time Illuminance (PITI)	
PITI June 21, noon (South-facing wall)	272 lux
PITI June 21, noon (Center of gallery)	396 lux
Average Annual Illuminance (AAI)	
Average daylight level (South-facing wall)	160 lux
Accumulated lux-hrs annually	469,200
Recommended total exposure target (480,000 lux-hrs annually)	Below
Useful Daylight Illuminance (UDI)	
Percentage daytime hours with daylight levels of 50–200 lux (South-facing wall)	73%
Daylight Dimming Potential (DDP)	
Percentage of daytime hours with daylight levels above 200 lux (Center of gallery, 8 a.m. to 6 p.m.)	64%

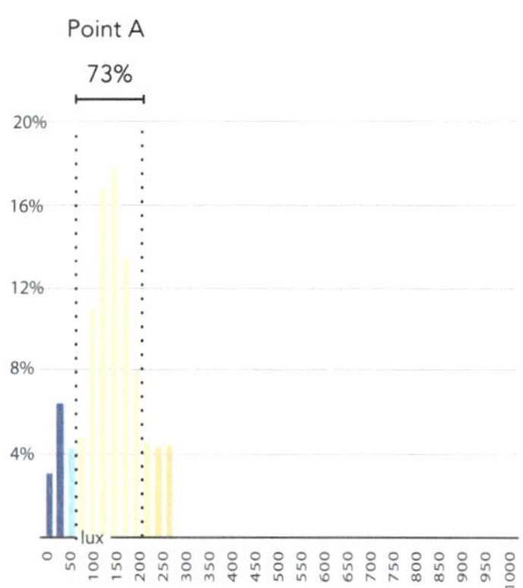

Illuminance at Point A (south-facing) falls within the target range 73% of the year with a peak hourly value of 272 lux and a cumulative annual exposure of 469,200 lux-hrs.

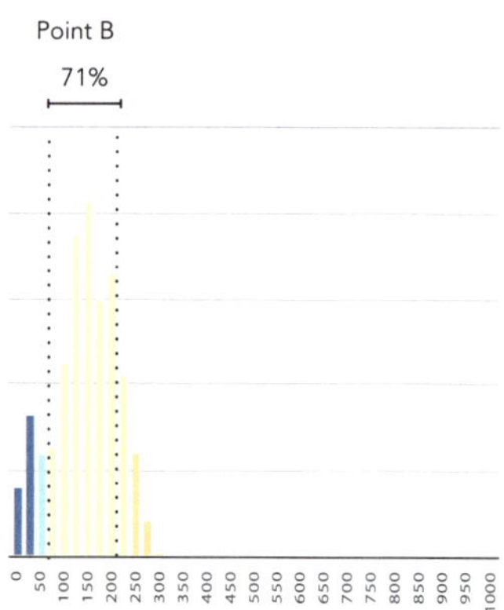

Illuminance at Point B (west-facing) falls within the target range 71% of the year with a peak hourly value of 280 lux and a cumulative annual exposure of 477,900 lux-hrs.

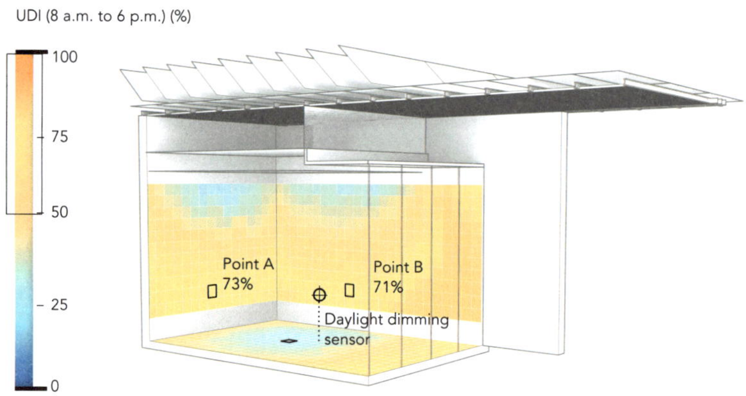

Useful Daylight Illuminance (UDI)
The spatial UDI map shows 71–73% of the operating hours receiving daylight illuminance levels of 50–200 lux.

Annual Illuminance Frequency (AIF)
The percentage values represent the annual daytime hours with illuminance within the target range.

1 Product description, performance characteristics: Saint-Gobain Sage Glass.

Qualitative Daylight Analysis
Glare and Visual Comfort

Physiological Glare
Annual Daylight Glare Probability (DGP)
Annual DGP simulation shows no direct or indirect glare on walls or floor.
Probability of disturbing glare: 16%.

Psychological Glare
Illuminance Value Contrast (IVC)
Point-in-time glare analysis shows luminance ratios for a gallery space. The contrast values are between 1:2 and 1:4 and show good contrast of luminance on the object.

Summary
The natural light penetrates through the multilayer roof system. The superior soft lighting condition in the gallery automatically adjusts to the desired luminance values. The thermal buffer zone helps to limit the effects of climatic extremes on the building and reduces radiance on mechanical systems.
The quantitative daylight analysis shows a dynamic lighting situation on the simulated walls and floor. The peak illuminance of 272 lux (PITI) and the accumulated annual total of 469,200 lux-hrs (AAI) are within the illuminance target recommendation.

The UDI and the AIF show that the center of the south-facing wall receives target daylight levels of 50–200 lux for 73% of the time annually.
The qualitative daylight analysis shows no perceptible glare (DGP) during the occupancy hours year-round. The lighting simulation (IVC) shows a dynamic contrast on the exhibit walls with contrast values of between 1:2 and 1:4 on most of the target zone. The annual daylight dimming potential is high, at 64% of the gallery operating hours.

Recommendations
The dynamic daylight system is excellent for sculptures, low and medium sensitive artwork. The daylighting values are within the recommended total exposure limits for moderately susceptible displayed artwork (textiles, oil paintings, leather etc.). The automated louvers are able to modulate or adjust the daylighting conditions according to desired lux values. Sun exposure to highly sensitive artwork needs to be addressed by closely monitoring the annual lux-hrs exposure. The sequence of diversified galleries features sideline windows with visual connections into courtyards, gardens and landscapes, as well as galleries with skylights as the only openings. This variation generates accentuated lighting scenarios and creates a stimulating visitor experience.

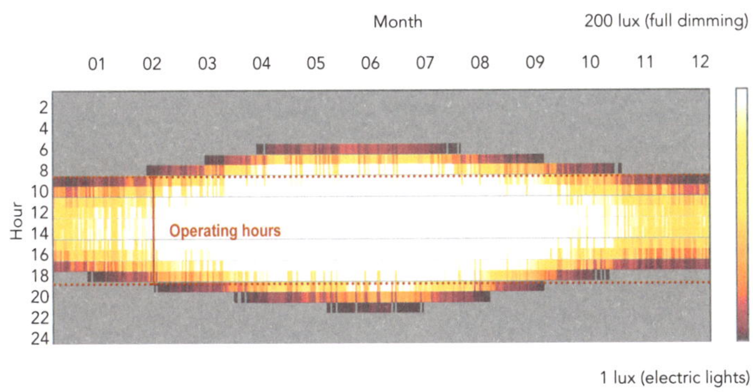

Daylight Dimming Potential (DDP)
Daytime hours when illuminance exceeds 200 lux (in white) indicate the potential to dim electric lighting 64% of the time annually.

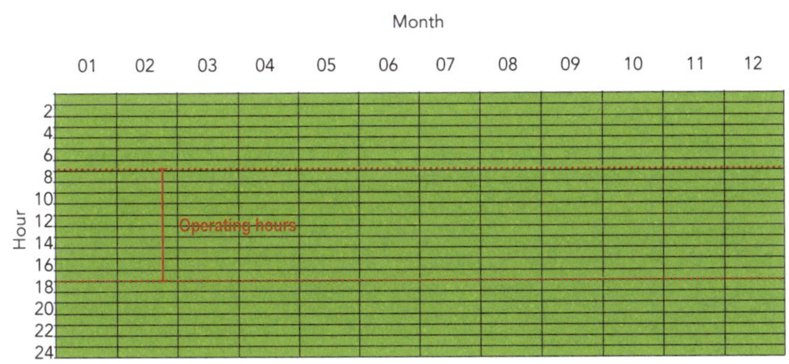

- intolerable glare, DGP ≥ .45
- perceptible glare, .4 > DGP ≥ .35
- disturbing glare, .45 > DGP ≥ .4
- imperceptible glare, .35 > DGP

Annual Daylight Glare Probability (DGP)
Annual hourly DGP from the camera viewpoint indicates no perceptible glare.

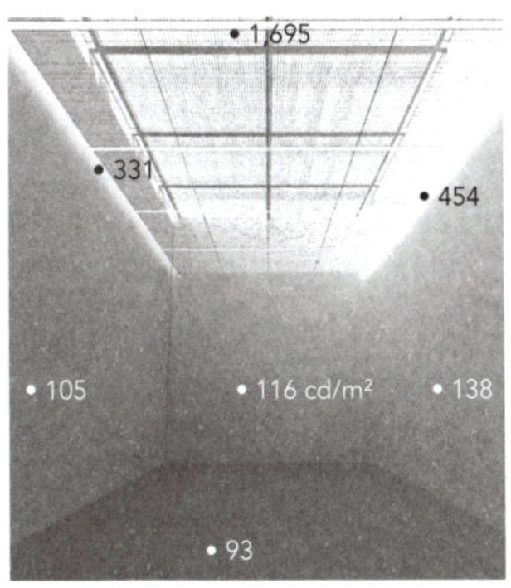

Illuminance Value Contrast (IVC)
The rendering shows highest contrast ratios when looking north on June 21 at noon.

Gallery View
View inside one of the gallery spaces. High-gloss flooring and white wall surfaces reflect light within the space.

Jean-Marie Tjibaou Cultural Center 1991–1998

Nouméa, New Caledonia
-22.256313°S, 166.481887°E

Exhibition Concept

Low light sensitivity of exhibit; sculptures. Illuminance threshold: 50 to 200 (300) lux; maximum lux-hours/year: 480,000.

Section Diagram

The section diagram shows natural light entering the building through the walls (in the southern hemisphere, the sun is in the north at noon).

Daylighting System

The daylighting system consists of a metal roof and a partly glazed curved wall. Aperture to Floor Area Ratio (AFR) is 0%.

Daylighting Control System

The exterior shell-like structure and the bamboo shading panels filter light into the interior spaces and shade the roof. The south sloping roof consists of metal panels.

Electric Illumination

Electric illumination complements the daylighting strategy and consists of spotlights underneath the roof structures.

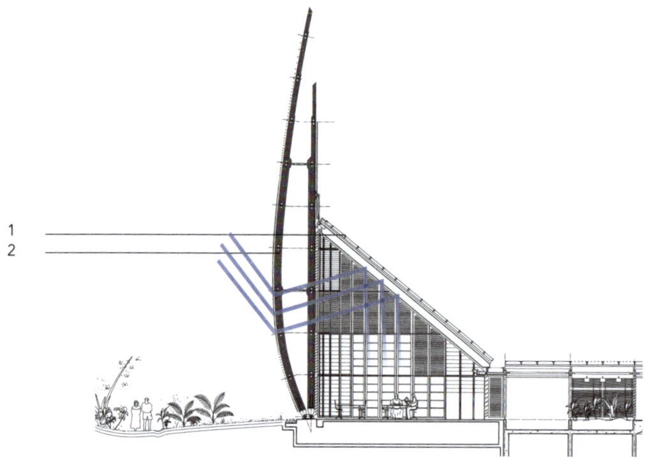

Section through Gallery Space

1 Exterior metal roof structure
2 Curved facade structure built from Iroko wood, glass, steel, and bamboo shading panels

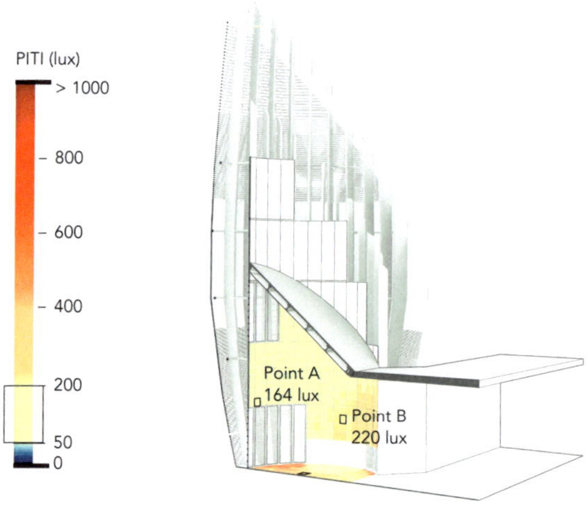

Point-in-Time Illuminance (PITI)
Summer solstice (Dec. 21, noon) light levels projected onto floor and wall surface

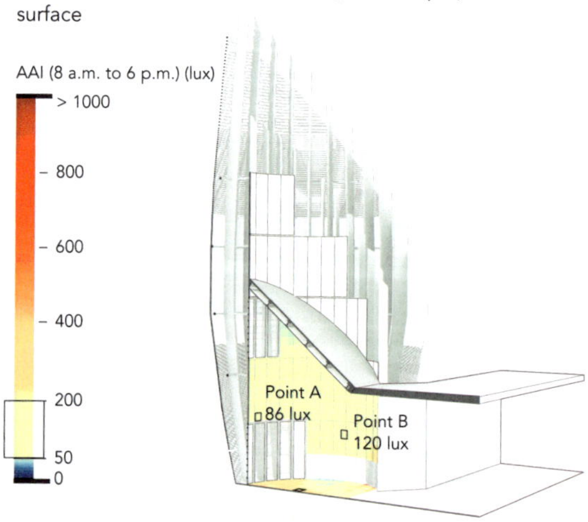

Average Annual Illuminance (AAI)
Light levels projected onto floor and wall surfaces

Location

Climate: Hot and humid

Building orientation: Southwest

Sunshading orientation: North facade shading screen

Material Properties

Walls and surface finishes

Wall: Iroko wood, LRV 35%

Floor: Coral and sand concrete topping, LRV 35%

Exposed structure: Anthracite gray paint, LRV 10%

Glass Facade

Window glass: VLT 50%, double pane low-e glass with UV coating

Reflection: Specular

Light-Guiding System – Control Logic

External shading: External shading: Static system, fixed bamboo louvers

Location of louvers: Vertical wall, wood, LRV 15%

Quantitative Daylight Analysis

Point-in-Time and Annual Illuminance

Point-in-Time Illuminance (PITI)	
PITI Dec. 21, noon (North-facing wall)	164 lux
PITI Dec. 21, noon (Center of gallery)	388 lux
Average Annual Illuminance (AAI)	
Average daylight level (North-facing wall)	86 lux
Accumulated lux-hrs annually	349,400
Recommended total exposure target (480,000 lux-hrs annually)	Below
Useful Daylight Illuminance (UDI)	
Percentage daytime hours with daylight levels of 50–200 lux (North-facing wall)	74%
Daylight Dimming Potential (DDP)	
Percentage of daytime hours with daylight levels above 200 lux (Center of gallery, 8 a.m. to 6 p.m.)	95%

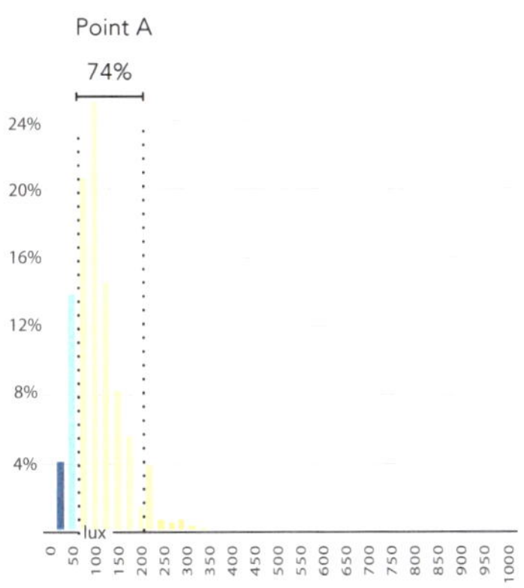

Illuminance at Point A (north-facing, southern hemisphere) falls within the target range 74% of the year with a peak hourly value of 344 lux and a cumulative annual exposure of 349,400 lux-hrs.

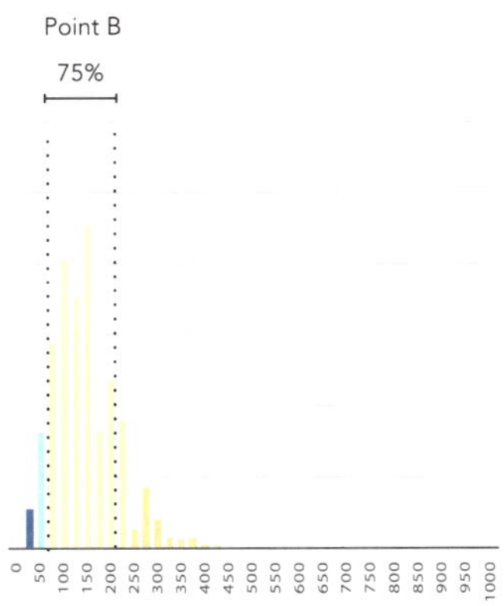

Illuminance at Point B (east-facing) falls within the target range 75% of the year with a peak hourly value of 412 lux and a cumulative annual exposure of 479,200 lux-hrs.

Annual Illuminance Frequency (AIF)

The percentage values represent the annual daytime hours with illuminance within the target range.

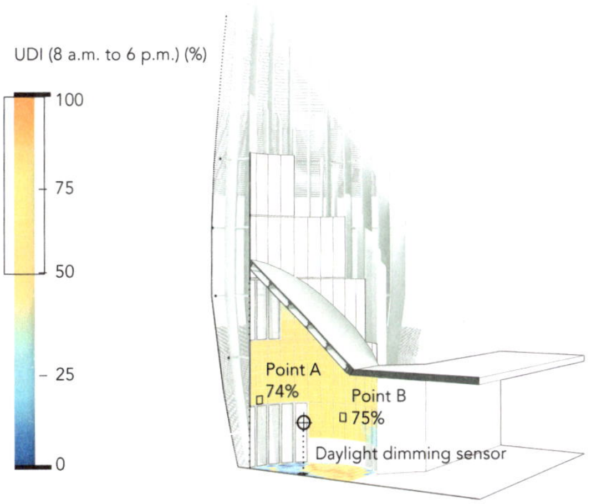

Useful Daylight Illuminance (UDI)

The spatial UDI map shows 74–75% of the operating hours receiving daylight illuminance levels of 50–200 lux.

Qualitative Daylight Analysis
Glare and Visual Comfort

Physiological Glare
Annual Daylight Glare Probability (DGP)
Annual DGP simulation shows no direct or indirect glare on walls or floor.
Probability of disturbing glare: 27%.

Psychological Glare
Illuminance Value Contrast (IVC)
Point-in-time glare analysis shows luminance ratios for one gallery space (hut pavilion). The contrast values are between 1:2 and 1:4 and show good contrast of luminance on the object. Partial direct sun though the vertical windows can cause veiling reflections as seen in the photo.

Summary
The wooden exterior shell-like structure and the shading panels filter light into the interior spaces and shade the roofs. The system of fixed shading panels allows for dynamic lighting scenarios suitable for low sensitive art work and sculptures. Medium and high sensitive art work or materials need additional daylight protection.
The quantitative daylight analysis shows a dynamic lighting situation on the simulated walls and floor. The peak illuminance of 164 lux (PITI) and the accumulated annual total of 349,400 lux-hrs (AAI) are below the illuminance target recommendation.
The UDI and the AIF show that the center of the north-facing wall receives target daylight levels of 50–200 lux for 74% of the time annually.
The qualitative daylight analysis shows no perceptible glare (DGP) during the occupancy hours year-round, although there is the possibility for glare between 6 and 8 a.m. during the spring and fall season, likely the result of direct sunlight through an east-facing window. The lighting simulation (IVC) shows a dynamic contrast on the exhibit walls with contrast values above 1:10 on most of the target zone. This is due to the lighting through sightline windows and potential veiling. The annual daylight dimming potential is high at 95% of the gallery operation hours.

Recommendations
The purpose of the gallery pavilions or huts was to house a permanent collection of sculptures. The concept of connecting the interior with the landscape through windows results in a dynamic daylight system, excellent for less sensitive artwork.
The daylighting values are within the recommended total exposure limits for low susceptible displayed artwork (wood, metal, glass etc.) and are below the target threshold of 50 to 200 lux. The structure extending above the roof lines and the shading panels act as external shading for the metal roofs. The fixed shading panels modulate the daylighting conditions accordingly to desired lux values for less sensitive artwork. The high contrast value is excellent for 3-D object viewing, but problematic for sensitive artwork or displays.

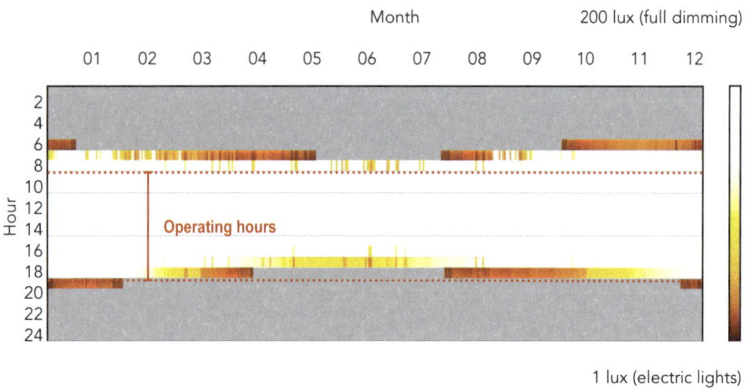

Daylight Dimming Potential (DDP)
Daytime hours when illuminance exceeds 200 lux (in white) indicate the potential to dim electric lighting, 95% of the time annually.

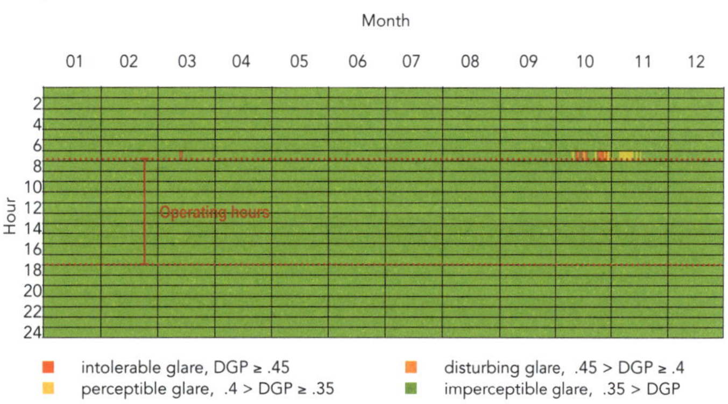

Annual Daylight Glare Probability (DGP)
Annual hourly DGP analysis indicates no perceptible glare during operating hours throughout the year.

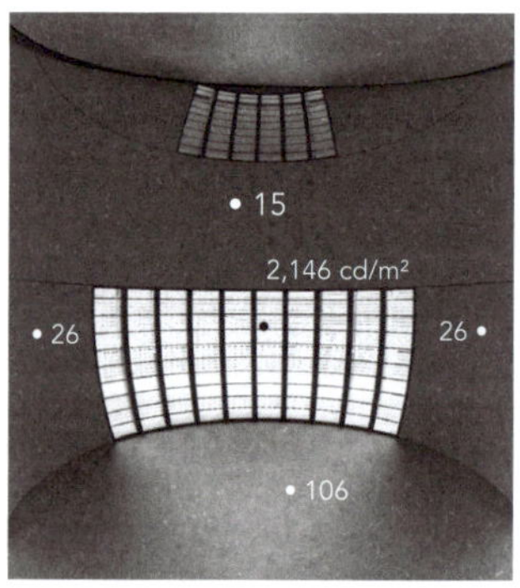

Illuminance Value Contrast (IVC)
The rendering shows highest contrast ratios when looking north on December 21 at noon, causing veiling reflections as seen in the photo.

Gallery View
Interior view of one of the cultural huts

Cy Twombly Pavilion 1992–1995

Houston, Texas, USA
29.736694°N, -95.397798°W

Exhibition Concept

Medium to high light sensitivity of exhibit; sculpture, paintings and drawings; permanent exhibitions. Illuminance threshold: 50 to 200 lux; maximum lux-hours/year: 480,000.

Section Diagram

The section diagram shows natural light entering the building through the roof. Light is bounced through four layers of roofing, which progressively diffuse the light. In addition, the structure, which supports the glass roof, acts as a solar deflector. As a result, light is evenly spread across the gallery space.

Daylighting System

Multilayer linear roof composition consisting of exterior non-adjustable horizontal sunshade louvers, a horizontal double-glazed glass roof, motorized interior horizontal aluminum louvers and a translucent fabric ceiling. Aperture to Floor Area Ratio (AFR) is 100%.

Daylighting Control System

The exterior horizontal louvers (1) and the steel canopy (2) shade the glass roof. The sloped glass roof (3) consists of double pane low-e glass and blocks UV light. Computer-motorized aluminum louvers (4) control light levels in each gallery. The translucent fabric ceiling (5) diffuses the light further, giving softness to the room and hiding all other light control elements and structure.

Electric Illumination

Electric illumination complements the daylighting strategy and consists of space lighting, located above the fabric ceiling, and spotlights on stems underneath the fabric ceiling.

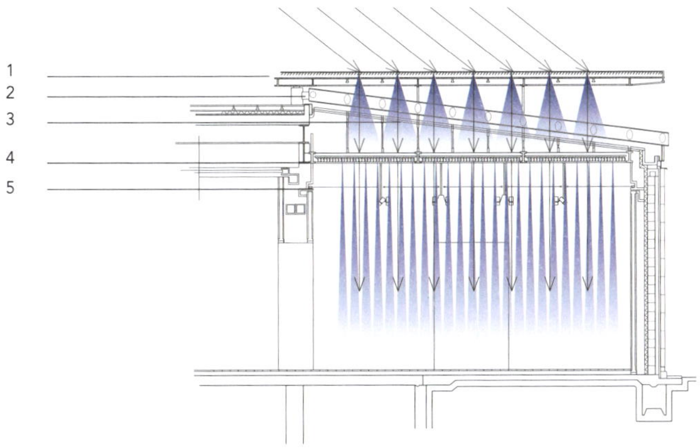

Section through Gallery Space

1. Non-adjustable sunshade louvers
2. Structural steel canopy frame
3. Double pane low-e glass with UV coating
4. Adjustable louvers
5. Translucent fabric ceiling

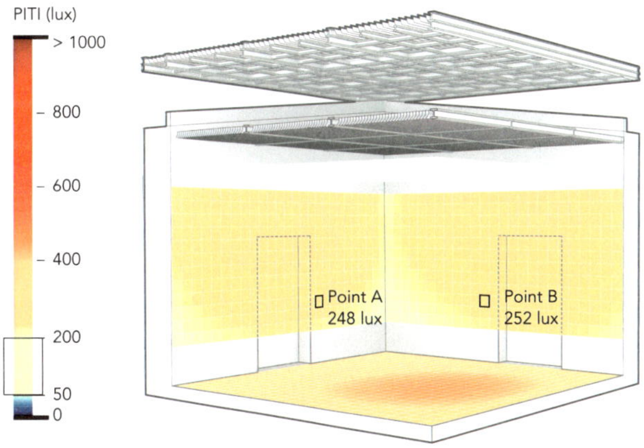

Point-in-Time Illuminance (PITI)
June 21, noon light levels projected onto floor and wall surfaces

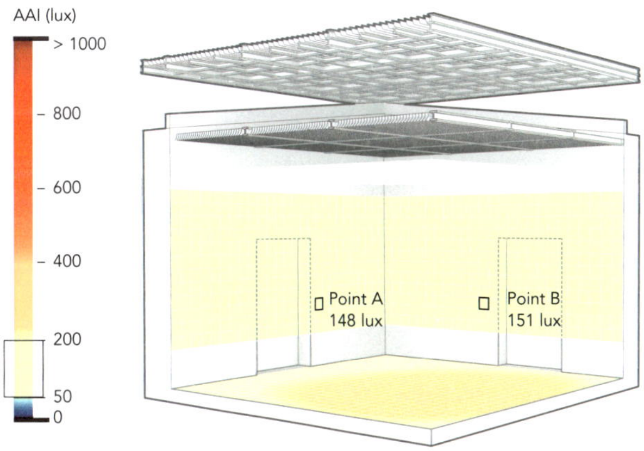

Average Annual Illuminance (AAI)
Light levels projected onto floor and wall surfaces

Location
Climate: Hot and humid
Building orientation: North-south
Louver orientation: East-west, north-south
Material Properties
Walls and surface finishes Wall: SW 7757 High Reflective White, LRV 92.6% Floor: Natural oak, LRV 37.9%
Exposed structure: White paint, LRV 80%
Overhead Skylight Glass
Skylight glass: VLT 40%, double pane low-e glass with UV coating, diffuse reflection, 80% silk-screened
Reflection: Specular
Light-Guiding System – Control Logic
External shading: Static louvers The roof structure is a significant part of the external shading.
Internal shading: Computer-motorized aluminum louvers "Velum" suspended ceiling: White cotton sheets diffuse the light. VLT 45%
Control logic for internal louvers: Sensors automatically adjust the louvers above each room independently.
Location of louvers: Under skylight, white, LRV 80%

Quantitative Daylight Analysis
Point-in-Time and Annual Illuminance

Point-in-Time Illuminance (PITI)	
PITI June 21, noon (South-facing wall)	248 lux
PITI June 21, noon (Center of gallery)	440 lux
Average Annual Illuminance (AAI)	
Average daylight level (South-facing wall)	148 lux
Accumulated lux-hrs annually	539,200
Recommended total exposure target (480,000 lux-hrs annually)	Above
Useful Daylight Illuminance (UDI)	
Percentage daytime hours with daylight levels of 50–200 lux (South-facing wall)	77%
Daylight Dimming Potential (DDP)	
Percentage of daytime hours with daylight levels above 200 lux (Center of gallery, 8 a.m. to 6 p.m.)	76%

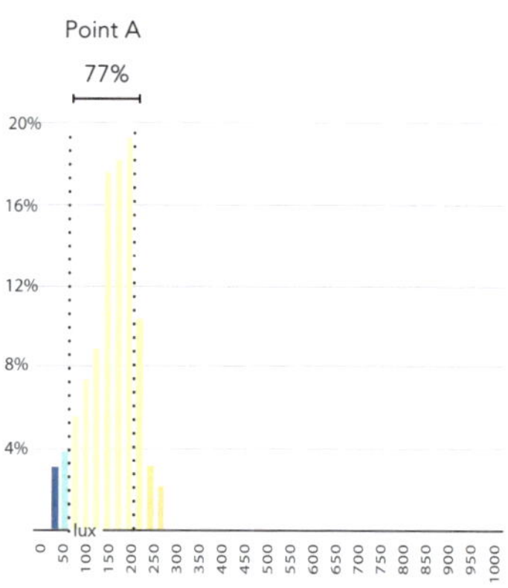

Illuminance at Point A (south-facing) falls within the target range 77% of the year with a peak hourly value of 272 lux and a cumulative annual exposure of 539,200 lux-hrs.

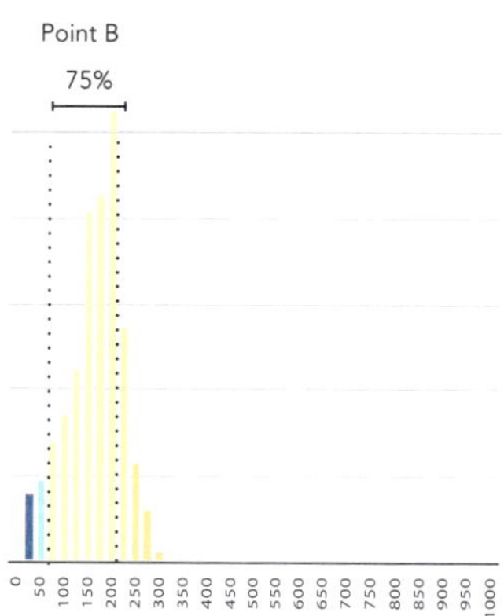

Illuminance at Point B (west-facing) falls within the target range 75% of the year with a peak hourly value of 280 lux and a cumulative annual exposure of 552,300 lux-hrs.

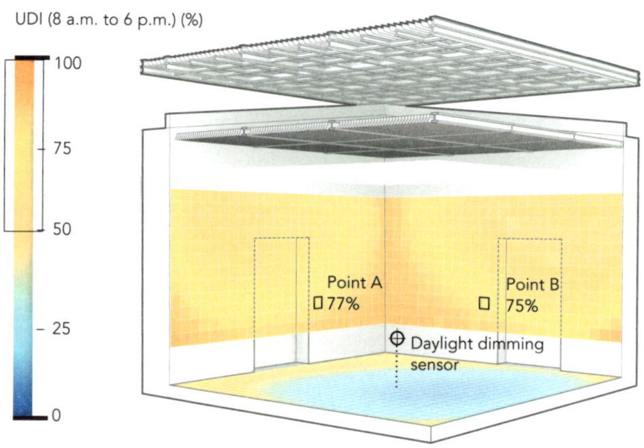

Useful Daylight Illuminance (UDI)
The spatial UDI map shows 75–77% of the operating hours receiving daylight illuminance levels of 50–200 lux.

Annual Illuminance Frequency (AIF)
The percentage values represent the annual daytime hours with illuminance within the target range.

Qualitative Daylight Analysis
Glare and Visual Comfort

Physiological Glare
Annual Daylight Glare Probability (DGP)

Annual DGP simulation shows no direct or indirect glare on walls or floor.
Probability of disturbing glare: 20%.

Psychological Glare
Illuminance Value Contrast (IVC)

Point-in-time glare analysis shows luminance ratios for a gallery space. The contrast values are between 1:2 and 1:4 and show good contrast of luminance on the object.

Summary

The roof system consists of exterior horizontal louvers and the steel roof structure shades the glass roof from direct sun exposure. The computer-motorized aluminum louvers automatically control light levels in each gallery. The translucent fabric ceiling diffuses the light further, giving softness to the gallery and hiding all other light control elements and structure. The quantitative daylight analysis shows a dynamic lighting situation on the simulated walls and floor. The peak illuminance of 248 lux (PITI) and the accumulated annual total of 539,200 lux-hrs (AAI) are above the illuminance target recommendation.

The UDI and the AIF show that the center of the south-facing wall receives target daylight levels of 50–200 lux for 77% of the time annually.
The qualitative daylight analysis shows no perceptible glare (DGP) during the occupancy hours year-round. The lighting simulation (IVC) shows a dynamic contrast on the exhibit walls with contrast values of between 1:2 and 1:4 on most of the target zone. The annual daylight dimming potential is high, at 76% of the gallery operating hours.

Recommendations

The initial concept for the galleries was to house a permanent collection of paintings by the artist Cy Twombly. The dynamic daylight system is excellent for low and medium sensitive artwork. The daylighting values are within the recommended total exposure limits for moderately susceptible displayed artwork (textiles, oil paintings, leather etc.). The automated louvers modulate or adjust the daylighting conditions accordingly to desired lux values. Because of the relative uniformity of the contrast value, spotlights are suggested for better viewing of 3D objects.

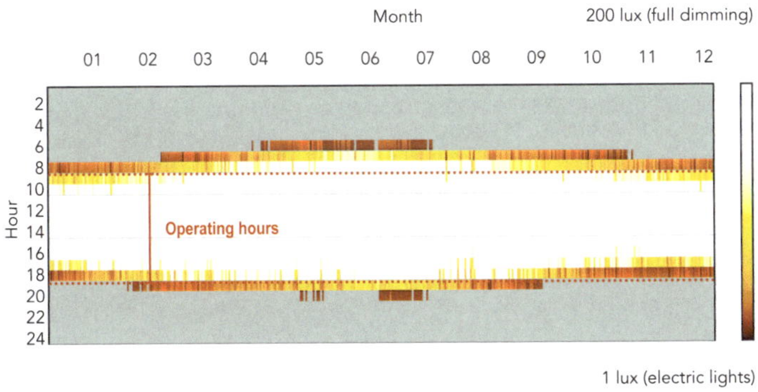

Daylight Dimming Potential (DDP)
Daytime hours when illuminance exceeds 200 lux (in white) indicate the potential to dim electric lighting 76% of the time annually.

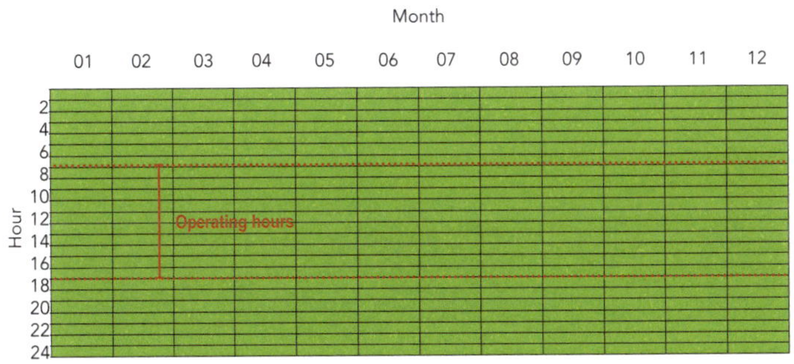

- intolerable glare, DGP ≥ .45
- perceptible glare, .4 > DGP ≥ .35
- disturbing glare, .45 > DGP ≥ .4
- imperceptible glare, .35 > DGP

Annual Daylight Glare Probability (DGP)
Annual hourly DGP from the camera viewpoint indicates no perceptible glare.

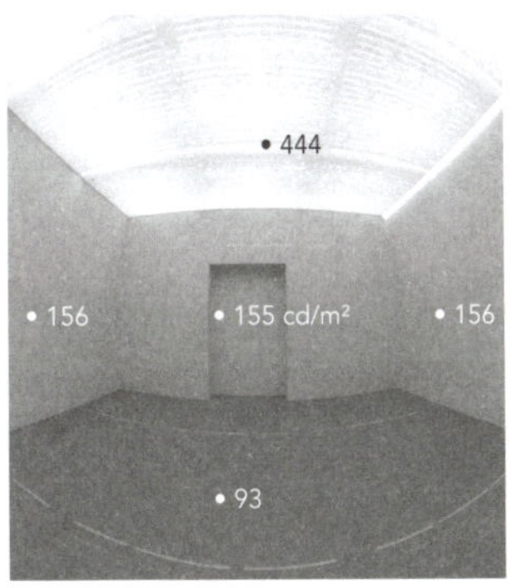

Illuminance Value Contrast (IVC)
The rendering shows highest contrast ratios when looking north on June 21 at noon.

Gallery View
View inside one of the gallery spaces. The light diffusing fabric aims to create the appearance of a floating roof plane.

Nasher Sculpture Center 1999–2003

Dallas, Texas, USA
32.788095°N, -96.800114°W

Exhibition Concept

Low light sensitivity of exhibit; sculptures. Illuminance threshold: 50 to 300 lux; maximum lux-hours/year: 480,000.

Section Diagram

The section diagram shows natural light entering the building through the roof. A single, curved roof shade (with light scoops) completely blocks out direct light when the sun is between the east, the south and the west. Direct sunlight will penetrate the shade in the sunrise hour and the sunset hour.

Daylighting System

Thin double-layer roof composite of shielding system consisting of aluminum sun-shading panels with three-dimensional shells and a slightly curved glass roof. Aperture to Floor Area Ratio (AFR) is 100%.

Daylighting Control System

The roof is composed of 912 cast aluminum sun-shading panels with 223,020 aluminum light scoops or "shells". Oriented to the north, the light scoops block direct south light and allow soft north light to penetrate the gallery space. The roof is supported by 322 steel tension rods, which tie back to the wide travertine walls and extend above the building. Each shell weighs 40 grams and is precisely cast in aluminum at the correct angle to exclude the sun's direct rays, while also maximizing and precisely controlling daylight as the sun tracks across the Dallas sky. The glass roof consists of double pane low-e glass and blocks the UV light.

Electric Illumination

Electric illumination complements the daylighting strategy and consists of spotlights on tracks underneath the glass roof structure.

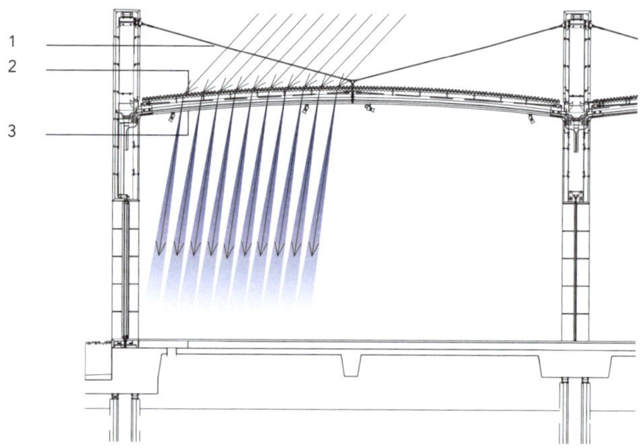

Section through Gallery Space
1 Exterior roof structure
2 Exterior cast aluminum panels with shell/light scoops
3 Curved glass roof of double pane low-e glass with UV coating

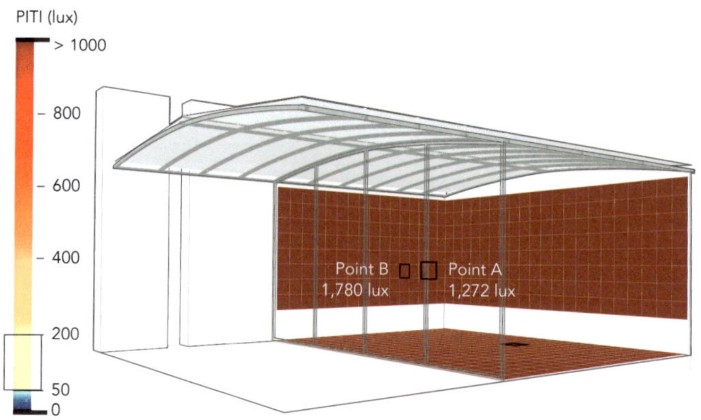

Point-in-Time Illuminance (PITI)
June 21, noon light levels projected onto floor and wall surfaces

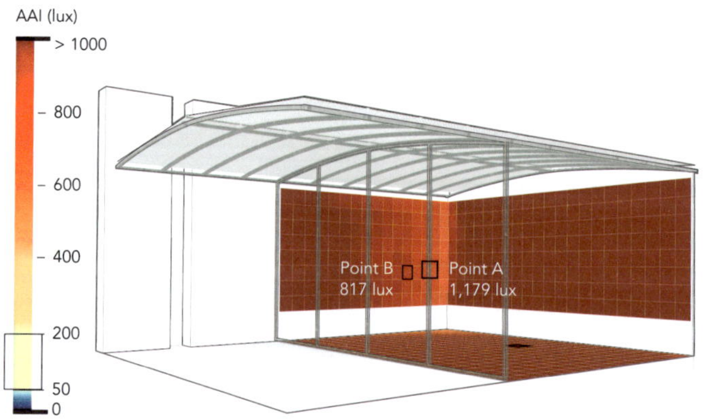

Average Annual Illuminance (AAI)
Light levels projected onto floor and wall surfaces

Location
Climate: Hot and humid
Building orientation: Northwest
Orientation of sun-shading waffle/light scoop: North
Material Properties
Walls and surface finishes
Wall: Travertine walls, LRV 40%
Floor: Lightwood (American white oak), LRV 31%
Exposed structure: White paint, LRV 80%
Overhead Skylight Glass
Skylight glass: VLT 50%, double pane low-e glass with UV coating
Reflection: Specular
Light-Guiding System – Control Logic
External shading: Static system, three-dimensional aluminum elements. The die-cast shielding elements diffuse the illumination and the glass roofing provides lighting levels of up to 2,000 lux.[1] This is only acceptable because the collection consists mainly of low light sensitive sculptures.
Location of louvers: Above skylight, white, LRV 80%

Quantitative Daylight Analysis
Point-in-Time and Annual Illuminance

Point-in-Time Illuminance (PITI)	
PITI June 21, noon (South-facing wall)	1,272 lux
PITI June 21, noon (Center of gallery)	2,372 lux
Average Annual Illuminance (AAI)	
Average daylight level (South-facing wall)	593 lux
Accumulated lux-hrs annually	2,165,000
Recommended total exposure target (480,000 lux-hrs annually)	Above
Useful Daylight Illuminance (UDI)	
Percentage daytime hours with daylight levels of 50–200 lux (South-facing wall)	8%
Daylight Dimming Potential (DDP)	
Percentage of daytime hours with daylight levels above 200 lux (Center of gallery, 8 a.m. to 6 p.m.)	96%

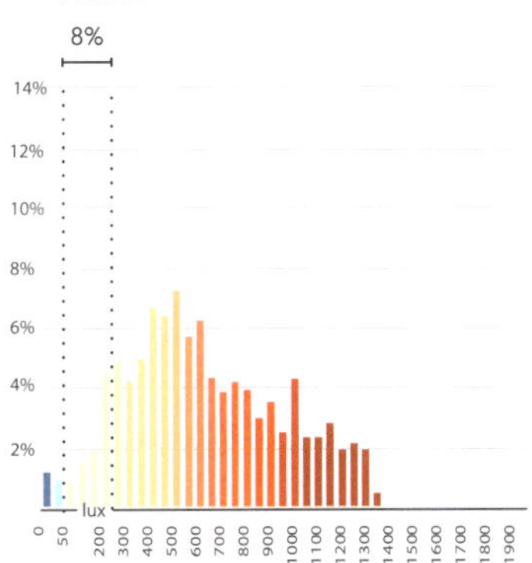

Illuminance at Point A (south-facing behind mullion) falls within the target range 8% of the year with a peak hourly value of 1,336 lux and a cumulative annual exposure of 2,165,000 lux-hrs.

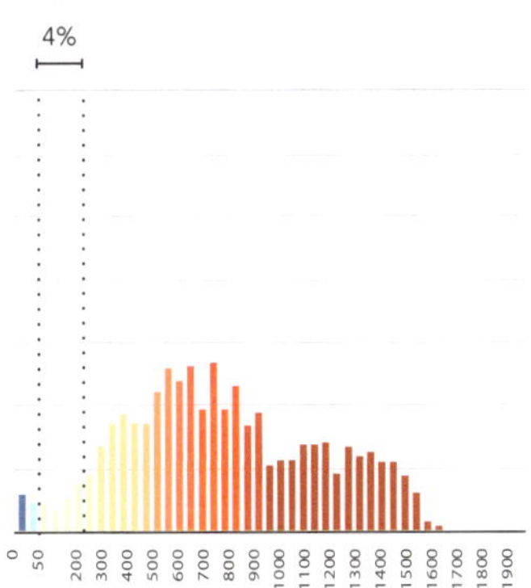

Illuminance at Point B (west-facing) falls within the target range 4% of the year with a peak hourly value of 1,780 lux and a cumulative annual exposure of 2,981,000 lux-hrs.

Annual Illuminance Frequency (AIF)
The percentage values represent the annual daytime hours with illuminance within the target range.

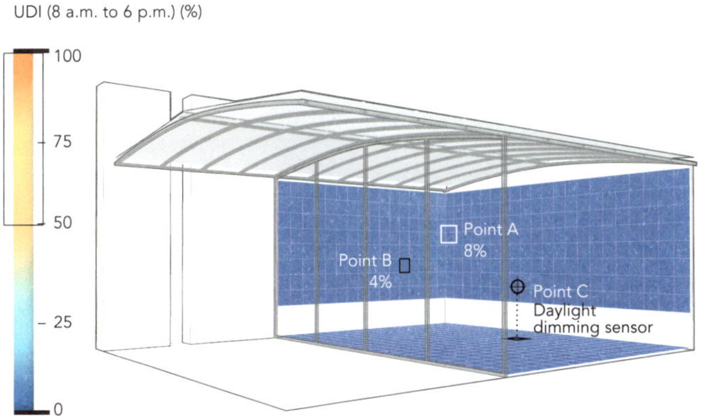

Useful Daylight Illuminance (UDI)
The spatial UDI map shows 4–8% of the operating hours receiving daylight illuminance levels of 50–200 lux.

1 http://www.rpbw.com/project/nasher-sculpture-center

Qualitative Daylight Analysis
Glare and Visual Comfort

Physiological Glare
Annual Daylight Glare Probability (DGP)
Annual DGP simulation shows periodic direct or indirect glare on walls and floor.
Probability of disturbing glare: 34%.

Psychological Glare
Illuminance Value Contrast (IVC)
Point–in-time glare analysis shows luminance ratios for a gallery space. The contrast values are above 1:10 and show high contrast of luminance on the object.

Summary
The cast aluminum shells form the unique shading system of the Nasher Sculpture Centre's glass roof and create optimum environmental conditions to display sculptures. Successfully filtered direct light results in a spectacular, naturally lit environment. Computational analysis of the sun's path at the gallery site was used to design and fabricate the shells and roof in a way that fulfilled Piano's ambition to create the thinnest roof possible.
The quantitative daylight analysis shows a dynamic lighting situation on the simulated walls and floor. The peak illuminance of 1272 lux (PITI) and the accumulated annual exposure of over 2 million lux-hrs (AAI) are significantly above the illuminance target recommendation.
The UDI and the AIF show that the center of the south-facing wall receives target daylight levels of 50–200 lux for only 8% of the time annually (4% for west-facing wall).
The qualitative daylight analysis shows perceptible *glare* (DGP). The annual hourly DGP analysis indicates glare from May to July in the evening. Glare hours are likely to be attributed to low-angle setting sunlight through the vertical glazing at the northwest end of the gallery. Internal blinds are provided at this location to prevent visual discomfort during these hours. The lighting simulation (IVC) shows a dynamic contrast on the exhibit walls with contrast values above 1:10 on most of the target zone. The annual daylight dimming potential is high at 96% of the gallery operation hours.

Recommendations
The concept was to house the permanent collection of sculptures on the daylit upper gallery floor. The dynamic daylight system is excellent for low sensitive artwork. The daylighting values are in the recommended total exposure limits for less susceptible displayed artwork (wood, metal, glass etc.). The fixed shading panels modulate the daylighting conditions accordingly to desired lux values for less sensitive artwork. The high contrast value is excellent for 3D object viewing.

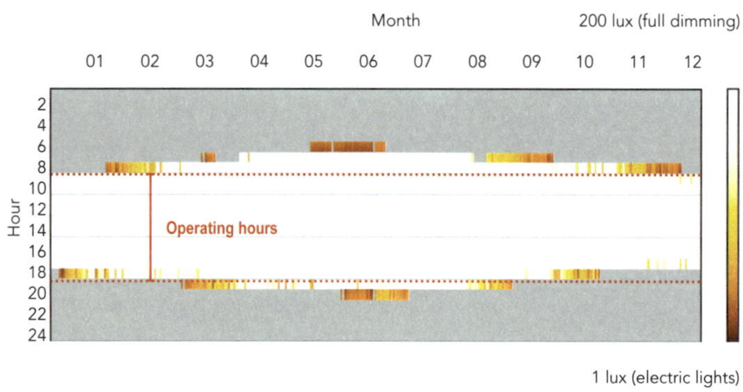

Daylight Dimming Potential (DDP)
Daytime hours when illuminance exceeds 200 lux (in white) indicate the potential to dim electric lighting 96% of the time annually.

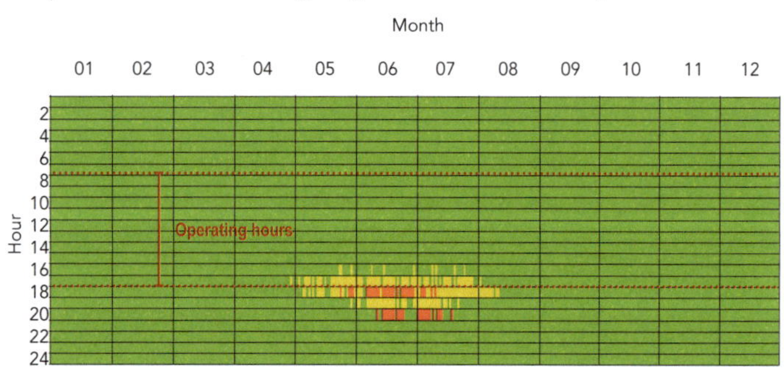

intolerable glare, DGP ≥ .45 | disturbing glare, .45 > DGP ≥ .4
perceptible glare, .4 > DGP ≥ .35 | imperceptible glare, .35 > DGP

Annual Daylight Glare Probability (DGP)
Annual hourly DGP analysis indicates glare from May to July in the evening, from the sun's low angle through the vertical glazing at the northwest end of the gallery. Internal blinds prevent visual discomfort (34% DGP).

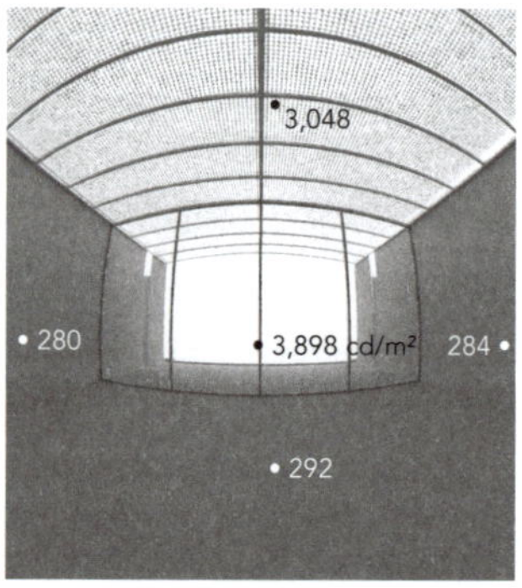

Illuminance Value Contrast (IVC)
The rendering shows highest contrast ratios when looking north on June 21 at noon.

Gallery View
View inside the gallery spaces. Sculptures are placed freely in the space for optimal viewing.

High Museum Expansion 1999–2005

Atlanta, Georgia, USA
33.789892°N, -84.386111°W

Exhibition Concept

Medium to high light sensitivity of exhibit. Illuminance threshold: 50 to 200 lux; maximum lux-hours/year: 480,000.

Section Diagram

The section diagram shows diffuse natural light entering the building through the roof cones/skylights.

Daylighting System

A total of 1,000 skylights (800 on the Weiland Pavilion and 200 on the Anne Cox Chambers Wing) consist of clear glass and are shadowed by shades on the roof facing north. These rooftop "sails" funnel soft north light into the galleries through cone-shaped openings. Each mini-skylight twists slightly to focus the light and diffuse it through the top floor galleries, which house the museum's permanent collection. Approximately 5% of the light entering each skylight is reflected from the sails. Aperture to Floor Area Ratio (AFR) is 25%.[1]

Daylighting Control System

The daylight system consists of exterior sun-shading sails approximately 1.8 meters (6 feet) high – round north-sloped glass skylights 60 centimeters (2 feet) above the main roof line – and a shaped tube below each skylight, 1.5 meters (5 feet) deep and integrated into the ceiling. The sails, curved around the southern side of the skylight, and the light tubes reflect and bounce indirect sunlight into the galleries.

Electric Illumination

Track lighting (iGuzzini fixture designed by Piano) supplements the daylighting. The track is on two circuits: one controlled relative to the amount of daylight and the other independently to meet the requirements of the artwork.

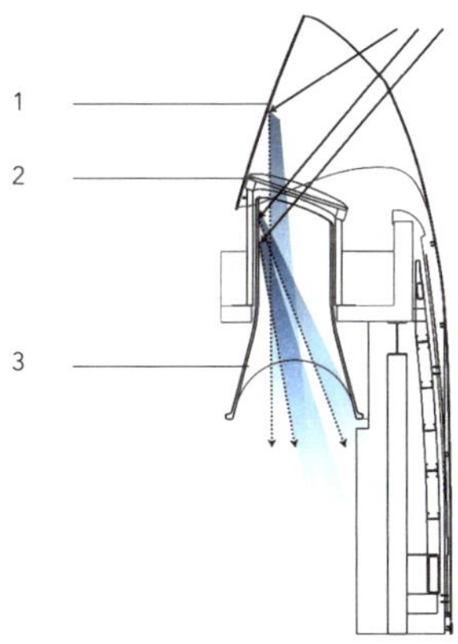

Section through Gallery Skylight

1. White exterior aluminum conical skylight visor sails, 3 mm (1/8") thick and approximately. 1.8 m (6 ft) high, curved around the southern portion of the skylight, blocking direct sunlight.
2. North-sloping skylights with a diameter of 67 cm (2 1/4 ft), shielded by the exterior sunshades; the laminated double pane glass unit features low-iron glass with a low-e coating and UV protection. This glass unit has a high Color Rendering Index (CRI) for natural color rendering.
3. The interior tubular units are constructed of glass fiber-reinforced gypsum on a square grid measuring 1.2 m (4 ft), diffusing and directing light from the skylight.

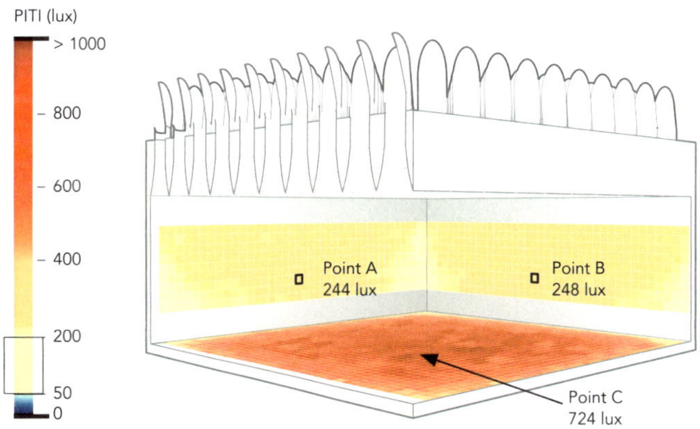

Point-in-Time Illuminance (PITI)
June 21, noon light levels projected onto floor and wall surfaces

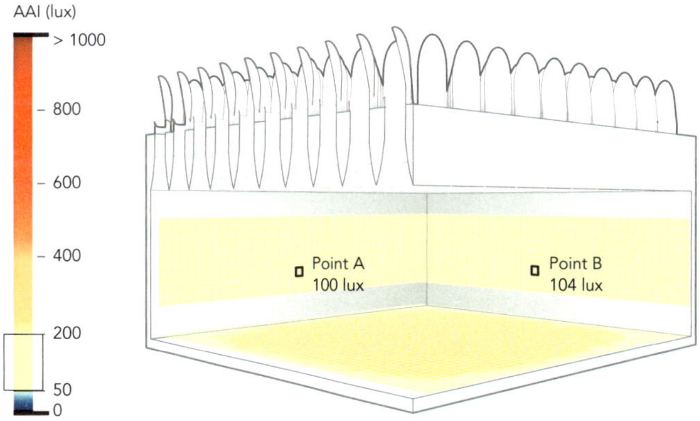

Average Annual Illuminance (AAI)
Light levels projected onto floor and wall surfaces

1 Christine Killory and René Davids (eds.), Detail in Process, "High Museum of Art," Princeton Architectural Press, New York 2008, pp. 150–157.

Location
Climate: Humid, subtropical
Building orientation: Northeast
Sun-shading waffle/light scoop orientation: North
Material Properties
Walls and surface finishes
Wall: SW 7757 High Reflective White, LRV 92.6%
Floor: Natural oak, LRV 37.9%
Exposed structure: White paint, LRV 80%
Overhead Skylight Glass
Skylight glass: VLT 50%, double pane low-e glass with UV coating, CRI greater than 97
Reflection: Specular
Light-Guiding System – Control Logic
External shading: External shading: Static system, fixed three-dimensional aluminum sunshades
Location of sunshades: Above skylight, white, LRV 80%

Quantitative Daylight Analysis
Point-in-Time and Annual Illuminance

Point-in-Time Illuminance (PITI)	
PITI June 21, noon (South-facing wall)	244 lux
PITI June 21, noon (Center of gallery)	724 lux
Average Annual Illuminance (AAI)	
Average daylight level (South-facing wall)	100 lux
Accumulated lux-hrs annually	346,400
Recommended total exposure target (480,000 lux-hrs annually)	Below
Useful Daylight Illuminance (UDI)	
Percentage daytime hours with daylight levels of 50–200 lux (South-facing wall)	75%
Daylight Dimming Potential (DDP)	
Percentage of daytime hours with daylight levels above 200 lux (Center of gallery, 8 a.m. to 6 p.m.)	70%

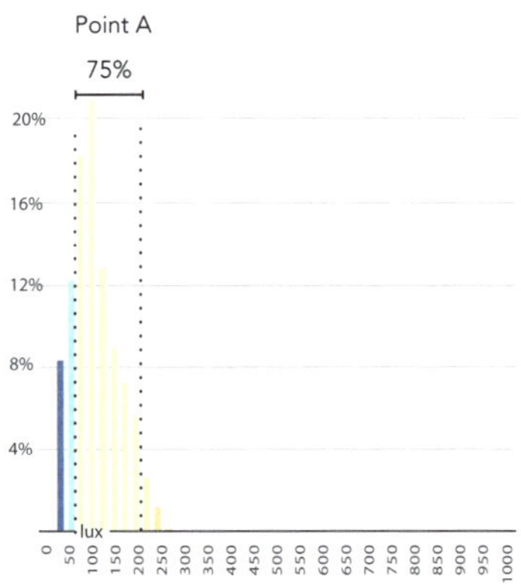

Illuminance at Point A (south-facing) falls within the target range 75% of the year with a peak hourly value of 252 lux and a cumulative annual exposure of 346,400 lux-hrs.

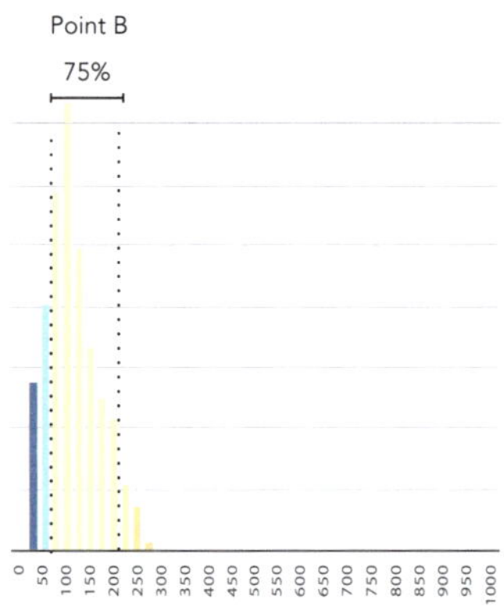

Illuminance at Point B (west-facing) falls within the target range 75% of the year with a peak hourly value of 260 lux and a cumulative annual exposure of 361,500 lux-hrs.

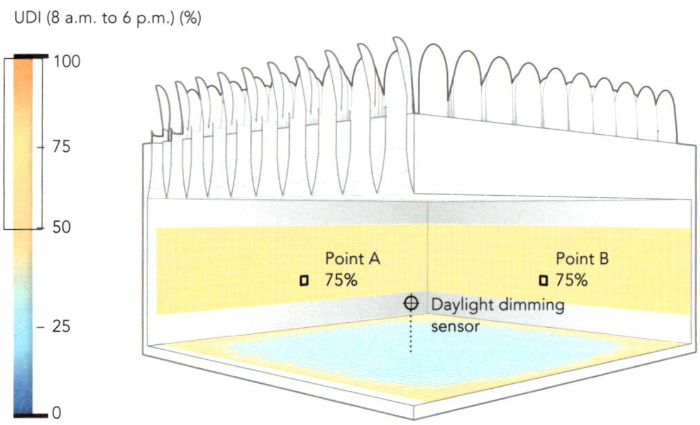

Useful Daylight Illuminance (UDI)
The spatial UDI map shows 75% of the operating hours receiving daylight illuminance levels of 50–200 lux.

Annual Illuminance Frequency (AIF)
The percentage values represent the annual daytime hours with illuminance within the target range.

Qualitative Daylight Analysis
Glare and Visual Comfort

Physiological Glare
Annual Daylight Glare Probability (DGP)
Annual DGP simulation shows no periodic direct or indirect glare on walls and floor.
Probability of disturbing glare: 19%.

Psychological Glare
Illuminance Value Contrast (IVC)
Point-in-time glare analysis shows luminance ratios for a gallery space. The contrast values are between 1:2 and 1:4 and show good luminance contrast on the object. The daylighting reveals the dynamic conditions.

Summary
One thousand circular skylights, evenly spaced above the 5.25-meter (17.25-foot) high galleries, fill the space with softly diffused light. The natural light levels, which can be supplemented by artificial light as required, are within the 160 to 323 lux required by the museum's curator. Low-iron glass with a low-e coating was selected to increase thermal performance and minimizes reduction in CRI.
The skylight roof system required the analysis of a series of computational models, physical models and a full-scale 4.8 by 12.2 meter (16 by 40 foot) gallery mock-up to verify simulated illuminance levels.[2] The skylight system design performs exceptionally and shows the desired range of properly colored indirect natural light, while excluding harmful UV radiation.
The quantitative daylight analysis shows a dynamic lighting situation on the simulated walls and floor. The peak illuminance of 244 lux (PITI) and the accumulated annual total of 346,400 lux-hrs (AAI) are below the illuminance target recommendation.
The UDI and the AIF show that the center of the south-facing wall receives target daylight levels of 50–200 lux for 75% of the time annually.
The qualitative daylight analysis shows no perceptible glare (DGP) during the occupancy hours year-round. The lighting simulation (IVC) shows a dynamic contrast on the exhibit walls with contrast values of between 1:2 and 1:4 on most of the target zone. The annual daylight dimming potential is high at 70% of the gallery operating hours.

Recommendations
The top gallery of the High Museum takes full advantage of daylight illuminance and provides optimum conditions for viewing the museum's permanent collection. The passive external sun-shading sails prevent any direct sunlight from entering the gallery spaces below and reflect a soft diffused light. The skylight glazing has a high color rendering index and provides excellent natural color reception. The passive shading strategy requires no mechanical systems or controllers and significantly less maintenance and service, in comparison to active mechanical shading systems. Extensive simulation and mock-ups of a skylight, including the internal light tubes, were tested using actual humidified air to ensure the design's environmental performance, including daylight, glare, air-temperature and condensation.

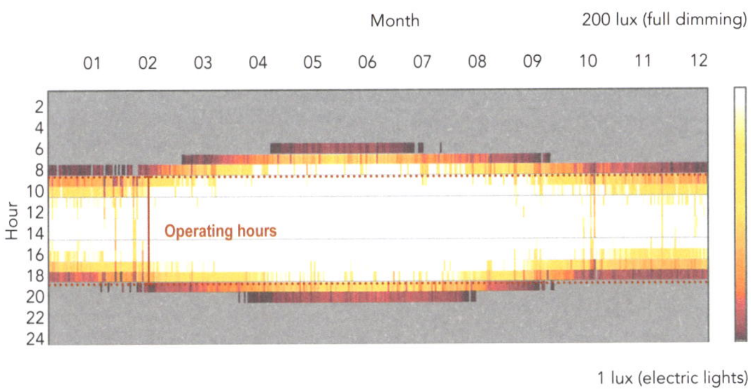

Daylight Dimming Potential (DDP)
Daytime hours when illuminance exceeds 200 lux (in white) indicate the potential to dim general electric lighting 70% of the time annually.

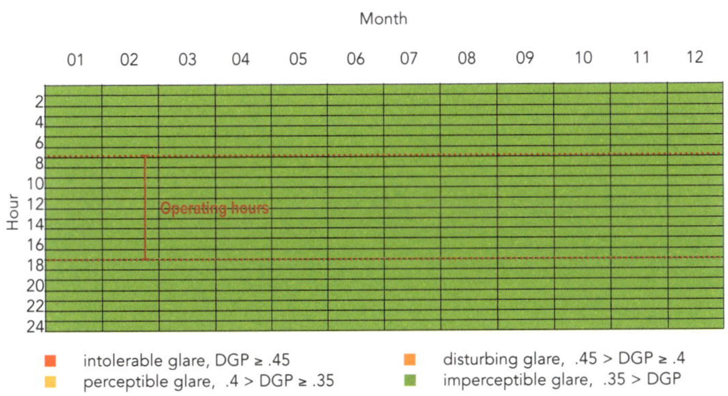

Annual Daylight Glare Probability (DGP)
Annual hourly DGP analysis indicates no perceptible glare during operating hours throughout the year.

2 Ibid.

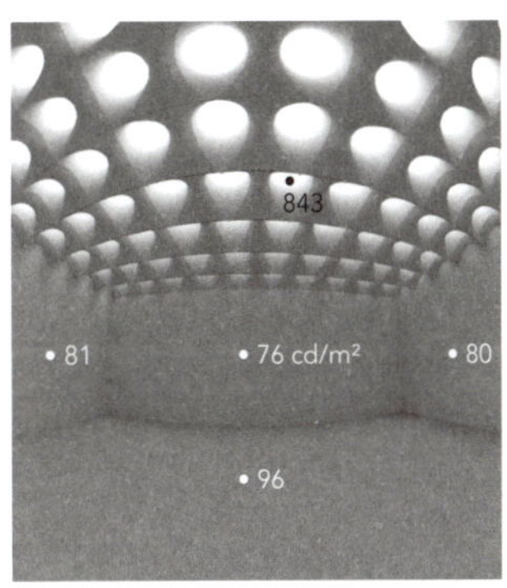

Illuminance Value Contrast (IVC)
The rendering shows highest contrast ratios when looking north on June 21 at noon.

Gallery View
View inside one of the gallery spaces. Light tubes capture and distribute light evenly into the space.

Renovation and Expansion of the Morgan Library and Museum 2000–2006

New York City, New York, USA
40.749269°N, -73.981545°W

Exhibition Concept

Low light sensitivity of exhibit; sculptures and lobby space. Illuminance threshold: 50 to 300 lux; maximum lux-hours/year: 480,000.

Section Diagram

The section diagram shows natural light entering the lobby space, dubbed the "Italian piazza," through a multilayered roof system. Each interior aluminum fin reflects light to lower the overall brightness. This reflection bounces the light and diffuses it across the gallery.

Daylighting System

Multilayer roof surface consisting of an external horizontal steel grid, a slightly tilted double-glazed roof, interior horizontal aluminum louvers and structural fins. Aperture to Floor Area Ratio (AFR) is 100%.

Daylighting Control System

The horizontal steel grid (1) prevents direct sunlight penetration, diffuses light during operating hours and allows access to the glass roof for maintenance. The glass roof (2) consists of double pane low-e glass with coating to block UV light. The computer-motorized aluminum louvers (3) sit below the glass roof and control light levels in the atrium. Structural steel fins (4) underneath the glass roof provide the structural support and act as internal louvers.

Electric Illumination

The lighting system is augmented with spotlights positioned on tracks.

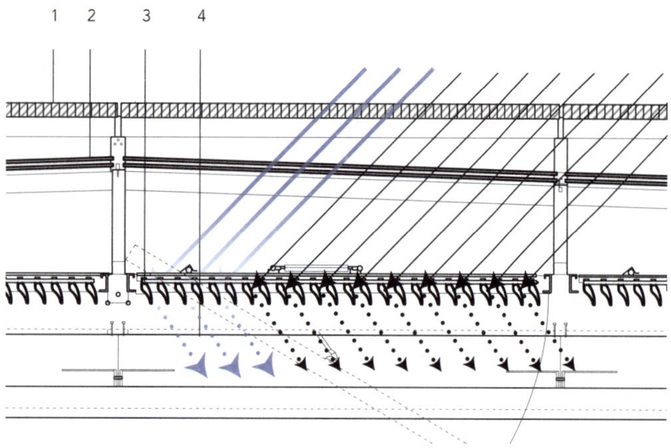

Section through Gallery Space

1 External shading: Steel grid
2 Weatherproof layer: Double pane low-e glass with UV coating
3 Aluminum louvers/fins: Computer-motorized to control light levels
4 Structural fins support the glass roof and function as louvers

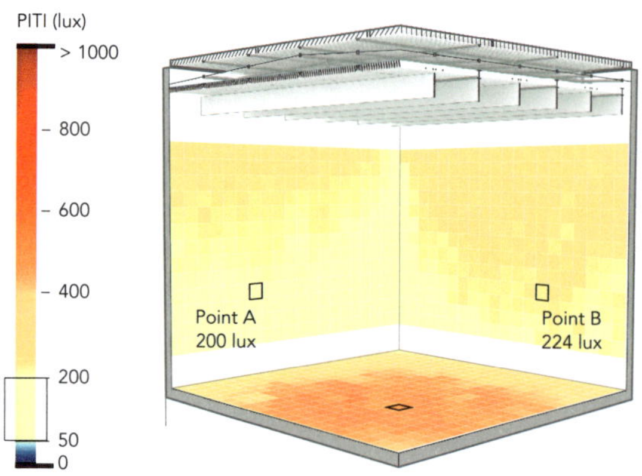

Point-in-Time Illuminance (PITI)
June 21, noon light levels projected onto floor and wall surfaces

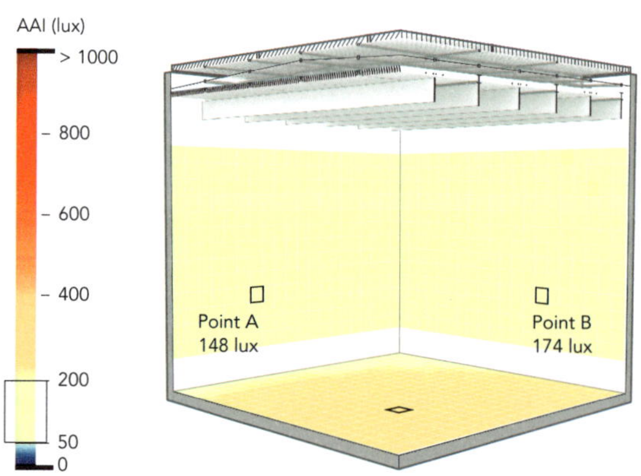

Average Annual Illuminance (AAI)
Light levels projected onto floor and wall surfaces

Location
Climate: Temperate
Building orientation: Northwest
Louver orientation: Southeast
Material Properties
Walls and surface finishes
Wall: SW 7757 High Reflective White, LRV 92.6%
Floor: Natural oak, LRV 37.9%
Exposed structure: White paint, LRV 80%
Overhead Skylight Glass
Skylight glass: VLT 50%, double pane low-e glass with UV coating
Reflection: Specular
Light-Guiding System – Control Logic
External shading: Static system, fixed horizontal steel grid, LRV 80%
Internal shading: Kinetic system, aluminum louver blades
Control logic for louvers: Computer-motorized
Location of louvers: Under skylight, white, LRV 80%

Quantitative Daylight Analysis
Point-in-Time and Annual Illuminance

Point-in-Time Illuminance (PITI)	
PITI June 21, noon (South-facing wall)	200 lux
PITI June 21, noon (Center of gallery)	452 lux
Average Annual Illuminance (AAI)	
Average daylight level (South-facing wall)	148 lux
Accumulated lux-hrs annually	510,600
Recommended total exposure target (480,000 lux-hrs annually)	Above
Useful Daylight Illuminance (UDI)	
Percentage daytime hours with daylight levels of 50–200 lux (South-facing wall)	62%
Daylight Dimming Potential (DDP)	
Percentage of daytime hours with daylight levels above 200 lux (Center of gallery, 8 a.m. to 6 p.m.)	71%

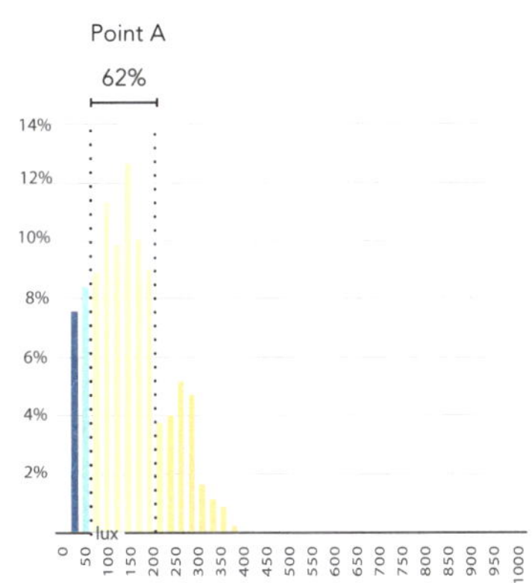

Illuminance at Point A (south-facing) falls within the target range 62% of the year with a peak hourly value of 400 lux and a cumulative annual exposure of 510,600 lux-hrs.

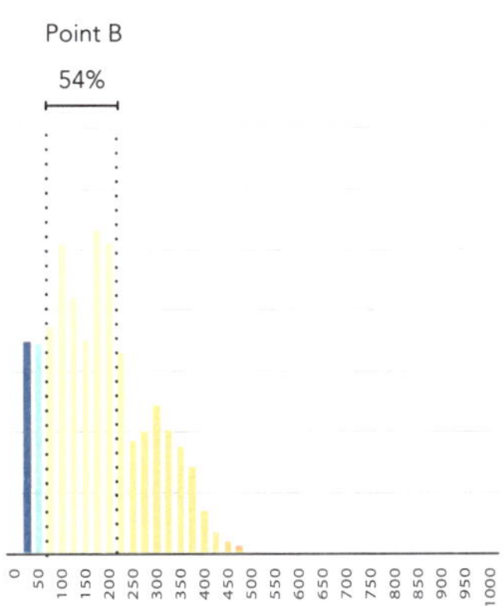

Illuminance at Point B (west-facing) falls within the target range 54% of the year with a peak hourly value of 468 lux and a cumulative annual exposure of 602,300 lux-hrs.

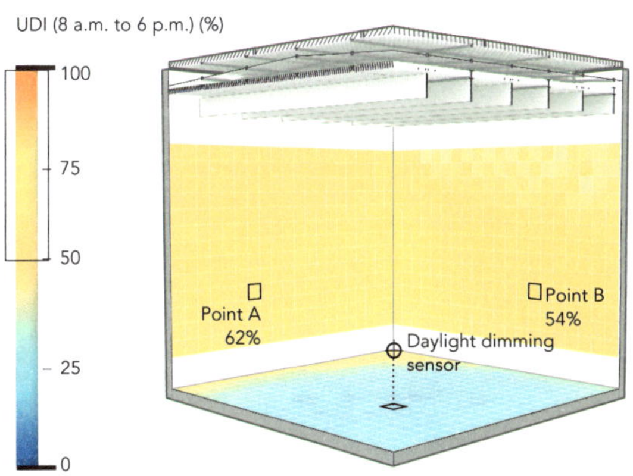

Useful Daylight Illuminance (UDI)
The spatial UDI map shows 54–62% of the operating hours receiving daylight illuminance levels of 50–200 lux.

Annual Illuminance Frequency (AIF)
The percentage values represent the annual daytime hours with illuminance within the target range.

Qualitative Daylight Analysis
Glare and Visual Comfort

Physiological Glare
Annual Daylight Glare Probability (DGP)
Annual DGP simulation shows no direct or indirect glare on walls or floor.
Probability of disturbing glare: 18%.

Psychological Glare
Illuminance Value Contrast (IVC)
Point-in-time glare analysis shows luminance ratios for a gallery and lobby space. The contrast values are within 1:2 and show good contrast of luminance on the object.

Summary
The natural light penetrates through the multilayer roof system and the glass walls. The lighting condition in the atrium is automatically adjusted to the desired luminance values. The central atrium space – the "Italian piazza" – is used as a lobby. The dynamic lighting scenario is suitable for low and medium sensitive artwork and sculptures.
The quantitative daylight analysis shows a dynamic lighting situation on the simulated walls and floor. The peak illuminance of 200 lux (PITI) and the accumulated annual total of 510,600 lux-hrs (AAI) are slightly above the illuminance target recommendation.

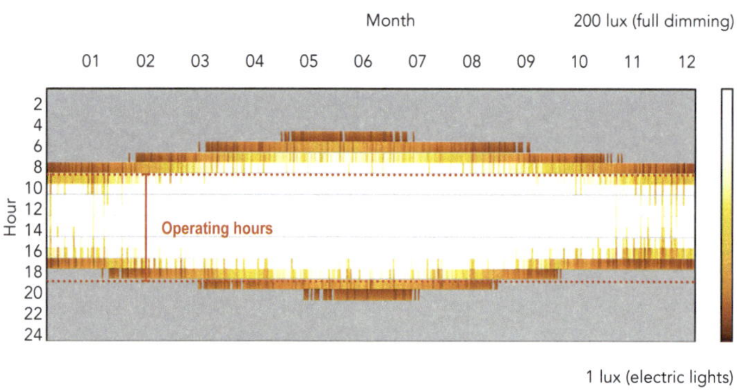

Daylight Dimming Potential (DDP)
Daytime hours when illuminance exceeds 200 lux (in white) indicate the potential to dim electric lighting 71% of the time annually.

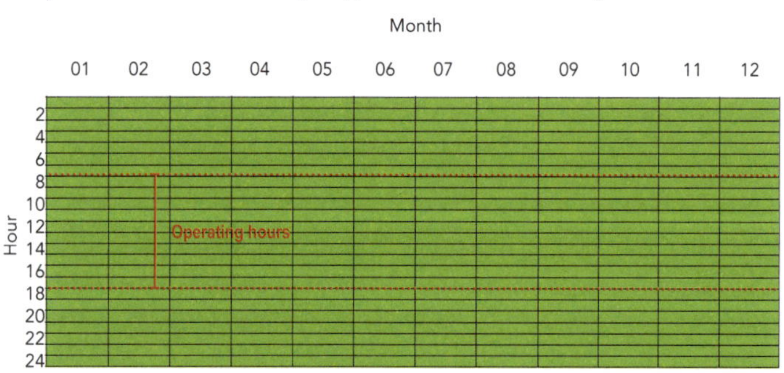

■ intolerable glare, DGP ≥ .45 ■ disturbing glare, .45 > DGP ≥ .4
■ perceptible glare, .4 > DGP ≥ .35 ■ imperceptible glare, .35 > DGP

Annual Daylight Glare Probability (DGP)
Annual hourly DGP analysis indicates no perceptible glare during operating hours throughout the year.

The UDI and the AIF show that the center of the south-facing wall receives target daylight levels of between 50 and 200 lux for 62% of the time annually.
The qualitative daylight analysis shows no perceptible glare (DGP) during the occupancy hours year-round. The lighting simulation (IVC) shows a dynamic contrast on the exhibit walls with contrast values within 1:2 on most of the target zone. Values can be higher closer to the glass facade. The annual daylight dimming potential is high at 71% of the gallery operating hours.

Recommendations
The dynamic daylight system creates an excellent lighting condition in the museum's lobby for sculptures and low sensitive artwork. The daylighting values are above the recommended total exposure limits for moderately susceptible displayed artwork. The automated louvers modulate or adjust the daylighting conditions, according to desired lux values.
The large number of sidelights in the glass facades and the glass roof creates a beautiful daylit piazza and a delightful atmosphere, perfect for exhibiting large sculptures and objects. The museum café is also situated in the atrium.

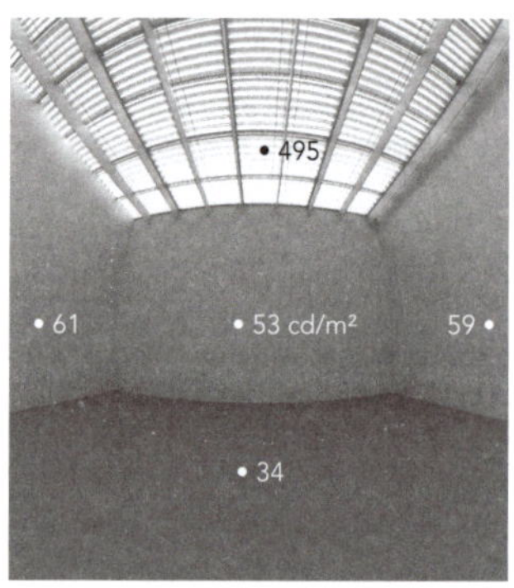

Illuminance Value Contrast (IVC)
The rendering shows highest contrast ratios when looking north on June 21 at noon.

Gallery View
View inside the museum's lobby space. The piazza-like space is beautifully lit and is perfect for exhibiting sculptures and objects.

Broad Contemporary Art Museum 2003–2008

Los Angeles, California, USA
34.063326°N, -118.359820°W

Exhibition Concept

Medium to high sensitive exhibit. Illuminance threshold: 50 to 200 lux; maximum lux-hours/year: 480,000.

Section Diagram

The section diagram shows diffuse natural light entering the building through the sawtooth roof skylights.

Daylighting System

The sawtooth roof comprises a series of ridges, pitched on the south-facing side, with vertical motorized blinds that channel north light into the third-floor galleries, excluding direct sunlight. Approximately 5% of the light entering each skylight is reflected from the sawtooth roof.[1] Aperture to Floor Area Ratio (AFR) is 80%.

Daylighting Control System

The inclined fixed external shading (1) consists of white panels, inclined at 45 degrees and open to the north. The orientation prevents direct sunlight for most of the year, but allows for reflected diffused sunlight. The external vertical motorized roller blinds (2) diffuse early morning and late afternoon summer sun that can pass the inclined fixed shading panels, control natural light levels within the galleries during opening hours and reduce the amount of daylight when the museum is closed, preventing unnecessary exposure of light to art. The horizontal roof glazing (3) provides a weatherproofing layer.
To maximize color rendering and minimize the distortion of natural light color, low-iron glass is used. The double pane low-e glass consists of a clear polyvinyl butyral (PVB) interlayer to filter UV radiation and a custom white fritted pattern on the glass to diffuse light and reduce sunlight transmission. A horizontal metal grate (4) is added to the ceiling, where no inclined fixed external panels provide shading.

Electric Illumination

Track lighting with integrated UV filters within the glazing mullions supplements the daylighting and provides spotlights for sculptures. The track lighting is daylight-linked and controlled through photocells connected to the electric lighting control system. The control system automatically adds electric light when daylight levels fall below 200 lux, decreasing the electric light to the target total illuminance level when natural light levels are sufficient, and provides transition from daytime to nighttime lighting conditions.

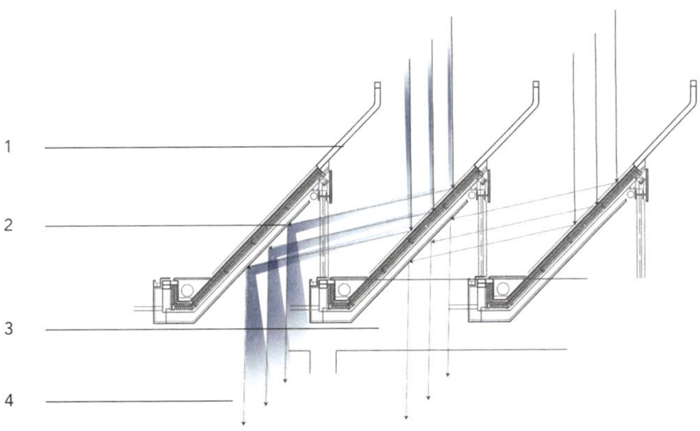

Section through Gallery Skylights

1 Inclined fixed external shading
2 External motorized roller blinds (shades)
3 Horizontal roof glazing (ceiling), double pane glass with low-e coating and UV protection
4 Horizontal metal grate, only where inclined fixed external shading is absent

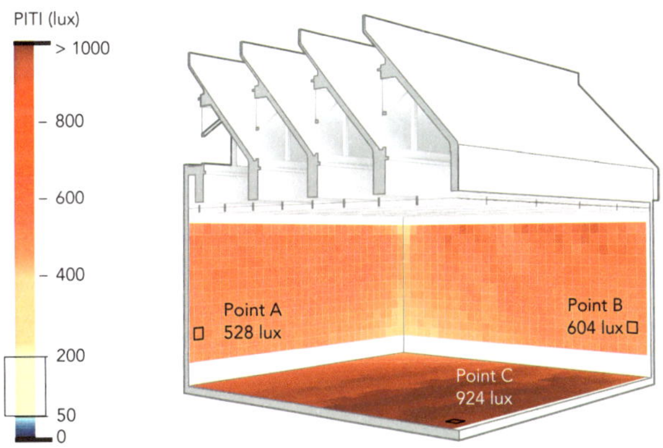

Point-in-Time Illuminance (PITI)
June 21, noon light levels projected onto floor and wall surfaces

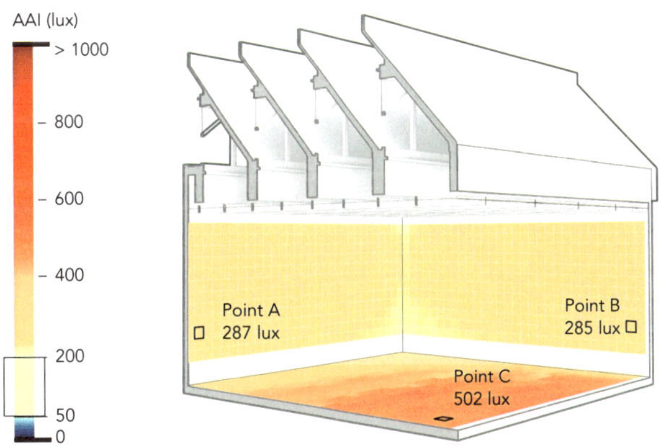

Average Annual Illuminance (AAI)
Light levels projected onto floor and wall surfaces

1 Mark Gilberg, Charlotte Eng and Frank Preusser, "Illuminating Art Using a Daylight System at the Broad Contemporary Art Museum," *WAAC Newsletter*, 32(2), 2010, pp. 10–15, 10.

Location
Climate: Mediterranean/maritime
Building orientation: North-south
Sunshading orientation: Sawtooth roof facing north
Material Properties
Walls and surface finishes
Wall: SW 7757 High Reflective White, LRV 92.6%
Floor: Natural oak, LRV 37.9%
Exposed structure: White paint, LRV 80%
Overhead Skylight Glass
Skylight glass: VLT 50%, double pane low-e glass with UV coating, custom white frit pattern, CRI greater than 97
Reflection: Diffuse
Light-Guiding System – Control Logic
External shading: Static system, sawtooth roof inclined at 45°
Location of external shading: Above skylight, matte white (two gloss units at 60° at angle of incidence), LRV 80%, diffuse reflection
External motorized roller blind: VLT 7% (6% diffuse, 1% direct), average annual operation: 54%

Quantitative Daylight Analysis
Point-in-Time and Annual Illuminance

Point-in-Time Illuminance (PITI)	
PITI June 21, noon (South-facing wall)	528 lux
PITI June 21, noon (Center of gallery)	924 lux
Average Annual Illuminance (AAI)	
Average daylight level (South-facing wall)	287 lux
Accumulated lux-hrs annually	999,800
Recommended total exposure target (480,000 lux-hrs annually)	Above
Useful Daylight Illuminance (UDI)	
Percentage daytime hours with daylight levels of 50–200 lux (South-facing wall)	26%
Daylight Dimming Potential (DDP)	
Percentage of daytime hours with daylight levels above 200 lux (Center of gallery, 8 a.m. to 6 p.m.)	83%

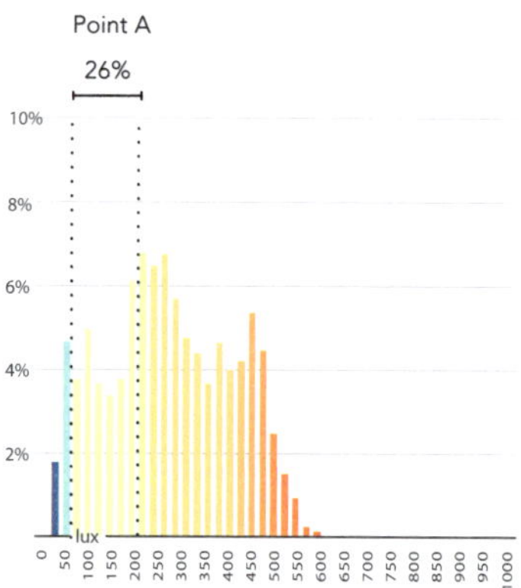

Annually, illuminance at Point A (south-facing) falls within the target range 26% of the year with a peak hourly value of 624 lux and cumulative annual lux-hour exposure of 999,800 lux.

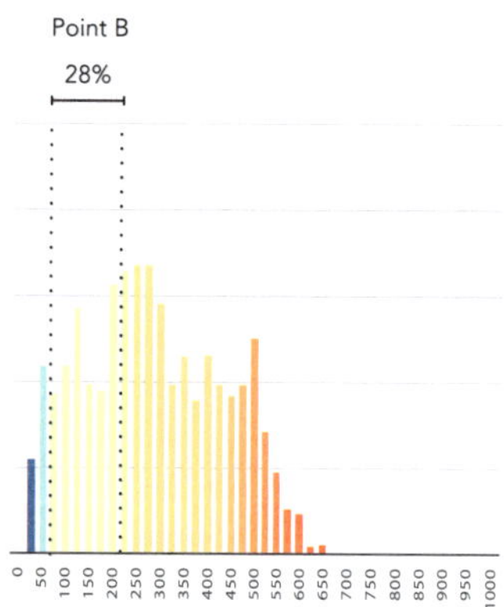

Annually, illuminance at Point B (west-facing) falls within the target range 28% of the year with a peak hourly value of 648 lux and cumulative annual lux-hour exposure of 993,500 lux.

Annual Illuminance Frequency (AIF)
The percentage values represent the annual daytime hours with illuminance within the target range.

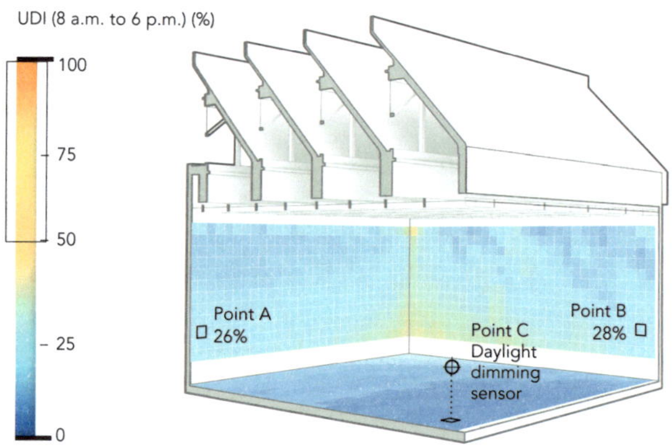

Illuminance (UDI)
The spatial UDI map shows 24–28% of the operating hours receiving daylight illuminance levels of 50–200 lux.

Qualitative Daylight Analysis
Glare and Visual Comfort

Physiological Glare
Annual Daylight Glare Probability (DGP)

Annual DGP simulation shows periodic direct or indirect glare on walls and floor.
Probability of disturbing glare: 45%.

Psychological Glare
Illuminance Value Contrast (IVC)

Point-in-time glare analysis shows luminance ratios for a gallery space. The contrast values are between 1:3 and 1:4 and show good contrast of luminance on the object. The daylighting shows the dynamic characteristics of the sun's conditions. Glare was detected by unfiltered sunlight entering through gaps between the roller shades and the roofing system. For a short period in the morning, values above 1:10 were detected.

Summary

Following the museum's opening, the recorded daylight levels in the galleries exceeded the predicted values. Even with the shades fully drawn, wall illuminance levels during the day were consistently above predicted light exposure and reached levels up to 600 lux.[2] This was due a gap between the roller shade tube and the roofing system and the lack of a hem bar on the bottom of each roller shade.

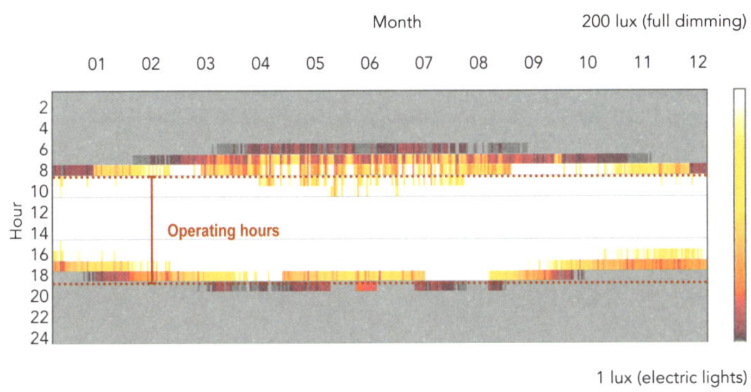

Daylight Dimming Potential (DDP)
Daytime hours when illuminance exceeds 200 lux (in white) indicate the potential to dim electric lighting 83% of the time annually.

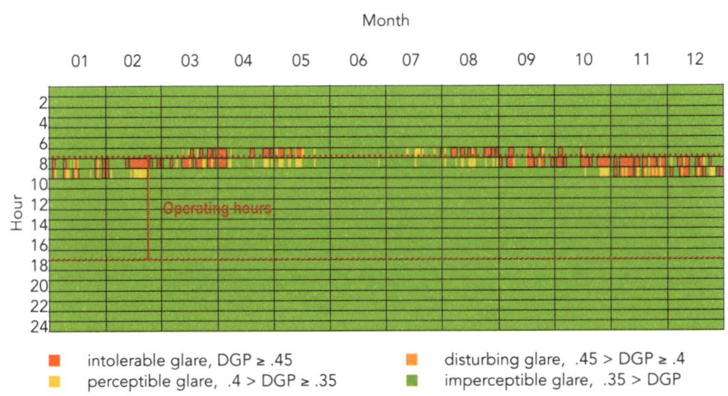

Annual Daylight Glare Probability (DGP)
DGP analysis indicates perceptible and disturbing glare between 7 and 9 a.m. throughout the year. Glare may be attributed to direct sunlight on the north-facing skylight aperture during the early morning hours (35–45% DGP).

To reach expectable illuminance levels, the roller shades (VLT 15–17%) were replaced with a fabric with a lower visual transmission (VLT 7%).
The quantitative daylight analysis shows a dynamic lighting situation on the simulated walls and floor. The peak illuminance of 528 lux (PITI) and the accumulated annual total of 1 million lux-hrs (AAI) are significantly above the illuminance target recommendation.
The UDI and the AIF show that the center of the south-facing wall receives target daylight levels of 50–200 lux for 26% of the time annually.
The qualitative daylight analysis shows perceptible glare (DGP) during the occupancy hours year-round. The lighting simulation (IVC) shows a dynamic contrast on the exhibit walls with contrast values of between 1:3 and 1:4 on most of the target zone. The annual daylight dimming potential is high at 83% of the gallery operating hours.

Recommendations

The top gallery of the BCAM takes full advantage of daylight illuminance. Actual light level readings in the galleries from May to December 2010 show considerable variation in illumination and a maximum light level exposure above the desired 200 lux.[3] The high maximum wall illuminance is primarily a result of the automated behavior of the roof shades. To protect the shades from wind damage, they automatically retract when wind speeds exceed 40 km/h (25 mph). Manual override roller blind schedules for roof maintenance or photography in the galleries also allows for direct light to enter the galleries.
The initial simulation carried out in the planning stage diverged significantly from the actual readings. This is due to differences in the planned versus the constructed skylight system and changes in the operational parameters. Post monitoring and evaluation is critical to ensure good correlations between the predicted and actual lighting situation.

2 Ibid.
3 Ibid.

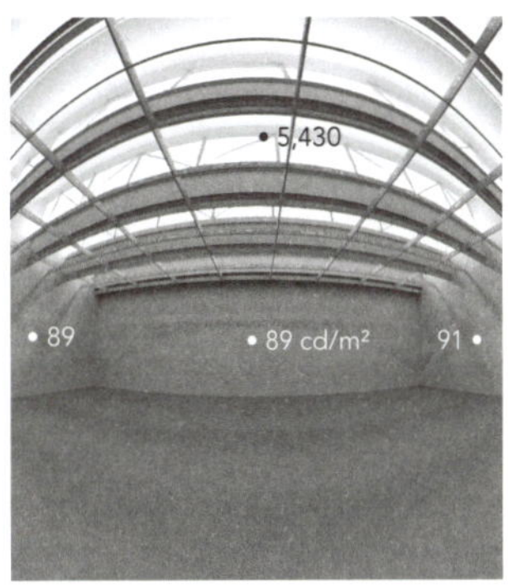

Illuminance Value Contrast (IVC)
The rendering shows highest contrast ratios when looking north on June 21 at noon.

Gallery View
View inside the upper floor gallery space.

Summary

Light from the sun is the primary agent of illumination. Through reflection, absorption and transmission, this becomes a secondary light source and reflects the light from a primary light source to our eyes. For example, the sunlight (primary) is reflected off the paintings (secondary) to our eyes, so that we are able to see the artwork. With sunlight as the primary source, the temporal nature of daylight and its continuous fluctuation affects the secondary light in a unique way that cannot be achieved under electric light.[1]

It is difficult for any designer to develop clear design guidelines for daylight performances. Daylighting in museum galleries encompasses multiple and sometimes contrary performance criteria. Conservational guidelines for the overall daylighting performance of the gallery space are needed to protect sensitive artwork on display. They also ensure optimum color rendering and contrast for best artwork reception and a visually stimulating visitor experience.[2] Good daylighting in galleries also contributes to the energy efficiency in museums by reducing the need for electric lighting.

Quantitative versus qualitative daylight evaluations

The quantitative illuminance evaluation uses objective performance matrixes and benchmarks. It is important to recognize that these matrixes are not as objective as they first seem; based on the definition of 'what is good lighting and a well-daylit space'. For example, the recommended illuminance targets[3] change with the age of the viewer and should double when the 'visual age of observers' is above 65 years. At the same time, the maximum illuminance for galleries is determined by the sensitivity of the exhibited artwork and target illuminance can only be changed by the exhibit concepts. Higher illuminance levels annually can be acceptable but only if the annual exhibit time of the individual artwork is shortened.

The qualitative illuminance evaluation is somewhat more subjective and perceptual; glare and object contrast, visual interesting spaces and lively daylighting are equally important for a positive art reception and visitor experience. A museum's atmosphere with changing lighting scenarios and dynamic light shifts, reflecting the sky conditions outside, are important for an exciting visitor experience. The illuminance levels and the quality of daylight are perceived differently by the viewer in the context of spatial composition, light contrast and viewing quality.

RPBW manages to fulfill both aspects of daylight – the quantitative and qualitative daylight evaluations – in his museums in an excellent way.

Daylighting System – Passive versus Active

RPBW developed a wide range of daylighting systems for optimal daylight use in museums and galleries. The projects presented show relatively simple system solutions by means of stationary and passive daylight systems, e.g., in The Menil Collection Museum or the Nasher Sculpture Center. There are also highly complex multilayer active daylight systems such as in the Beyeler Foundation or the Cy Twombly Pavilion. A comparative analysis of different daylight systems confirmed that passive daylight systems with fixed shading devices are able to present excellent lighting solutions. Active shading systems are inherently more complex in design and construction; they must also be continuously maintained. Moreover, active systems are able to completely eliminate unwanted daylight when the exhibition is closed to visitors. This is particularly important from a conservational point of view because light cumulatively affects photosensitive materials.

Top-lighting with Surface, Linear and Point Skylights

The preferred daylighting concept in museums is top-lighting through skylights, although solar radiation falling on a roof can be very significant. Surface skylights and glass roof systems require external shade. The quantity of lumens and radiation falling

1 Mohamed Boubekri, *Daylighting Design: Planning Strategies and Best Practice Solutions*, Birkhäuser, Basel 2014.
2 Christoph Reinhart, *Daylighting Handbook I: Fundamentals – Designing with the Sun*, Building Technology Press, Cambridge 2014.
3 The Museum and Art Gallery Lighting Committee of the Illuminating Engineering Society of North America, *Recommended Practice for Museum Lighting*, ANSI/IES RP-30-17, Illuminating Engineering Society, New York 2017, errata 1.

on the glass and entering the building would over-light and heat up the gallery space. External shading has proved to be a better system solution for cutting out unnecessary light and heat gain. Linear skylights and especially polar-oriented skylights avoid direct sunlight because of its north-facing orientation. The benefits of blocking unwanted direct radiation through the geometric orientation of the skylights present a simple solution for a daylight system (The Broad Museum). Point skylights are typically arranged in checkerboard patterns across a larger roof area (High Museum). Floor to skylight ratio can vary depending on the skylight's purpose. It can be used for ambient lighting and animating a space by having light levels change as clouds pass, or for generally lighting walls and artwork. To illuminate a gallery space efficiently using skylights, only 15% of the aperture to floor area ratio (AFR) is needed (High Museum),[4] while the number of skylights can be tuned to the desired illuminance levels. In contrast, all glass roofs or surface skylights need extensive shading, while point skylights allow only the necessary daylight into the gallery space below.

Good daylight design in museums involves more than adherence to specified parameters for light intensity or light levels and goes far beyond purely physiological visual requirements. These guidelines are a prerequisite for good lighting, but exceptional daylight design also includes psychological, aesthetic and emotional aspects. These play a major role in the visitors' perception of light and the objects they are viewing. Aesthetic room and object lighting, the spectral composition of the light, the right lighting contrast, the necessary (adapted) light intensity, a dynamic light distribution and a natural color rendering are key for a successful lighting concept. The interaction of these aspects in relation to the perception of space, the representation of the object and the reception of the viewer is not yet fully understood. In this sense, RPBW goes far beyond fulfilling pure technical requirements. It builds spaces of experience in which the art and the object are in the foreground and the space becomes a living "art space" that supports the works of art.

4 Barry Lord and Gail Dexter Lord (eds.), *The Manual of Museum Exhibitions*, AltaMira Press, Walnut Creek 2001, p. 169.

List of Abbreviations

AAI	Average Annual Illuminance
AFR	Aperture to Floor Area Ratio
AIF	Annual Illuminance Frequency (AIF)
CRI	Color Rendering Index
DDP	Daylight Dimming Potential
DGP	Annual Daylight Glare Probability
IVC	Illuminance Value Contrast
LRV	Light Reflectance Value
PITI	Point-in-Time Illuminance
SW	Sherwin-Williams Paint
UDI	Useful Daylight Illuminance
UV	Ultraviolet
VLT	Visible Light Transmittance

Project Details

1982–1986
The Menil Collection
Houston, Texas, USA

Client: The Menil Foundation

Piano & Fitzgerald, architects

Design Team: S. Ishida (associate in charge), M. Carroll, F. Doria, M. Downs, C. Patel, B. Plattner C. Susstrunk

Consultants: Ove Arup & Partners (P. Rice, N. Nobel, J. Thornton – structure); Hayne & Whaley Associates (services); Galewsky & Johnston (local services); R. Jensen (fire prevention)

www.menil.org

1991–1997
Beyeler Foundation
Riehen, Basel, Switzerland

Client: Beyeler Foundation

Renzo Piano Building Workshop, architects in association with Burckhardt + Partner AG, Basel

Preliminary Design, 1992
Design Team: B. Plattner (senior partner in charge), L. Couton (architect in charge), with J. Berger, E. Belik, W. Vassal and A. Schultz; P. Darmer (models)
Consultants: Ove Arup & Partners (structure and services)

Phase One, 1993–1997
Design Team: B. Plattner (partner in charge), L. Couton (architect in charge), with P. Hendier, W. Matthews, R. Self and L. Epprecht; J. P. Allain (models)
Consultants: Ove Arup & Partners, C. Burger + Partner AG (structure); Bogenschütz AG (plumbing); J. Forrer AG (HVAC); Elektrizitäts AG (electrical engineering); J. Wiede, Schönholzer + Stauffer (landscaping)

Phase Two, 1999–2000
Design Team: B. Plattner, E. Volz (partner and associate in charge)
Consultants: C. Burger + Partner AG (structure); Bogenschütz AG (plumbing); J. Forrer AG (HVAC); Elektrizitäts AG (electrical engineering); Schönholzer + Stauffer (landscaping)

www.fondationbeyeler.ch

1991–1998
Jean-Marie Tjibaou Cultural Center
Nouméa, New Caledonia

Client: Agence pour le Développement de la Culture Kanak

Renzo Piano Building Workshop, architects

Competition, 1991
Design Team: P. Vincent (partner in charge), A. Chaaya (architect in charge), with F. Pagliani, J. Moolhuijzen, W. Vassal and O. Doizy, A. Schultz (models)
Consultants: A. Bensa (ethnology); Desvigne & Dalnoky (landscaping); Ove Arup & Partners (structure and ventilation); GEC Ingénierie (cost control); Peutz & Associés (acoustics); Scène (scenography)

Preliminary Design, 1992
Design Team: P. Vincent (partner in charge), A. Chaaya, D. Rat (architects in charge), with J. B. Mothes, A. H. Téménidès and R. Phelan, C. Catino, A. Gallissian, R. Baumgarten; P. Darmer (models)
Consultants: A. Bensa (ethnology); GEC Ingénierie (cost control); Ove Arup & Partners (structural and MEP engineering concept); CSTB (environmental studies); Agibat MTI (structure); Scène (scenography); Peutz & Associés (acoustics); Qualiconsult (security); Végétude (planting)

Design Development and Construction Phase, 1993–1998
Design Team: P. Vincent (partner in charge), D. Rat, W. Vassal (architects in charge), with A. El Jerari, A. Gallissian, M. Henry, C. Jackman, P. Keyser, D. Mirallie, G. Modolo, J. B. Mothes, M. Pimmel, S. Purnama, A. H. Téménidès, J. P. Allain (models)
Consultants: A. Bensa (ethnology); Agibat MTI (structure); GEC Ingénierie (MEP engineering and cost control); CSTB (environmental studies); Philippe Délis (exhibit design); Scène (scenography); Peutz & Associés (acoustics); Qualiconsult (security); Végétude (planting); Intégral R. Baur (signage)

www.adck.nc

1992–1995
Cy Twombly Pavilion
Houston, Texas, USA

Client: The Menil Foundation

Renzo Piano Building Workshop, architects

Design Team: M. Carroll (partner in charge), S. Ishida (partner), with M. Palmore and S. Comer, A. Ewing, S. Lopez

Consultants: R. Fitzgerald & Associates (local architect); Ove Arup & Partners, Haynes Whaley Associates Inc. (structure); Ove Arup & Partners (services); Lockwood Andrews & Newman (civil engineering)

www.menil.org/campus/cy-twombly-gallery

1999–2003
Nasher Sculpture Center
Dallas, Texas, USA

Client: The Nasher Foundation

Renzo Piano Building Workshop, architects

Design Team: E. Baglietto (partner in charge), B. Terpeluk with S. Ishida (partner), B. Bauer, L. Pelleriti, S. Scarabicchi (partner), A. Symietz, E. Trezzani and G. Langasco (CAD), Y. Kashiwagi; F. Cappellini, S. Rossi (models)

Consultants: Peter Walker & Partners (landscape architect); Ove Arup & Partners (structure and services); Interloop A/D (consulting architect); Beck Architecture (local consulting architect)

General Contractor: HCBeck

www.nashersculpturecenter.org

1999–2005
High Museum Expansion
Atlanta, Georgia, USA

Client: High Museum of Art + Woodruff Arts Center

Renzo Piano Building Workshop, architects in collaboration with Lord, Aeck & Sargent Inc., architects, Atlanta

Design Team: M. Carroll (partner in charge), E. Trezzani (associate in charge), S. Ishida (partner), S. Colon, D. Patterson, A. Symietz, with F. Elmalipinar, G. Longoni, M. Maggi, A. Parigi, R. Sproull, E. Suarez and J. Boon, J. Silvester, S. Tagliacarne, B. Waechter, M. Agnoletto, S. Chavez, D. Hlavacek, R. Supiciche, A. Vrana; M. Ottonello, G. Langasco (CAD operators); D. Cavagna, F. Cappellini, S. Rossi (models)

Consultants: Ove Arup & Partners + Uzun & Case + Jordan & Skala (structure and services); Arup Acoustics (acoustics); Arup Lighting (lighting); HDR/WLJorden (civil engineering); Jordan Jones & Goulding (landscaping); Bergmeyer Associates (interiors/restaurant); Brand+Allen Architects (interiors/retail)

www.high.org

1999–2005
Zentrum Paul Klee
Bern, Switzerland

Client: Maurice E. and Martha Müller Foundation

Renzo Piano Building Workshop, architects in collaboration with arb Architekten, Bern

Design team: B. Plattner (partner in charge), M. Busk-Petersen, O. Hempel (architects in charge), with L. Battaglia, A. Eris, J. Moolhuijzen (partner), M. Prini and F. Carriba, L. Couton, S. Drouin, O. Foucher, H. Gsottbauer, F. Kohlbecker, J. Paik, D. Rat, A. Wollbrink; R. Aebi, O. Aubert, C. Colson, F. de Saint-Jouan, P. Furnemont, Y. Kyrkos (models)

Consultants: Ove Arup & Partners, B+S Ingenieure AG (structure); Ove Arup & Partners, Luco AG, Enerconom AG, Bering AG (services); Emmer Pfenninger Partner AG (facade engineering); A. Walz (geometry studies); Ludwig & Weiler (special structural elements); Grolimund+Partner AG (bauphysik); Müller-BBM (acoustics); Institut de sécurité (fire prevention), Hügli AG (security); M. Volkart (food service); Schweizerische Hochschule für Landwirtschaft, F. Vogel (landscaping); Coande (signage)

www.zpk.org

2000–2006
Renovation and Expansion of the Morgan Library and Museum
New York City, New York, USA

Client: The Morgan Library

Renzo Piano Building Workshop, architects in collaboration with Beyer Blinder Belle LLP, New York

Design Team: G. Bianchi (partner in charge), K. Doerr, T. Sahlmann, with A. Knapp, Y. Pages, M. Reale and P. Bruzzone, M. Cook, S. Abe, M. Aloisini, L. Bouwman, J. Hart, H. Kybicova, M. Leon; Y. Kyrkos, C. Colson, O. Aubert (models)

Consultants: Robert Silman Associates (structure); Cosentini Associates (services); Ove Arup & Partners (thermal performance and lighting); Front (facade consultant); Kahle Acoustics (acoustics); Harvey Marshall Associates (A/V consultant); IROS (elevator design); HM White (landscape); Stuart-Lynn Company (cost consultant)

www.themorgan.org

2003–2008
Broad Contemporary Art Museum (LACMA expansion – Phase I)
Los Angeles, California, USA

Client: Los Angeles County Museum of Art (LACMA)

Renzo Piano Building Workshop, architects in collaboration with Gensler Associates, Santa Monica

Design Team: A. Chaaya (partner in charge), with J. Boon, D. Graignic-Ramiro, A. Knapp, S.Joly, B. Malbaux G. Perez, M. Pimmel, D. Prasilova, M. Reale and A. Jankovic, A. King, K. Ramirez, E. Vélez, M. Watabe; O. Aubert, C. Colson, Y. Kyrkos (models)

Consultants: Arup (structure and services); Advanced Structures Incorporated (facade); Davis Langdon (cost consultant); KPFF (civil engineering)

www.broadartfoundation.org

Bibliography

Renzo Piano Building Workshop

A + U Architecture and Urbanism, *Recent Projects: Renzo Piano Building Workshop*. no. 568, 2018/1, pp. 146–153.

ANY: Architecture New York, *Renzo Piano Building Workshop*. no. 13, 1996, pp. 46–51.

Barandun, Ursina, and Nathalie Gygax Huber (eds.), *Zentrum Paul Klee, Bern: Die Architektur*. Hatje Cantz, Ostfildern 2005.

Buchanan, Peter, *Renzo Piano Building Workshop: Complete Works*, Volumes 1–5. Phaidon, London 1994–2008.

Ciccarelli, Lorenzo, *Renzo Piano before Renzo Piano: Masters and Beginnings*. Fondazione Renzo Piano/ Quodlibet, Genoa 2017.

Cuito, Aurora, *Renzo Piano*. teNeues, Düsseldorf 2002.

Dal Co, Francesco, *Renzo Piano*. Mondadori Electa, Milan 2014.

Fernández-Galiano, Luis (ed.), *Renzo Piano Building Workshop, 1990–2006*. Arquitectura Viva, Madrid 2006.

Fernández-Galiano, Luis, *Renzo Piano: Building Workshop*. Arquitectura Viva, Madrid 2017.

Fondation Beyeler (ed.), *Renzo Piano – Fondation Beyeler: Ein Haus für die Kunst*. Birkhäuser, Basel 2001.

Fondazione Renzo Piano (ed.), *Piece by Piece, Renzo Piano Building Workshop*. Exhibition catalogue, 2015.

High Museum of Art (ed.), *Renzo Piano's Village for the Arts: Expansion of the High Museum of Art and Woodruff Arts Center*. High Museum of Art, Atlanta 2005.

Hofmeister, Sandra (ed.), *Renzo Piano Building Workshop: Architecture and Construction Details*. Edition Detail, Munich 2018.

Ito, Miwako, and Yumiko Fujimaki (eds.), *Renzo Piano Building Workshop: In Search of a Balance*. Process Architecture Co., Tokyo 1992.

Lampugnani, Vittorio M., *Renzo Piano 1987–1994 (Series)*. Birkhäuser, Basel 1995.

Nakamura, Toshio (ed.), *A+U Renzo Piano Building Workshop: 1964–1988*. A + U Architecture and Urbanism, Tokyo 1989.

Piano, Renzo, *Beyeler, Fondation Beyeler*. Fondazione Renzo Piano, Genoa 2008.

Piano, Renzo, *Logbook*. The Monacelli Press, New York 1997.

Piano, Renzo, *Menil: The Menil Collection*. Fondazione Renzo Piano, Genoa 2007.

Piano, Renzo, *Nouméa: Centre Culturel Jean-Marie Tjibaou*. Fondazione Renzo Piano, Genoa 2011.

Piano, Renzo, *Renzo Piano: Buildings and Projects, 1971–1989*. Rizzoli, New York 1989.

Piano, Renzo, *Renzo Piano: Sustainable Architectures / Arquitecturas Sostenibles*. Gingko Press, Berkeley 1999.

Piano, Renzo, *The Poetics of Construction (The Pietro Belluschi Lectures)*. School of Architecture and Planning, MIT, Boston 2002.

Piano, Renzo, and Kenneth Frampton, *Renzo Piano: The Complete Logbook, 1966–2016*. Revised and expanded edition, Thames & Hudson Ltd, London 2017.

Piano, Renzo, and Victoria Newhouse, *Renzo Piano Museums*. The Monacelli Press, New York 2007.

Pizzi, Emilio, *Renzo Piano*. Birkhäuser, Basel 2003.

Ranzani, Ermanno, "Ampliamento dell'IRCAM a Parigi: Renzo Piano Building Workshop." Domus 713, 1990, pp. 38–47.

White, Elizabeth (ed.), *Renzo Piano Museums*. The Monacelli Press, New York 2007.

Daylight in Buildings

Boubekri, Mohamed, *Daylighting Design: Planning Strategies and Best Practice Solutions*. Birkhäuser, Basel 2014.

Brandi, Ulrike, *Light Design*. Edition Detail, Munich 2006.

Druzik, James, "Illuminating Alternatives: Research in Museum Lighting." *Getty Conservation Institute Newsletter*, 2004, 19(1).

Fördergemeinschaft Gutes Licht – FGL (ed.), *Museums-beleuchtung: Strahlung und ihr Schädigungspotenzial – Konservatorische Maßnahmen, Grundlagen zur Berechnung*. FGL, Frankfurt am Main 2006.

Illuminating Engineering Society of North America, *Museum and Art Gallery Lighting: A Recommended Practice*, ANSI/IESNA RP-30-96, Illuminating Engineering Society of North America, New York 1996.

Köster, Helmut, *Tageslichtdynamische Architektur: Grundlagen, Systeme, Projekte*. Birkhäuser, Berlin 2004.

Lull, William P., and Paul N. Banks, *Conservation Environment Guidelines for Libraries and Archives*. Canadian Council of Archives, Ottawa 1995.

Mardaljevic, John, Lisa Heschong and Eleanor Lee, "Daylight Metrics and Energy Savings." *Lighting Research & Technology*, 2009, 41(3), pp. 261–283.

Merritt, Elizabeth, *National Standards & Best Practices for U.S. Museums*. AAM PRESS, Arlington 2010.

National Park Service, *Museum Handbook*, "Museum Collections Environment." NPS, Washington, D. C., 1999.

Phillips, Derek, *Daylighting: Natural Light in Architecture*. Elsevier, Amsterdam 2004.

Rea, Mark Stanley (ed.), *The IESNA Lighting Handbook: Reference and Applications*. Illuminating Engineering Society of North America, New York 2000.

Reinhart, Christoph, John Mardaljevic and Zack Rogers, "Dynamic Daylight Performance Metrics for Sustainable Building Design." *Leukos*, 2006, 3(1), pp. 7–31.

The Museum and Art Gallery Lighting Committee of the Illuminating Engineering Society of North America, *Recommended Practice for Museum Lighting*. ANSI/IES RP-30-17, Illuminating Engineering Society, New York 2017.

Thomson, Garry, *The Museum Environment*. Second edition, Routledge, London 1994.

Tregenza, Peter, and Michael Wilson, *Daylighting: Architecture and Lighting Design*. Routledge, London and New York 2011.

RPBW Websites

Renzo Piano Building Workshop: www.rpbw.com

Fondazione Renzo Piano: www.fondazionerenzopiano.org/en/

About the Author

Edgar Stach writes on technology and design, structure and form as well as energy and performance. Currently professor of architecture at Thomas Jefferson University in Philadelphia, USA, he previously taught at the Bauhaus University in Weimar, Germany, the University of Tennessee, USA, and Delft University of Technology, the Netherlands. He teaches architectural design, technology and methods of construction.

Educated in Germany and Austria, he studied architecture at the RWTH Aachen University, Germany, and the TU Wien, Austria. He received his Dr.-Ing. (PhD) from the TU Braunschweig in Germany for his thesis on design principles for daylighting systems in museums. As a licenced architect, his practice focuses on synthesizing science, research and technology that embraces energy efficiency, ecological sensitivity and environmental responsibility. He is the author and co-author of over 50 articles and book chapters published in IASS, Springer, WTI, ACSA and other peer-reviewed journals and publications. His book *Mies van der Rohe. Space – Material – Detail*, was published by the Swiss publishing house Birkhäuser in October 2017.

Illustration Credits

© ADCK – Centre Culturel Tjibaou © RPBW – Renzo Piano Building Workshop Architects. John Gollings – Gollings Photography: 43 (top, bottom), 47 (left), 155 (right), Pierre Alain Pantz: 44, 47 (middle, right), 50 (left), 51 (left, right), William Vassal: 48 (top, bottom), 49

© Alte Pinakothek, Munich, Germany: 112 (top)

bpk Bildagentur / Nationalgalerie, Staatliche Museen, Berlin, Germany / © 2017 Artists Rights Society (ARS), New York / VG Bild-Kunst, Bonn. Christian Gahl 2005: 13 (bottom)

Chicago History Museum, Hedrich-Blessing Collection: HB-18506-D: 13 (top)

© Fondazione Renzo Piano. 22, 58 (right), 61(top), Hickey & Robertson Photography: 16 (bottom), 17 (top), 53 (bottom), 53 (top), 54–55, 58 (left), 61 (left), 61 (right), 139 (right), 156 (left)

Gianakos, D. Jules: cover, 12 (top)

Iwan Baan Photography B.V.: 14 (bottom)

Kimbell Art Museum, Fort Worth, Texas / Art Resource, NY / Architectural Archives, University of Pennsylvania: 10

Kimbell Art Museum; Fort Worth, Texas. Nic Lehoux: 11 (top), 17 (below) Robert Wharton: 11 (bottom), Robert LaPrelle: 123

© Marc Riboud: 24 (middle)

© Michel Denancé: 15 (top, bottom), 33, 37 (top, bottom), 38 ,39, 50 (right), 64, 66 (right), 68 (right), 69 (bottom), 69 (top right), 70 (left, middle), 72, 73, 75, 76 (left, bottom), 78, 80, 83, 84 (top), 85, 86, 87 (bottom), 87 (top), 88 (left, middle), 91, 93 (left, middle, right), 95, 97 (top, bottom), 99 (left, middle, right, bottom), 100 (left, right), 101 (left, right), 106 (left), 109, 112 (bottom), 133 (right), 136 (right), 142 (right), 145 (right), 148 (right), 151 (right), 155 (middle), 156 (right), 157 (left, middle)

© Museum Associates, dba LACMA: 106 (right)

© Nasher Sculpture Center. Timothy Hurley: 14 (top), 63, 66, 68 (left), 70 (right), 156 (middle)

© Niggi Brauning: 35

© Piano & Fitzgerald, architects © Fondazione Renzo Piano. Richard T. Bryant – Richard T. Bryant Photography: 9, 155 (left), Ben Smusz: 21, Hickey & Robertson Photography: 23, Paul Hester – Paul Hester Photography: 24 (top, bottom), 31, 130 (right), Shunji Ishida: 29

© RPBW – Renzo Piano Building Workshop Architects. 34, 45, 69 (top left), 81, 92, 105 (left), 108, Christian Richters: 7, 12 (bottom), Enrico Cano: 84 (bottom), Enrico Cano: 88 (right), Nic Lehoux: 103, 104, 105 (right), 157 (right)

© RPBW – Renzo Piano Building Workshop Architects © Fondazione Renzo Piano. Fulvio Roiter: 16 (top)

Schezen, Roberto / Esto, Daylight and Architecture Magazine: 117

Stach, Edgar / Esposito, Michael: 128 (top right, bottom right), 129 (left, right), 130 (top left, bottom left, middle), 131(top right, bottom right), 132 (left, right), 133 (top left, bottom left), 134 (top left, top right, bottom right), 135 (left, right), 136 (top left, bottom left, middle), 137 (top right, bottom right), 138 (left, right), 139 (top left, bottom left, middle), 140 (top right, bottom right), 141 (left, right), 142 (top left, bottom left, middle), 143 (top right, bottom right), 144 (left, right), 145 (top left, bottom left, middle), 146 (top right, bottom right), 147 (left, right), 148 (top left, bottom left, middle), 149 (top right, bottom right), 150 (left, right), 151 (top left, bottom left, middle)